Praise for
Never Mind the Bullocks

*Terrific and terrifying in equal measure: a life-affirming,
death-welcoming journey around the world's most
dangerous roads in a wheeled toaster oven.*
**Tim Moore, author of *Do Not Pass Go, Gironimo!* and
*French Revolutions***

*Vanessa is a gem – her writing is as effervescent and
refreshing as diving naked into a lake of champagne.*
Olly Smith, TV presenter and author

The proverbial English dry wit.
Time Out

*Travelling has never been this tough, never been this
enjoyable and entertaining as Able takes you on a
remarkable journey of humour through her scathing
comments and lucid writing… A hilarious book, from an
author that pulls no punches.*
Postnoon

*Vanessa Able is doggedly intrepid, deliciously acerbic, keenly
inquisitive and quite possibly mental.*
Jaideep VG, *Time Out India*

*A witty account of riding the Nano over 10,000km across
India, braving dust and grime, risking accidents and
flouting driving rules.*
Livemint India

Never Mind THE BULLOCKS

One girl's 10,000 km adventure around India in the world's cheapest car

VANESSA ABLE

NICHOLAS BREALEY
PUBLISHING

London • Boston

First published by
Nicholas Brealey Publishing in 2014

3–5 Spafield Street	20 Park Plaza
Clerkenwell, London	Boston
EC1R 4QB, UK	MA 02116, USA
Tel: +44 (0)20 7239 0360	Tel: (888) BREALEY
Fax: +44 (0)20 7239 0370	*Fax: (617) 523 3708*

www.nicholasbrealey.com

ISBN: 978-1-85788-612-2
eISBN: 978-1-85788-928-4

British Library Cataloguing in Publication Data
A catalogue record for this book is available from the
British Library.

Printed in the UK by Clays Ltd, St Ives plc.

For the Ghost who came alive

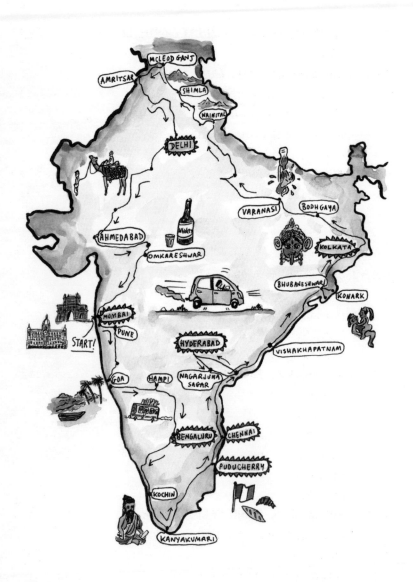

CONTENTS

START ME UP – Bagging the £1,000 car

'et me get this straight: you're planning to drive all the way around India in a Tata Nano?' Naresh Fernandes, editor of *Time Out Mumbai*, asked me in a voice that sounded like disappointment. 'Are you going to be planting lots of trees in your wake to compensate for the emissions?'

It was not the reaction I had hoped for. I sat across from him in his office, pathologically thumbing the retractor button of my biro and thinking of something witty to dredge me out of the mire of his opinion.

'Umm, not exactly. No trees. But it is a fuel-efficient car, so I doubt it'll cause too much… damage…'

'Oh. Is it electric?'

'No.'

'Hybrid?'

'No.'

'Diesel?'

'No. But it goes a fair distance per litre.'

'How far?'

Folding under the pressure of the interrogation, my brain knocked random numbers around before drawing a blank and retreating with a whimper into the dank warren of its own inadequacy.

'I'm not sure exactly,' I said, trying to mask my inner dullard with an unconvincing veneer of cockiness, 'but I know it's a lot.'

'What's your route?'

'A big circle around the country. Going south first. 10,000 kilometres.'

'Why 10,000?'

'Um. It's a challenge?'

The chat was not going as planned.

I had come to *Time Out Mumbai* as part of a media out-reach strategy intended to generate a level of hype and enthu-siasm among the press similar to the one aroused in my loyal circle of support (namely my mum and my two best friends). I didn't exactly imagine being drowned by a press tsunami, but I thought at least a little corporate nepotism might come into play with Naresh, given that I was a former *Time Out* editor myself. But this particular fish wasn't in the least impressed by my plan and was most certainly not biting.

What I was too embarrassed to tell Naresh was that what had really drawn me to the Nano was one of my less virtuous traits, namely my limitless capacity for being motivated by a bargain. The car recently launched by Tata Motors – the com-pany that had bought Jaguar Land Rover in 2008 – was officially the world's cheapest, and as such it had me at first sight: a hopeless sucker for marketing campaigns aimed at hopeless suckers bent on expanding their collection of easy electronic comestibles, I immediately added the vehicle (four doors, two cylinders and 624 cc of oomph, which, I was vaguely aware, was tantamount to a motorbike with a roof) to the tally of delecta-ble gadgets that were within reach of my credit card limit. It was the first time a new car had ever featured on that list, an event that inspired in me the warm rush of consumer anticipation.

'What's that, a Smart Car?' asked my mum, squinting into the screen of my laptop.

'Actually, Mum, it's a Tata Nano. It's the cheapest car in the world.'

'I haven't seen any about.'

'That's because we don't have them here in Jersey.'

'So where are they, then?'

'India.'

'India?'

This was the other part of the story. Although Tata had plans for releasing the Nano globally at some point in the future, for now the only place one could buy a model was in India. I was gutted: it had never occurred to me that, unlike laptops and phones, cars were not altogether international products.

'So, yeah. I'm thinking of going over there to get one. Drive it around a bit.'

My mother didn't flinch. In the last few weeks she had become accustomed to my reactionary rhetoric, a horrible regression in behaviour that followed my move back home after the sticky end of a four-year relationship.

'Haven't you been to India enough? What about getting a job instead?'

With the vexation of a vilified teen, I inhaled and slowly reeled off the same speech I had been laying on my parents for the last decade, namely that freelance travel writing *was* a job and a noble one at that. If she had the impression that my time was not sufficiently consumed by the pursuit, it was only because the publishing world was currently in crisis and work was thin on the ground. I had come here to my childhood home – nay, *refuge* – on the Channel Island of Jersey as an interim measure, to consider my future in the light of the current global climate and to decide what to do next. And whatever that was, I indignantly assured her, it would certainly not involve any *job* of the nine-to-five variety. I was a free soul, a wanderer; a leaf that floated in the breeze and submitted hotel and restaurant reviews to paying publications. My wings might have been clipped, but I wasn't about to let that stop me.

'Anyway, it's about to be my Jesus Year,' I reminded my mother.

'Your what?'

'My Jesus Year. Thirty-three. It's when you make things happen in your life. When you make decisions and change things.'

'Why not make it the year you decide to finally enter a legitimate workforce?'

I opted not to comment.

'Besides, Jesus *died* when he was thirty-three. That's so morbid.'

Mum was right, as she often is, in her assertion that I'd been to India a lot. And that a proper paying job would be something of enormous benefit. This was true: but since I'd started thinking about the Nano, a thought process that coincided with other ideas of immediate escape from the rock of my birth that was now holding me emotional prisoner, I had become possessed by the idea of returning to India. A decade earlier, it had been the land of opportunity for me: a paradise for the youthful, adventurous and relatively broke. It was an anarchic, volatile, often squalid place where my conceited young soul could play out the illusion of influence with as little as a few quid in my back pocket. A world of easy drugs and full moon parties set against a blurred and (for me then) only fleetingly interesting background of social hardship, where for the western traveller hippie type virtually anything could be made possible for the right price, and that figure was a fraction of what it was back at home.

Would those things really still hold any appeal? I knew I was definitely a few years over that level of decadence, but the urge to explore India was still in my veins. My savings account contained several times more than it ever had during my student days when the vacation coffers were only scantly furnished with the proceeds from a job pulping oranges at a doomed juice bar on Charing Cross Road. Now I had the kind of money that could buy me three months in India. I could, I reasoned, purchase myself one of these cheap cars and take it all the way around the country on the drive of a lifetime. What better way, I mused, to take on newly single life and embark on another, more daring chapter?

While I was indulging in these fantasies, hype around the Nano was ballooning globally, as the international media caught on to what the car actually meant in a country with a booming economy and a ballooning new middle class. *USA Today* echoed the popular opinion that the car 'may yield a transportation revolution', while *Time* magazine pegged it as 'one of the most important cars ever designed'. 'Indian streets may never be the same again,' declared the BBC, and *Newsweek* asserted that the Nano was 'changing the rules of the road for the auto industry and society itself'. But it was the *Financial Times*' claim that the Nano encapsulated 'the dream of millions of Indians groping for a shot at urban prosperity' that really caught my imagination. This was my chance to partake in what was destined to be legend.

I was sold. All that remained was to figure out how to get my hands on one.

'Hello! Mr Shah?' I yelled into my computer. *'I'd – like – to – buy – your – Nano!'*

'Something something *Nano*?' Mr Shah shouted back.

'Yes, your Nano! I want to buy it! *How much for your Nano*, Mr Shah? Your – Nano – that – is – for – sale?'

Silence, followed by a low churning noise.

It turned out that trying to buy the most wanted car in India off a bloke in Mumbai from an island in the English Channel was not as easy as I had anticipated. Spurred on by an internet ad I had come across earlier, I had dialled Mr Shah with the aim of coming to some agreement about the sale of his car, and in the hope that he might take credit cards. But I soon discovered that such high-stakes negotiations were not suited to debilitated internet telephony. All I could hear from my laptop speaker was a series of crackles and the voice of a man-bot who sounded like he was trying to physically project his voice 9,000 km into my ear.

'Mr Shah? How much is it, the car?'

'Something something *two-lakh four*.'

I had no idea what he was talking about. 'Sorry, could you repeat that, please?'

There was no response and I couldn't tell if he'd heard me. I gave my laptop a caustic shake as though jiggling it might help clear the crud that was blocking the line or the satellite beam somewhere between me and Mumbai. But with Mr Shah's voice still only coming through in barely fathomable fits and starts, my patience expired and I finally hung up to rethink my strategy.

When Tata launched the Nano at the Delhi Auto Expo back in 2008, it was not yet ready to go on the market. Due to a controversy surrounding the acquisition of land for its proposed factory in West Bengal, production of the car had been delayed. To keep buyers interested, Tata nonetheless opened the brand up for business and began to take orders. There was a deluge towards dealership offices, as forms were hastily filled out and hefty deposits paid. Around 200,000 orders were placed before Tata decided it would be best to close the lines, as the number was higher than it could realistically produce in the coming months. It eventually accepted half of the orders, which it chose through a lottery, and pledged that the cars would all be delivered by October 2010. In a time of global recession, 2010 was still looking bright for India's economy, which had been on the rise ever since the liberalization of the country's financial system in 1991. The advent of the Nano was just another symptom of the boost in trade and industry that was providing hundreds of thousands of people with their first taste of material might, and, for now at least, it seemed they all wanted to buy the same car.

So in January 2010, nine months before the delivery deadline, it transpired that simply snapping up a Nano was an impossible task. Dealerships were only distributing the car to people on Tata's waiting list, and it was predicted that new buyers might have to hold out for a whole year before getting their hands on one.

As far as I was concerned, this wouldn't do. I had made up my mind to leave Jersey and circumvent India in the World's Cheapest Car, and every day I spent getting narky with my mum, or huffing when my dad asked me to close the garage door, was another day of lessening self-worth. In order to bag a Nano, I realized I would need an accomplice in India; a person on the ground, a local, a savant, someone who could pull strings and get me what I damn well wanted. I needed an Indian genie of sorts, so I called on the only person I knew who could fulfil that role, who also happened to be the only person I knew in India at the time. My saviour was Akhil Gupta, a friend of my American cousin who I had met some years ago at a birthday party in Vermont. All I really knew about Akhil was that he lived in Mumbai and was the chairman of a private equity firm called Blackstone India. Our link was tenuous to say the least, so it was with some hesitation that I sent him an email one day out of the blue asking if he could help me buy a car.

Gentleman and inveterate yes-man that he is, he didn't flinch and responded immediately in the affirmative, as though I'd asked him to pop round the corner for a pint of milk. A few days later, however, he came back to me with grim tidings. After some extensive research, he confirmed that it was not possible to buy a Nano at a dealership anywhere in India.

The project looked on the verge of being shelved, and Akhil was showing signs of relief. He tactfully put some more sensible recommendations on the table: a Toyota Innova, he suggested, would be a far more suitable vehicle in which to tour India, and for £350 a month I could hire the car and the driver. Clearly concerned for my safety, Akhil outlined the following reasons in neat bullet points as to why I should definitely not attempt to cross India in a Nano:

- Nano is not meant for highway driving.
- If the car breaks down, you are in trouble, as there is no AAA, and may not have service stations which have Nano parts.
- Single beautiful girl like you travelling alone will be worrisome.

I wasn't worried about hiring the driver that Akhil suggested. I'd been at the wheel since before I was legal, the only daughter of parents desperate to desist from their roles as my personal chauffeurs, and in particular a father bent on passing down his driving skills to the son he never had. Many a Sunday afternoon in my mid-teens was spent stalling my dad's car around various parking lots. 'Be one with the machine,' he would intone with uncharacteristic Yoda-ness that made me suspect he had been preparing for this moment for many years: 'Feel the rise of the car when you take your foot off the clutch. It's not a car you are driving; it's a machine you're fusing with.'

And fuse I did. Within days of my seventeenth birthday I had passed my driving test (of which I can only recall performing an Olympic-grade three-point turn in yet another car park) and was the proud owner of a Parish of Grouville driver's licence.[1] It didn't take me long to catch the road bug: at eighteen, I devoured Kerouac's *On the Road* like every other teenage Beatnik wannabe. It was the stimulus that inspired my first solo road trip at the age of nineteen: an ambitious, though somewhat less degenerate, voyage that spanned the length and breadth of New Zealand in a Vauxhall Viva purchased for $300 from a Japanese woman in Auckland. In the years that followed, I rented a Yugo and drove through the villages of Serbia, a Tofaş Şahin over the eastern plains of Turkey, a Chevy through the American deserts to the Pacific coast, and a pimped-out Jeep Grand Cherokee in the abysmal traffic of Mexico City. I once even co-drove a behemoth eight-bed caravan through France, Italy and over to Greece, redefining the laws of Newtonian physics round Kefalonian hairpin bends. In short, I was no wet-eared neophyte: my driver's CV was extensive and for the most part spotless (barring the one-time orchestration of a three-car pile-up on Ladbroke Grove in London, of which I shall not speak here).

But Akhil was not the only person with consternation for my wellbeing. Soon his assistant Prasad, who was charged with the execution of my request, also began trying to coax me into curbing my plans. He extolled the virtues of India's other much-loved indigenous vehicle, the Maruti, reiterating that in his opinion, the brand had a much more reliable national support network than Tata.

Undeterred and feigning staunch oblivion to the butterflies this lack of confidence in the Nano was inspiring in me, I went back online and decided to consult Google. I searched for 'second-hand Tata Nano for sale, India' and within seconds was returned a search result informing me that a certain Mr Shah of Mumbai was selling his newly delivered yellow Nano LX with only 300 km on the clock.

My phone call with Mr Shah having miserably failed, I entreated Prasad to contact him to try to seal the deal. Prasad came back to me within hours with the happy news that the car was still for sale at the price of two-lakh four or Rs 240,000. That was exactly double what I had expected to pay. It turned out the reason was that there were three models of Nano and not just one: the cheapest model was indeed Rs 100,000, or one lakh, but the more expensive version, the one that listed air conditioning and electric windows among other perks, was a damn sight more. And Mr Shah, being in possession of the latter model, was reselling it, of course, at a premium. At double the price of the cheapest car in the world, it was no longer a bargain, but by that point I was so entrenched in the idea of a road trip that it seemed I had no choice: the cheapie version was nowhere to be seen in my subsequent trawl through Indian used-car classifieds. Needs must when the devil drives, and in the knowledge that this could be my only shot at bagging a Nano, I called Prasad and gave him the go-ahead.

The speed at which things moved after that was a little daunting. Within a couple of days, I received an email from Prasad that bore the triumphant words 'Nano bought' in the subject line. Accompanying the email was a trio of shakily framed, steamed-up photos of the car taken from his cell phone at varying angles. I sat down to reassess what was to be my trusty steed for a one-woman road trip around India.

The plan now had to be hiked up from a flight of fancy to something that was definitely going to happen. As such, I branded it: I started a blog called The Nano Diaries and set a distance challenge of 10,000 km, which was what India's circumference roughly measured. I made a tentative map of the ensuing journey: a hand-drawn circle around the country that started and ended in Mumbai and took in all the major cities like Bangalore, Chennai, Calcutta and Delhi, as well as passing through the Nilgiris hills of the south, right down to Kanyakumari at the southernmost tip, before heading back up the east coast all the way to West Bengal. From there I'd head over to the northern plains, to the cradle of Buddhism in Bihar and India's most holy city, Varanasi, before going north into the foothills of the Himalayas. My trajectory in that direction ended at the Kashmiri border where the mountains looked a little too Nano-unfriendly. Instead, I would work my way back down through Delhi and Gujarat to finish up again in Mumbai.

It was only at that moment – having set up the blog and committed to 10,000 km in the Nano – that I went back to Prasad's photos and was struck by just how unroadworthy the car looked: it had no discernible front bonnet or boot, and it was painted a ridiculous, attention-drawing bright yellow. It did not in any way resemble the fantasy compact, all-terrain vehicle I had created on the drawing board of my mind that was somewhere between a Smart Car and a Suzuki Vitara. With four doors, and an undercarriage about eight inches off the ground, this was neither a particularly compact car, nor did it look fit for the miles of off-roading I suspected lay ahead. I began to think that the Toyota Innova might not have been such a bad idea after all.

My mum peered at the triptych of yellow cars on my computer screen. 'Gosh, it's tiny!' she exclaimed. 'Are you sure that's not a Smart? And where's the engine?'

Determined not to ignite her incendiary maternal scrub, I tried to sound like I knew what I was talking about and parroted off the specs I had lifted from the Nano website minutes earlier. It might seem small, I began to explain with an air of technical authority, but in fact this particular model boasted a host of luxury features stripped from the mid-range (CX) and standard models in the name of economy. Had she not noticed the beaded roof, the spoiler, the ever-so-subtle tint across the windows, the front and rear fog lamps, the fabric upholstered seats, the – ahem – *electronic* trip meter, power windows, double cup holder and locks on the passenger side? And of course, it was impossible to tell from these photos, but the car also had air conditioning. Glossing over the scantier safety features and the fact that the front bonnet's foreshortened size looked like a driver's legs might take a drubbing from something as light and likely as a bicycle collision, I kept a perfectly straight face when Mum hammered in the final nail.

'As long as it's got airbags. Traffic's a bit hairy over there, isn't it?'

1

TRIAL BY RUSH HOUR – Girl Meets Traffic

MUMBAI; KM 0

What's the worst thing about driving in India-
aaaaaaarrrrgggghhh?' I asked Puran from the back
seat, my question trailing off into a startled squawk as he
narrowly avoided scraping a bus on the left. He didn't blink
before promptly answering, 'The traffic, madam. Never drive in
Mumbai from 8 until 10 morning time.'

I took a mental note, but didn't really believe that morning traffic was the absolute worst thing about driving in the
city. As far as I could see from our little jaunt along the seaside
road, every second spent in one's vehicle here had the flavour
of an exhilarating movie car chase, packed with stunts, terror
and close calls. Puran drove as though he were auditioning for
Mario Cart the Movie: swerving one way then the other, speed-
ing up and slowing down with effortless dexterity in order to
overtake, dodge and thread into a gap that looked about half
the size of our Skoda. It felt like we were kissing the wing mirrors of every vehicle we passed.

Akhil had instructed Puran to collect me from Chhatrapati
Shivaji International and take me to the Gupta residence,
where his cook would be waiting for me with toast, tea and, I
was starting to hope, plenty of sympathy. My morning landing
in Mumbai coincided perfectly with the early rush hour, and
within two hours of disembarking into the tepid humidity of a
February morning, I sat sweating in the back, tending to a bruise

on my lower calf that was the consequence of a trolley skirmish at baggage reclaim. The incident, a split-second pile-up after a luggage belt mix-up, had given me my first insight into how conflicts over right of way were resolved in India. Now I was watching the same principle play itself out on a larger scale.

'It's your first time in India?' Puran chirped from the driver's seat, clearly trying to distract me from the visceral fear I must have been emitting in waves from behind.

'Er, no,' I replied, though from my bewilderment at what I was seeing out of the window, it might as well have been. I'd always known India's reputation for manic driving, but the detail had somehow faded from my memory. It was as though, through the rose-tinted filter of my recollection, I had hung on to the country's more charming images – the sunsets, the smiles, the smoke-filled temples – while discarding the chaff of urban congestion and batty driving.

We were in the eye of a tornado of vehicles expanding out to every last inch of available road space, weaving, swerving, revving, braking, doing just about anything in their capacity to execute their objective, which was to keep on moving forward, no matter what. Lorries rushed past in shades of scarlet, orange and blue; yellow and black taxis barged through barely available gaps; sleek-looking coaches cruised proudly through the fray like metal maharajas; while rickety three-wheelers apparently held together by masking tape and string laced a wobbly path along any available breach.

We bolted past an elegiac road sign that read 'Speed Thrills But It Also Kills'. Speed Kills: the words burned with the power of a dozen stadium lights into my cortex as I contemplated how was I going to negotiate this traffic quagmire alone. I had already had a taste of suicidal trolley drivers and I had a throbbing leg as evidence. If a trolley could impart such a large bruise, I balked at the thought of what the blood-red lorry

– momentarily sat beside us at a traffic light – would be capable of inflicting.

Sitting behind Puran as he ploughed through the relentless throng, I wasn't sure my nerves could take the quick-fire weaving of two-wheelers between cars that were moving at surprising speeds. Many of the motorbikes were loaded with entire families. Old men on rickety bicycles at the side of the road were overtaken within an inch of their lives by lumbering lorries farting clouds of black smoke. A very knackered-looking bullock pulled a cart piled with hay and topped with six lads taking in the view from the top of the unsecured load. How was it possible, I thought, that hundreds of people weren't dying in this unholy mess every day?

The simple answer to this is that they were. In India, a person dies in a road accident every five minutes.[2] That works out to around 288 deaths per day and over 110,000 per year,[3] the highest number of road fatalities for any country. I reflected that it was more than the entire population of my home island of Jersey being snuffed out annually by crashing lorries and colliding buses. How in the name of Dick Dastardly was I going to survive this?

We pulled up outside the gates of Akhil's apartment building in Breach Candy and I relaxed my grip on the edge of the seat. As we swung into the parking lot, I saw what at first glance looked like a giant lemon stationed under a tree. There she blew (instantaneously a she, a feminine adventurer and sprightly vessel, a she in the way boats and mares are, imbued with womanly dignity and prowess): my Nano, my trusty yellow steed. She was Silver to my Lone Ranger, K.I.T.T. to my Knight Rider, the Tardis to my Dr Who; she was to be my transport, home and confidante for the next three months. I felt like a bride meeting my betrothed for the first time, and I'll admit to a few tummy tingles as my eyes met her headlights.

I stood back to inspect my Nano in the flesh. At first sight, she was funny looking, sort of awkward and boxy. Her front and back foreshortening made her seem as though someone had sliced off her bonnet and trunk. But what she lost in length, she made up for in height, and from a certain angle she almost looked as tall as she was long. Up close, the tyres appeared smaller even than in the photographs, as did the steering wheel, which you could almost substitute with a large button and not lose much in the way of design or engineering.

Like the several online testimonies I'd read had said, the interior was indeed very spacious. There was legroom galore in the front and a fair amount in the back, with a high roof and wide-span windscreen adding to the sense that a cat could safely be swung without too much damage to either the car's interior or the spinning moggie.

In terms of the dashboard, a good salesman would exhort its simplicity and straightforwardness of purpose and design. To me, it looked more like I'd been given the factory demonstration model before anyone had thought to put dials on. There was a speedometer, a petrol gauge, an engine thermostat, an air-conditioning switch, two electric window buttons – and that was pretty much all. The radio and speakers I had secretly been hoping for were nowhere to be found, even after I obstinately performed three or four searches inside the doors and under the steering wheel. Neither was there a cigarette lighter/charging socket, an omission that was to be my undoing on several legs of the trip to come.

I took a moment to contemplate the cheapest car in the world. Costs had indeed been cut. Looking at the little Nano, I had the impression that you couldn't subtract much more from her and still call her a car. I was already extremely uncomfortable with the absence of a passenger-side mirror, and was still fairly stumped as to exactly where the engine could be, as having taken down the rear backrest I found only a small storage space instead of the expected motor.

I sat in the driver's seat and turned the key. The elusive engine rumbled into life from somewhere behind me and I pushed down on the accelerator to give it a few revs. It growled back with a satisfying snarl, signalling that all was in order and she was ready to go. Relief: against the odds, I'd bought a car in India that I'd never seen before, and it appeared to work. And that was all that mattered. You could put as many ribbons and bells on a car as you like (or not, in this case) in the form of heated leather seats, a mahogany dashboard, built-in GPS, even a flux capacitor. But what was most important was that it ran, and that it would get me from my point of departure – Mumbai – to my intended destination – Mumbai – via a series of exploits all around the country. I had most definitely scored.

'Why are you buying this car?' Puran asked me with disarming frankness as he took an inaugural photograph of me standing proudly next to the Nano, one proprietary hand placed on her rear haunch.

'What do you mean?'

'Nobody is buying this Tata Nano,' he said with confidence. 'Driving it on the highways is very dangerous.'

I couldn't believe I was hearing these words from a man who minutes earlier could have passed for James Bond's driving stunt double. He continued, 'Ma'am, if you crash on the highways in the Nano, you will not be going to hospital. You will be going straight to heaven.'

I shot him a look of annoyance, which must have more truthfully resembled an expression of abject terror, as he immediately followed up with a vindication, mumbling something about how brave I was.

Still, the line between brave and gormless is a thin one. In order to err well on the side that would maximize my chances of survival, I figured I needed to swallow my pride and take some tips from the pros. I handed Puran the Nano keys and asked him to show me how it was done. He couldn't have looked happier had I gifted him a gold-plated Ferrari occupied by a trio of beauty queens. He grabbed the keys out of my hand and installed himself in the driver's seat with a sombre sense of authority. In a flash, his consternations about the car's safety evaporated and were replaced by a boyish euphoria.

'Ma'am, it's my first time driving a Nano,' he beamed as he turned on the engine.

I got in the passenger side and we reentered the chaos of Mumbai. Puran handled the car perfectly, thrusting the gear stick around and performing all manner of sharp U-turns and overtaking, while beating out a short tattoo on the horn to accompany each move. At one point we stopped at a traffic light and got a taste of the Nano's superstar status, becoming the source of intense scrutiny to the other road users gathered around us.

Not used to being the centre of attention, Puran shifted uncomfortably in his seat. 'Ma'am, everybody looking,' he said, staring with intense will at the red lights up ahead.

Within the space of ten minutes, we had swerved, ducked, blown our horn and been honked at more times than I could count. And yet Puran executed all these manoeuvres with impressive ease. He'd give a motorbike in front a terrifying rapid-fire blast of the horn before flooring the accelerator to overtake him within inches of hitting an oncoming truck, while simultaneously pointing out to me the rows of leather shops on the outskirts of the infamous Dharavi slum, where he used to work before he landed a job as a company chauffeur.

Mumbai's drivers, I concluded, had to be stout-hearted mini-Buddhas. Only a Zen-like ability to detach oneself from this chaos, coupled with the reflex capacity of a Shaolin monk, could pull someone like Puran through years of sitting behind the wheel. And yet, if unflappability was the requisite for professional road users here, then where the heck was all this aggression coming from?

From the safety of my bed that night, far from the revs and horns and exhaust fumes of the great urban road beast outside, I decided that only hard facts could comfort and reassure me. As enchanted as I was at the prospect of discovering India by car, I had no intention of doing so at the cost of my life. I went online to try to find a silver lining in the cloud of my potential annihilation.

It turned out that although the odds of my making it back alive were not great, there was some comfort to be gained at the prospect that they could be worse. The World Health Organization's Global Status Report on Road Safety told me that India clocked up 16.8 road traffic deaths per 100,000 people in 2007. It was a hell of a lot more than Britain's impressive figure of 3.59, but then it was also less than countries like Iraq, Afghanistan and Libya, which were losing between 38 and 40 people per 100,000 to road accidents each year.[4] Cheer up, I thought; at least you're not in a war zone.

Puran called me the next morning, offering his driving services for another day. This time, I was forced to decline gracefully. 'Today, Puran,' I said, trying hard to hide the wobbles in my voice, '*I* will be doing the driving.'

Puran protested. 'Ma'am, please, it is really no problem for me to come.'

'No, no really. It's fine, thanks. I need to start somewhere, don't I? I'll be just, um, fine.'

And I was. For the first part, anyway. From when I put the keys in the ignition right up to the bit when I drove up to the front gate of Akhil's building – Michael Schumacher himself couldn't have done it better. But slowly, the gates opened and the reality of a late Wednesday-morning Mumbai revealed itself to me.

This was it: I was going head first into an initiation by fire. My first instinct was to pray. I noticed there was a small plastic figurine of Ganesha stuck to the dashboard, which I presumed had been put there by Mr Shah. I knew little about Ganesha barring that he was an important Hindu god with the head of an elephant and that he was particularly revered for being a skilled remover of obstacles. It followed that he was popular with drivers in India and was to be seen fronting many a dashboard or hanging from a large number of rear-view mirrors. Although I wasn't a Hindu, I figured it could do me no harm to post a protection request at the door of the local divinities. After all, I was on their territory now.

Ploughing forward at the mercy of weekday traffic, I realized that my appeal to Ganesha was not so much a prayer to preserve me as a plea to spare me the embarrassment of writing off the car on our first excursion. That would be just awful.

A lane led from the gates to the intersection of Bhulabhai Desai Road and August Kranti Marg. I stopped the Nano at the threshold of the main road and took in the sight before me. Mumbai's cars were out in force, and they were pissed. There was a nasty snarl-up at the crossroads accompanied by a nerve-clenching dissonance of horns. At the junction, I watched the traffic speed past me. The vehicles were moving at about 30 kmph, bumper to bumper, then stopping dead in their tracks when the lights turned red and filling up every square inch of the road. I took a deep breath. How the hell was I going to infiltrate this mass? Whether moving or still, it was solid, impenetrable.

My one secret hope had been that the Nano's celebrity status might work in our favour in such situations, and that fellow drivers, roused by the glory of India's new darling, would politely step aside and let us go wherever we wanted. But India's love for the Nano didn't stretch as far as gratuitous chivalry. We were no better or worse than all the other vehicles that vied for the tiny space the road afforded us. It wouldn't have mattered if I were a Porsche or a rickshaw: the struggle was the great equalizer, and I was on my own. This was, after all, the world's largest democracy.

The thought gave me a warm, fuzzy feeling inside, which was immediately shattered by a sharp klaxon from behind. I looked in my rear-view mirror to see the face of an irate taxi driver, egging me on to take the plunge. Now I had nowhere to go but forward. Shit.

First things first, I went for the indicator, a token gesture given my options. I was stalling for time, hoping that a huge, gaping hole would open its jaws in the middle of the road and swallow me up, thus sparing me the trauma and inevitable humiliation of what I was about to do. Another blast came from behind. I winced and put the gear stick into first. I tapped the accelerator and let up the clutch ever so slightly. We moved forward about an inch to the sound of another, much longer and angrier horn from behind. I snapped back at him. 'Give it a rest will you, asshole! What the hell do you expect me to do here? Just ram into the traffic?'

He responded with another beep and moved forward enough that the Nano could surely feel him breathing down the back of her bumper.

I put out another inch, and another, holding my breath and hunching my shoulders, bracing for what would be the inevitable impact of metal at my side. No one was relenting, but neither was anyone crashing into me. I didn't stop to think about it, I just kept going, edging the Nano's flattened nose further and further out into the road. There were angry-sounding beeps and honks but, as if by a miracle, the other cars started circumventing us. How was this possible? Within seconds I had pulled out completely and joined the flow towards the traffic light, which quickly turned red and forced us to another stop.

I had done it, I thought. I had negotiated my first merge into a main road and had lived to tell the tale. The sky was the limit; Mumbai was my oyster. I was born to do this, born to be the traffic doyenne of… My roll of elation was interrupted by the light turning green again and I realized that in order to go in the direction I had planned, I needed to make a U-turn at the junction. Feeling nothing less than superhuman after my exit from Akhil's road, I swung to the right and began to dig my way into the crowded lane that was moving the other way. Thinking on my toes, I took advantage of a couple of metres' space in front of a bulky bus that was hobbling towards us and clearly having trouble gathering speed. I let rip, hauling my button-wheel to the right and getting in the space right before the bus, much to the driver's annoyance, which he expressed with a succession of galled horns.

'Bite me!' I imagined calling back over my shoulder.

My first U-turn. I was on fire. I released a reserved whoop, and another – ten minutes later – after cranking the gearstick into third for the first time. Ebullience manifest in the driver's seat; this was it, I was doing it. Our first foray into the Mumbai traffic, the Nano and I, and here we were, minutes later, still rolling and definitely not wrapped around a lamppost. And if we could get through Mumbai unscathed, the rest of India would be a breeze. In a rush of maternal tenderness, I smacked the wheel with congratulatory ardour. 'Nice going, Abhilasha!'

Abhilasha. It was a name that my now ex-boyfriend had suggested to me when he caught wind of my purchase. It meant desire, wish, aspiration and affection in Sanskrit. I had initially spurned the idea of naming the car, never having been much into the practice of anthropomorphizing inanimate objects. Yet since he had offered up the token with such sincere poignancy, I felt compelled to bring it along. A bit of my past mixed in with my present; something old to mix in with this something new.

Despite this epiphany, that night I lay in bed under the flickering ceiling fan while images from the day's traffic returned in post-traumatic flashback sequence. My brain was trying to process the abundance of incomprehensible and counterintuitive events I had witnessed from behind the wheel. The worst, and most embarrassing of all, had been my attempt at a parallel park. Stopping outside a street stall to buy a bottle of water, I figured I'd give the manoeuvre a whirl, just to see how I could handle it with my pint-sized steering wheel and no passenger-side window. The results had not been encouraging.

The space that had opened itself to me was bookended by a grey Maruti and a bullock cart carrying a menacing-looking gas tank. The spot was Nano-sized, which is to say it was tight. Unfamiliar with the dimensions of my new car and somewhat inhibited by the explosive potential of the nearby gas tank and the judgemental gaze of its guardian bullock, the operation took me several attempts to execute, though my efforts did provide an amusing diversion for a group of taxi drivers on their tea break. Finally a couple of the guys for whom the pain of the tragi-comedy was too much to bear broke off from their mates and came to help me wiggle my way in. There was a flurry of raised hands, beckoning me in every direction, then sporadically making me slam down the brakes with horrified expressions on their faces and urgent beats on the Nano's posterior as I came close to blemishing her perfect yellow paintwork. Cars were passing at very close quarters, honking their horns in outraged protest at my blocking the road, and I broke out in a sweat as I heaved the wheel from one side back to the other.

The whole dire episode almost ended in another disaster as a passing teenage boy came so close to the side of the car that I actually clipped his elbow with the wing mirror. Mortified at having caused my first human casualty, I rolled down the window in haste, ready with heartfelt apologies. The lad was frozen to the spot, fixing me fearfully before embarking on a soliloquy of regret. I tried to reassure him it had been my mistake, but he wasn't having any of it. We parted, awkwardly.

So, back in Naresh Fernandes' office, I was being served my backside.

'The last thing India needs is another 100,000 cars on the road,' he said, continuing his tirade against the automobile industry, the private sector and scum like me that were needlessly polluting and congesting his country for nothing short of apparent larks. He was currently referring to the Nano's famous pre-order list and gesturing at the jammed-up Keshav Rao Khadye Marg four storeys below, whose upwardly wafting cacophony of klaxons and horns provided a grumbling backdrop to our conversation.

I started to flush: in my eagerness to take my new Nano on the journey of a lifetime, I had turned a blind eye to the opinions of the car's detractors. There was, of course, a whole counter-Nano community whose slant on the car ranged from its being a bit shabbily made to its being an unmitigated disaster for Indian society.

The first peeps of dissent I uncovered came, unsurprisingly, from the e-pages of Topgear.com. Its review of the car ran under the headline 'Cheap Trick' and could be summed up in the quote: 'What can you get for the price of a sofa? Not a lot, in all honesty.' The article drew particular attention to what *Top Gear* perceived to be the car's cloudy safety aspects, concluding, 'Exactly what those [safety] requirements are remain unclear, but at least the Nano should be safer than a scooter. Or, say, hopping.'[5]

The eco-activists were also pitching in on the matter: 'This car promises to be an environmental disaster of substantial proportions,' proclaimed Daniel Esty, professor of environmental law at Yale, just after the Nano's release.[6] Dr Rajendra Pachauri, chairman of the UN Panel for Climate Change and director-general of the Energy Resource Institute, made his position clear by stating he was 'having nightmares' about the car,[7] an attitude that was echoed by environmental activist Sunita Narain of the Centre for Science and Environment, who asked the stinging question: 'Cars cost us the earth. Can we afford it?'[8] In an article in her environment fortnightly, *Down to Earth*, she launched an attack on government subsidies for the auto industry that completely disregarded the public transport sector. 'As the Nano rolls out, think about how we subsidize the car and tax the bus,' she said, illustrating her point by reminding her readers that in many Indian states, buses paid twelve times the tax of cars.[9]

So, despite the fact that there were masses of people desperate to get their hands on a Nano, there was also a large number of Indians for whom the car didn't stand as a liberator of the low-income belt, but rather as a giant pain in the ass that would add more traffic to the already over-congested roads.

Naresh Fernandes was one of these people. It was becoming clear to me that he was not, like me, a driving enthusiast. He was a public transport kind of guy, and as far as he was concerned, an army of shiny new Nanos flooding the market and seducing the country's emerging new middle class could only spell congestion doom.

I asked Naresh how he got around the city and he replied by train – like the 6.3 million other Mumbaikars who choose to commute via the suburban rail network every day to avoid the traffic clogging the city's arteries. It might be an environmentally friendly, socially responsible alternative, but Mumbai's trains were also straining under the weight of their passengers. A staggering 3,700 people die on their way to work in the city each year[10] – by being pushed out of overcrowded carriages, electrocuted by hanging cables when sitting on the roof or crossing the tracks and getting flattened by an oncoming locomotive. Naresh argued that rather than piling its roads up with more vehicles, India needed first to resolve the existing issues with its public transport system.

'The situation we now have in India is a lot like what happened in pre-war America, when the motor lobby effectively blocked all prospects of a public transportation network,' Naresh explained. I was nodding like a plastic St Bernard. He continued, making the popular comparison of the Nano to the Ford Model T, America's own 'people's car', a century earlier. It was a historical moment that not only initiated the modern concept of the production line but also marked the genesis of the United States as a nation of cars and not trains. The resulting impact on society, urban planning and the environment, not to mention a foreign policy driven in large part by the politics of oil, has been immense. Could India go the same way? Was the country really at such a significant crossroads? Surely the railway system in India – admittedly outdated and flawed in many aspects – was extensive and functional in a way that it had never been in the US? And should we expect a private company like Tata to care about issues of public transport? Was it not doing India a favour by furnishing its people with an alternative to asphyxiation by overcrowded train carriages, high-octane roof surfing and a gruesome flattening on the railway tracks?

I began to spin with the symbolic consequences of the task I was about to undertake. I was in over my head and probably should have taken advantage of a break in the conversation to make my excuses and leave. I felt like a bumbling Englisher, a parachute hack of the worst variety, an opportunist about to contribute nothing but another (fuel-efficient) death machine to the people of India. What had until this moment been a harmless voyage of discovery in the only vehicle I could really afford had suddenly evolved into a brutal crusade of devastation and destruction. I was kicking myself. Nano Schmano. I should have constructed a biodegradable windsurf with wheels that was partially fuelled by recycled waste and the tears of children. Now that would have been a worthier pitch; virtuous even. I could have gotten Bono or Bob Geldof or Arundhati Roy on board. They could have helped me plant some trees in my wake to make up for the tarmac erosion for which I would inevitably be responsible.

But the fact remained that I was the owner of a (nearly) new Tata Nano and only days away from embarking on a three-month drive around India. And all I needed was just a hint of encouragement.

Now it was finally time to make a dent in the 10,000 km journey, I suddenly found my safe, burrowed, Queen of Sheba–like existence in Akhil's apartment very appealing. It had been more than a week since I had arrived, and I hadn't lifted a finger in the direction of self-sufficiency. There was Mohan who cooked, and his younger brother who cleaned, washed my clothes and returned them to me ironed and interleaved with pages from a month-old copy of the *Times of India*. There was Puran who still called every day to see if I needed his services, clearly sceptical of my assertions that I was now self-driven.

And then there was the marvellous Akhil, who made intermittent appearances between meetings and business trips, only materializing for an early breakfast or late at night. I had awoken groggy and jetlagged on my second morning in Mumbai to an enthusiastic rapping on my bedroom door. I opened it to find my beaming friend dressed in British Airways pyjamas, suggesting I accompany him for a series of yoga stretches and pranayamic breathing exercises on his terrace. A platter of eggs and toast was then laid out before me, while Akhil munched away on a bowl of chilled sprouts, insisting that his was the breakfast of champions. The same evening he returned with a bottle of red wine, a local product he had just discovered and maintained was excellent. We had a glass to the amplified notes of a Mozart piano concerto that he blasted at top volume to demonstrate the power of his new surround-sound system that ran through the whole apartment, terrace and all. Mohan then brought each of us a cup of Horlicks, and Akhil retired to his desk for more work.

When he wasn't there, I padded around the marble floors of his apartment, inspecting his book collection under Mohan's watchful eye. There was no doubting it: I was ensconced in the lap of luxury, living in an India that belonged to only a tiny minority, and the longer I stayed, the harder it would be for me to get out and see the rest. Large city apartments inhabited by upper- and middle-class citizens with a significant disposable income were the domain of only about 6% of the country's population. Akhil's place was a world away from the standard of living endured by the majority of India's people who continue to subsist below the poverty line, something I figured would become clear as soon as I worked up the bottle to leave and see what lay beyond the sugar-coated gates of Breach Candy.

This cloistered time was conducive to reflection. If I stuck around for too long during the day, the empty flat would start to amplify my own feelings of solitude and disorientation at having come so far in such a short time. Under the steady gaze of a collection of Chopra novels, my thoughts began to stray from matters of the road to matters more interior. A bombshell attack of nostalgia for my previous stable couple-life in Mexico City would assail me from time to time and I would go out onto Akhil's terrace to contemplate the muggy Mumbai skyline and try to exhale the weight that hung between my ribs. The bewildering space that remains after the departure of a partner is a gap that's hopelessly difficult to fill. The only thing to do was dig in and wait for the other parts of my life to expand and dissolve the hole by means of slow erosion; in the meantime, I would bury my emotions under the avalanche of this all-consuming mission.

Looking south from Akhil's terrace, I could see a recession of skyscrapers lining the coast. They disappeared into the miasmic cloud of mist or pollution that's on perma-hover around the city, masking the horizon, so I couldn't quite see the point where the sky and the earth came together. And whatever that obscured point in the distance, be it road trip heaven or hell, that was my target. It was time to leave.

Waiting for me in the car park was Naresh's evil corporate death machine. I was still grappling to navigate the sea of moral iffiness and doubt my meeting with him had set me off on, and the only way to do that, I concluded, was to pretend his challenge to my integrity had never happened. I called on my trusty inner broom to sweep away the dust of bad feeling under my carpet of denial as I shoehorned my bags into Abhilasha's backseat and set out for India in the little yellow anti-hero that was about to carry this clueless wench across the length and breadth of an infinite country.

RULE OF THE ROAD #1
There Are No Rules

Or, to be more precise, no sanctioned written rules. Despite all my best efforts, I could find no such thing as an official Indian Highway Code. Initially, I began to fret: after my first few days of highly focused driving, I felt the need for relief in the form of some guidance, a document of commonly accepted rules and practice by which to measure transgression and misdeed.

I came from a place of one-way systems and yellow grids; of no-parking areas, dedicated bus and cycle lanes, and a terrifically courteous roundabout system particular to the island of Jersey called 'Filter in Turn'. But I was not in Jersey any more. Its unhurried, polite civility was a world away from the mobocracy of India's roads; this was a country where it seemed every man, woman and Nano had to fight for survival or risk annihilation.

I was convinced that a set of instructions had to exist somewhere, a tome that ordained correct lane driving, overtaking rules, guidelines for the interaction of animal and machine, of two-, three-, four- and eight-wheeled vehicles. Surely someone had to have sat down and created a manifesto by which all of India's incredibly diverse road beings could live together in harmony. If there was no right, how could there be any wrong, and vice versa? World order as I knew it began to crumble as I contemplated the grim eventuality that, if it couldn't be found on Google, it was possible that India might not have a national highway code. If it didn't, what then?

Pulling myself together, I went to the search engine with my request: 'Indian Driving Rules'. The results that came from more unofficial sources were mildly encouraging: the first couple sprouted from a site called indiadrivingschools.com, whose homemade list of pointers for the road was propelled by the notion that drivers 'should primarily focus on ways to control aggressiveness'.

Of the 27 commandments that followed, a surprising number were concerned with anger management: 'Avoid creating a situation that may provoke another motorist' instructed rule number two, while rule four ordained against 'inappropriate facial and hand gestures'. It was a bit like reading a driving manual from Edwardian England, more concerned with manners and etiquette than actual skills. I half expected to see some pointers as to what action to take in the event of a fault with the hand crank, or a rip in the overhead canopy. Even more uncannily antiquated was the complete disregard for women's lib demonstrated in rule 22, which was concerned with pedestrians and emphasized the need for special regard to be given to 'senior citizens, handicapped and ladies'.

The Delhi Traffic Police's initial approach was similar, in that its primary goal appeared to be keeping drivers calm behind the wheel. 'Maintain your cool, even in adverse situations,' the site read, adding rather compassionately, 'you may be burdened with unending number of problems at the home or office, but keep them aside before you venture on to the roads'.

The following section dealt with genuine road rules and featured a couple of fuzzy directives that in my opinion wouldn't stand up in court in the event of a collision between, say, a Nano and a lorry thundering towards it in the wrong lane. The first rule was concerned with the implementation of left-hand driving. One vestige of the Raj had been to employ British driving principles in India, so the British standard, left, also became the Indian rule of thumb. Thumb was the operative term, in particular according to the Delhi Traffic Police, which was all thumbs in its description of exactly where drivers should try to place their vehicles: 'How far from the left side of the road you should drive depends upon the road condition and the type of traffic on it. But, as a driver you must drive sufficiently to the left.' I reflected that from a legal point of view at least, 'sufficiently to the left' was painfully insufficient to cover the spectrum of eventualities. One man's suf-ficiently left might be another's way too far to the right, and the road was surely no backdrop for the volatility of such subjectivi-ties to play themselves out against.

Another rule endorsed by the DTP was lane driving. 'Every road has lanes, whether marked or not,' the web page stated. So if lanes are there, you drive between them. Easy peasy. But what if they're not? Drive sufficiently to the left? Call your local coun-cil works department and inform them of a substandard road? Choose another route? All sensible suggestions, but in fact the Delhi Traffic Police had an even more ingenious plan where absent lanes were concerned: 'When they are not marked, divide the road mentally into appropriate lanes.'

Divide the road mentally... I lingered on this one. So what the Delhi Traffic Police was asking of the capital's drivers was that in the absence of sanctioned road signs and signals, they insert the necessary guidelines by use of their imagination. It was a fascinating principle and one sure to shave a few rupees from the annual road maintenance budget. Indeed, why stop at lane mark-ings? Think of all the money that could be saved by the simple act of imagining traffic lights at busy junctions. Drivers could save minutes upon minutes by imagining a red signal to be green and so zipping straight through. Or what about fantasizing the speed limit? Dreaming up warnings for slippery surfaces or impending dangerous curves in random places where they may or may not occur? It was a near-perfect plan for smoothly running roads, the only danger being that in the unlikely event of two drivers contra-dicting one another, overlap might occur. But, with more than 10 million vehicles on the road in the city, realistically, what would be the chances of that happening?

2

TAKE-OFF – Down the NH66

MUMBAI to NAGAON; KM 0–118

What do you mean you don't have an address? How do you receive post?' I asked Russell Korgaonkar, my old school friend from London whom I was going to visit along with his wife Alexia at his family home in the village of Nagaon, about 150 km south of Mumbai. It was to be a gentle immersion into rural India, a buffer to help ease the transition of my delicate frame from the high life of staying with Akhil to what was inevitably in store over the next 10,000 km.

Russell had already made no secret of the fact he disapproved of my quest. 'I think you're mad,' he said in his customary deadpan tone. 'Why would you want to drive around India in that ridiculous car?' He followed up his admonitions with gloomy forecasts like 'It'll take you a month to leave Mumbai' and, more bluntly, 'You'll probably die, you know that, right?'

In all the years I've known Russell, a second-generation Indian and dyed-in-the-wool Londoner, he's shown very little enthusiasm for exploring his ancestral lands beyond the vacations at his family villa in Nagaon, and has admitted to never having so much as touched the wheel of a car in India for fear of an instant meltdown.

'Don't worry about the road name,' he advised me over the phone as I sat in thick traffic on Mumbai's Eastern Expressway, headed towards the six-lane Vashi Bridge crossing Thane Creek, the massive inland harbour that defines the eastern edge of

Greater Mumbai. 'Just get to Nagaon. I'll meet you somewhere on the road.'

I knew from the start that navigation would be an issue. Before leaving London, I had procured a £5.99 map of India that I packed in with my other indispensable navigational aids: an outdated edition of *Lonely Planet India* and a copy of a book called *Beginner's Hindi*. I casually figured that in any eventuality this triumvirate of travel tools couldn't help me with, the gods would surely intervene. I had opened up the map for the first time at Akhil's place, my second attempt to do so after I had wrestled with and loudly ripped the display copy in London when trying to sneak a not-so-subtle peek at its scale. And what I slowly began to realize as I studied the great triangular outline of the Indian subcontinent on my hands and knees was that this document might serve me better as emergency loo roll than as any useful implement for planning a road trip. Flapping under the sheer size of the map in a corner of Stanfords, I'd been convinced it was big enough to show every junction, pothole and chai stall from Kashmir to Kerala. But straining my eyes to see the little dot that was Mumbai and the thick, snaky road that emanated to its right and headed a whole centimetre over to Pune, I became aware that this was simply not going to fly.

Maps, schmaps; if I was driving a vehicle of the new millennium, I needed the navigational technology to match. I needed a GPS. The next day, I called Akhil's assistant Prasad for guidance on the best place to buy one. He answered (and I'm sure he was stifling a laugh here) that there was no such thing in India. The country was so vast and the roads so numerous and often, well, unofficial, that there would be no possible way to catalogue them successfully. 'Most roads don't even have names,' he informed me cheerily. 'Don't waste your time with this.'

I might well have taken Prasad's word for it, but I was bent on doing as much damage limitation as possible. The few hours I had spent holding my breath as I drove around the city with Puran had shown me just how much of my attention would need to go to the basic act of driving; I suspected there was no way I could concede even an ounce of concentration to unfolding and squinting at maps while at the wheel. This hunch, coupled with the overarching concern that I might not even be able to find my way out of Mumbai, let alone all the way around India and back again, convinced me to disregard Prasad's advice completely and head to a Croma electronics store – India's answer to Best Buy – in a search for nothing short of a miracle.

And indeed, the marvel showed itself in the form of a Mio Moov 200 Satellite Navigation unit. I was overcome.

'Really? And it, umm, works?' I asked Sunil, the smiling, badge-wearing shop assistant who was holding the blessed item up before my disbelieving eyes.

'Yes, ma'am. Perfectly. I will demonstrate.' He jabbed his finger at the screen. Within a minute he had me going 1,200 km to the Taj Mahal and arriving by the following evening. I was sold. Sunil packed the gadget back into the box and waved a cable at me.

'In-car charging,' he beamed with pride.

Half an hour later, from the darkness of the subterranean car park of Mumbai's Phoenix Mills shopping centre, I let out the long, despairing cry of consumer dreams cruelly dashed against the rocks of impracticality. The Nano had no charging outlet: no cigarette lighter, nowhere to plug in the damn GPS. Again, I refused to accept defeat and began to tug at two circular plastic discs down by the gear stick, which, due to their size and positioning, looked like prime candidates for a slyly concealed charging port. However, the discs failed to budge and I lost a portion of a fingernail in the process.

Injured digit hanging limply in mouth, I consoled myself with the wall-plug power charger that also came with the GPS. With languid optimism I mused that the Mio Moov would have at least three or maybe even four hours of life at full charge. With diligent use of battery power and assiduous advance route planning, we'd make it around the country with the efficiency of a well-oiled machine. What could possibly go wrong?

'Roger, Russ. Nagaon. I'll just feed that into the GPS.'

I reached over to the Mio Moov – which I had suctioned onto a small triangular section of window to my right – and punched in N-A-G-A-O-N. The Moov mulled over a little egg timer for several seconds before triumphantly presenting me with a result: Nagaon was 2,800 km away with an estimated journey time of 40 hours.

Huh? No, not Nagaon, Assam, you fool, I need Nagaon, Maharashtra. I tried again, with no joy. It seemed the only Nagaon in India the Moov wished to sanction was up in the hills somewhere near Bhutan. So I tried the next largest town, Alibag, and was relieved that it came up with the correct distance and a projected arrival time of 8 pm.

Surely not. Six blimming hours to cover just over 100 km? Impossible. That would mean an average speed of around 17 kmph. There had to be a mistake. I jabbed at the settings options on the Moov; clearly it had been preprogrammed for Sunday afternoon strolling speed and not highway driving. But there was nothing I could do to correct the estimate, and looking at my watch I got the sinking feeling that there might be an element of truth to the Moov's preposterous assertion: it had already been an hour and a half since I had left Akhil's place to embark on the Great Journey Around India and we'd barely clocked up 20 km. Not quite the cork-popping, flag-waving parade I had envisioned; the scene that surrounded us on the northbound NH3 more closely resembled a biblical exodus ground to a standstill.

We were crammed into a tiny gap between a gleaming white space-age Ashok Leyland coach with tinted windows and an Acer truck loaded with cement bags. As I grumpily prodded the Moov's screen for a way out of this unholy jam – a secret road leading from Mumbai, perhaps, that no one else knew – I noticed that Abhilasha and I had become a source of breathless mirth for a group of schoolchildren literally overflowing from the back of a Tempo shoehorned into a crack in the traffic ahead of me. The kids, pre-teen and dressed in baby-blue uniforms – the boys lanky with home-cut crops, the girls with white-ribboned pigtails – were gesturing eagerly at the Nano and shouting out its duosyllabic name again and again till I thought they might go hoarse. Smiles were shot out through the windscreen at me as they waved their hands with glee and brought them to up to their foreheads. 'Hello madam! Madam! Madam! Hello madam! Nano, madam, Nano! Na-no, na-no-na-no-na-no! Hello madam! Nano!' And then squeals – deep-throated howls – of laughter.

Feeling like a chimp at London Zoo, I awkwardly raised my right hand in a salutary gesture. I smiled, flattered by the children's attention and pleased finally to be garnering some enthusiasm, albeit inadvertently. But as the spectacle continued and I realized we weren't going anywhere fast, I began to melt in the limelight. My jaw was starting to hurt from my 'hello children' perma-grin and I began wondering exactly how long the kids could maintain so much enthusiasm for a small yellow car. I went back to fiddling with the GPS, this time with a far sterner expression on my face that I intended to resemble exaggerated concentration. But the children failed to interpret my facial 'do not disturb' sign and continued to shake and quiver in the direction of the Nano. We were rock stars, celebrities, VIPs stuck in a traffic jam on the road to nowhere.

A horn parped from behind and a motorbike appeared in my side mirror, squeezing itself through the space between the Nano and the Ashok Leyland. Ten tiny fingers and then a larger pair of hands walked their way across Abhilasha's back window, steadying the bike that was already wobbling under its hefty load. From what I could see, the vehicle was being steered by a five-year-old girl with braided pigtails. She was gripping the handlebars from between the legs of her father, who was deeply involved in some kind of transaction via his cell phone. Behind him sat a woman, presumably his wife, who was holding to her chest a baby, recognizable as such only by the appearance of a set of minute toes that peeked from under a blanket. The woman was wearing a pink and yellow sari that flapped around her and beat against the number-plate, while the tail end of the fabric danced teeth-clenchingly close to the spokes of the back wheel. She was sitting side-saddle with a look of nonchalance more appropriate to the resigned boredom of a doctor's waiting room than to moving among large vehicles along a main road with nothing to hold on to. The hands that should have been clutching her husband or a pillion bar were instead occupied with clinging onto her newborn child with the kind of relaxed composure I could only replicate embedded in an armchair, sleepily thumbing a remote control. They were like a campaign family for suicidal bike riding. As they wobbled past Abhilasha, they took a swift right in front of the Ashok Leyland and scooted off into the distance, joining the flow of two-wheelers hurtling past the disgruntled vehicles that were ground to a halt on the NH3.

As I watched the motorcycle disappear, I moved Abhilasha forward another few centimetres and began to wonder whether manning up and getting my hands on an Enfield would have been a better idea after all. How much time was I destined to lose sitting in congestion like this over the next few months? Still, after a quick chew over some simple statistics, I figured it was worth the wait: more people die on motorbikes than on any other form of transport in India, including all car, bicycle and rickshaw deaths combined.[11] It was a damn dangerous form of transport made all the more menacing by the acrobatics of those intent on using it as their family vehicle.

According to legend, it was this very image of an overloaded motorbike making its way through a city jam that sowed the seed of the Nano in the mind of Ratan Tata, who originally conceived of the car one day back in 2001 while idling through Bangalore traffic. His revelation was that motorbike accidents could be considerably reduced if the vehicles were not used for gravity-defying configurations of humans, children, animals, furniture, farm produce and building materials. However, the financial gap between an affordable motorbike and the cheapest available car was huge, and it occurred to Tata that there was a niche in the market for something in between: a cheap car that was only a bit more expensive than a motorbike, but that could safely accommodate whole families without the danger of losing a child to a sharp bend in the road, or of Mum being garrotted by her sari. This was the story that would be quoted again and again in accounts of the Nano's legendary rise, that of a socially responsible answer to a straightforward and very urgent need.

It's a heart-warming tale, and from all the accounts I had read of Tata's various philanthropic projects, I had no doubt the fellow had people's best interests at heart. However, being a rather astute businessman, there was no way he wouldn't have snuck at least a little peek at the figures before committing to a project that finally required an investment of Rs 1,800 crore ($320 million).

As in most Asian countries, motorbikes have a huge market share in India: something like three-quarters of all vehicles on the road are a motorized two-wheeler (which would also of course explain the hideously inflated death rate). Cars, on the other hand, account for only about 13% of India's vehicles.[12] What with the country's fast-expanding economy hitching up standards of living and providing hundreds of thousands of families who had previously lived hand to mouth with disposable income, the future looked bright for the car market, especially if those cars were priced just a smidgen higher than a good motorbike. In order to start making profits on the huge investment in the Nano, economists predicted that Tata would need to sell about one million cars. And if he was aiming to nick some of his customers from the two-wheeler segment, he'd need about 10% of them to reach his targets. It was a gamble, but it appeared to be a pretty good one. With the economy up in India, and with more and more people emerging with the financial resources to realize their aspirations, one of the first places I imagined they'd go would be straight to the car dealership.

So it seemed to me that Tata's vision made sense both on an economic level and a humanitarian one. And despite being stuck in excruciating traffic, I was still able to draw some comfort from my situation and appreciate what a luxury the four-wheeled vehicle really was. The late-afternoon sun burned outside while an air-conditioned breeze blew through my hair; my steering hands were free to concentrate on turning the wheel and occasionally checking my phone, unencumbered as they were by the weight of an infant; my bags were piled safely on the backseat and were not jiggling precariously between my knees.

But then there was the other consideration: traffic. As I and thousands of other drivers waited in line to shuffle out of Mumbai at a funereal pace, the motorbike family was long gone into the distance, as were the scores of other two-wheelers that passed me a dozen a minute. If Abhilasha were a bike, we'd be joining them, and by now, I fantasized, we'd be cruising an open country road. After all, if motorbikes really did count for three-quarters of all India's vehicles, then surely it was they that kept the country from coming to a nationwide standstill? I looked around at all the vehicles that were crowding around me in a bid to get out of the city, imagined our number amplified three times over and winced. How could India's roads ever stand such an escalation?

In theory, they should be able to. India has one of the lowest car densities in the world, meaning its car-to-kilometres-of-road ratio is very small indeed: 5,[13] to be precise, as opposed to the US's 38 and the UK's 77.[14] This is a shocking figure that basically attests to the fact that there are fifteen times fewer vehicles in proportion to the length of roads in India than there are in the UK. And although I had frequently been stuck in traffic in London, I had rarely seen gridlock of these proportions back home. So what was going wrong? What were the Indian authorities doing, or rather not doing, such that so few cars could cause this much congestion? The answer was not forthcoming, but I had 10,000 km to try to figure it out.

Landfall finally came in the form of a McDonald's whose golden arches appeared between the towers of Navi Mumbai, Bombay's[15] high-rise residential suburb. Three hours into the journey and we hadn't even crossed the city limits – it beggared belief. I needed an incentive, a reason to continue pushing through the morass. Caffeine, processed protein, carbohydrates – anything would do. I nosed the Nano's flat-packed beak into the parking lot and went inside to find that this unremarkable roadside fast-food chain was in fact *the* place for the swinging youth of Navi Mumbai. It was mobbed with hipsters, kids in drainpipe jeans and gelled hair, who sat sipping coke floats and giving me the occasional 'you're not from around here' side glance during lulls in their conversations.

I shuffled towards the counter with the furtive sheepishness of the new girl at school and ordered a cappuccino, which I half expected to be bullied off me by a gang of Big Mac–wielding hipsters. I could almost feel the conversation restart as the door closed behind me, and with a sigh that felt like I'd just had a brush with a hiding, I took out my phone to call Russell.

'You're where?'

'The Maccy-Dees in Navi Mumbai. You must know it. It's where all the cool kids hang.'

'What the hell are you doing still in Mumbai? It's quarter to six.'

Russell was nervous, and for good reason. Daylight was fading and I had another 80 km to go to Nagaon. Driving at night appeared to be something that all Indians, or at least the ones I had spoken to – like Russell, Akhil, Prasad, Puran, Naresh and even Sunil the Sat Nav whizz in Croma – feared like the Bogeyman. Once the outlandish and idiotic idea that I was taking the Nano past the limits of Navi Mumbai was absorbed into the individual psyches of my advisers, all that usually remained was to utter grimly, 'Be careful.' And then, 'But whatever you do, just don't drive at night.'

Their words resounded through my guts and stirred a family of gremlins that resided deep inside. When I dared to ask why, I was fed a litany of disaster scenarios and horror stories that ranged from the sheer paralysis of not being able to see a thing on an ill-lit, unmarked road, blinded by the full beams of oncoming traffic, to the apparent notoriety of long-distance truck drivers who aided their road concentration not through the traditional methods of stimulants like coffee, tea or the indigenous rocket fuel, Thums Up, but rather through the ingestion of copious alcohol. Not much fancying the prospect of a Mahindra lorry–Bagpiper whisky combo, I decided that this advice was best heeded and that all journeys would and must be completed by sunset. All, except of course this first one.

'Holy – effing – shit.'

I was straining up a steep incline, my foot flooring the accelerator, causing Abhilasha to bleat indignantly. I was wedged between an unknown bushy darkness to my left on the edge of the road, a doddery truck up front, and another truck to my right that was attempting to overtake us by accelerating its lard-arse up the hill, heralding its laboured ascent with its thunderous horn. I was inches, seconds, decibels away from death by unpleasant squishing.

I scoured my driving databanks for possible bailout options, but there was nothing I had ever experienced to provide a solution to this truck sandwich: the only alternatives that seemed feasible were slamming on the brakes, or swerving left into the bushes where I could take respite and possibly cry. But a quick glance in my rear-view mirror assured me quickly that neither plan was going to work: the incandescent yellow glare told of an angry corpus of vehicles on my tail, salivating at the prospect of taking a punt at my posterior.

The bright side of being wedged at right angles between two metal giants was that the one on my right was temporarily shielding me from the stream of traffic coming from the opposite direction. The procession, which I presumed had been forced off the road due to the presence of a large lorry in their own lane, had been burning headlight-shaped troughs into my retina in a carpet-bomb succession of nuclear explosions for the last hour. I wasn't sure if they all had their high beams on, or if it was the quality of the air, the dust, the humidity, or smoke from evening fires that diffused, reflected and even magnified the photons, but each time a set of lights came into my field of vision, it annihilated everything else around it, including the vehicle in front. This would force me to negotiate my way along the road, according to the principle of keeping the bastard bright beams always on my right and the truck in front in a state of cloudy near-visibility.

Jesus, this is not a joke, I thought, as I sat up straight, gripped the wheel and put every inch of my being and focus into keeping the car on an even keel and out of the way. Although the Nano's speedometer was reading a meagre 30 kmph, I actually felt more like I was negotiating a Formula One circuit with Vaseline in my eyes, against a cast of raving truck drivers who were all jumped up on some rather mettle-enhancing crack.

There was no choice but to keep up, although even this was soon an insufficient strategy. The truck in front of me began to bear sharply to the right, pushing into the truck next to it and forcing that further back into the oncoming lane. The manoeuvre was accompanied from all sides with a doleful roar of horns, including from the line of traffic in the opposite direction that was once again propelled off the road by the obstinate truck hogging their own god-given thoroughfare.

'What could he possibly be...' I started to mutter incredu-lously, before it became clear that what I was witnessing, and indeed was in the vortex of, was a daredevil double overtake: the truck in front that was already being so painfully passed by another was executing an overhaul of its own. Through the grey cloud of the accelerating vehicle's exhaust fumes, the hind legs of some large black animal came into view to my left, then another pair, and then another, all of which were soon accompanied by torsos, tails and lolling heads. They were bullocks – bulls without balls – and, as I was set to find out, as common a form of transport in India as the village tractor.

Within a few seconds, the bunch of bullocks had turned into a veritable herd, plodding contentedly at the command of a tiny man with a dirty-white turban who walked in their midst holding aloft a cane as though he were a tourist guide herding a sightseeing flock. I felt the thwack of a couple of shit-caked tails hitting the Nano's bodywork as we crawled past the indifferent beasts in a respectful and silent cortege. The last bullock behind us, the horns restarted, as did the efforts of the big fat lorry to get ahead of his counterpart. It was harrowing to watch, but he ultimately made it in front, with a left-ways wiggle that elicited a surprise whoop of relief from me.

Within minutes that particular party was over and traffic on the road thinned out. Then it was just me and the huge truck I'd been trailing for over an hour now; I'd been overtaken by every member of the impatient mob that had been straining behind me, leaving in their wake an eerily quiet instant of res-pite. Deciding the moment was ripe to try a little overtaking of my own, I shifted down into third gear and hit the gas. We were still on a bit of an incline and the Nano didn't pick up speed with quite as much gusto as I hoped, but after some gentle encouragement and motivation tricks ('Come on girl, you know you can do it. Let's show fatty here what we're made of') we finally edged past the behemoth and had nothing but a dark, open road ahead of us.

The NH66, my route from Navi Mumbai down to Maharashtra's seaside Nagaon, stretched ahead of us into the darkness. But the Nano's headlights, not a jot on the stadium-strength peepers of its peers, were not doing the best job lighting the way, and while I was fumbling with the switches to try to activate the full beams, I became aware that the dividing tracks of the road were shifting to the left underneath me. For some idiotically naive reason, I put this down to the road having widened to two lanes in either direction and congratulated myself for having passed through the eye of the storm and the worst part of the road unscathed. Now we'd be cruising all the way to the ocean.

This assumption turned out to be a very bad error of judgement. I rounded a bend only to be immersed in an explosion of light coupled with an outraged honk somewhere right in front of me. I instinctively swerved to the left and missed the oncoming vehicle by inches. It transpired that my two-lane fantasy was just that; in the end the road was only one lane in each direction, and I had been driving, quite evidently, in the *wrong* one. Within hours of my first auto outing in India, I had come close to being trouser-pressed by lumbering lorries, had my eyeballs fried, and then nearly annihilated myself by way of sheer stupidity, almost dragging the Mother Ship down with me into the jaws of hell. Was this what the next 10,000 km would look like?

The following hour passed in a blur while I maintained the concentration of a tightrope walker. The calm that had been broken by my earlier veering-off into the wrong lane turned out to be something of an oddity. The traffic was back in full monsoon-level flow on both sides, headlights blazing, horns blaring. I assumed a stiff, white-knuckled position behind the wheel, my nose almost touching the windscreen, my eyes squinting into the approaching glare. I hardly dared blink: one wrong move and I'd be tinned meat in a little yellow can.

The GPS was frustratingly impervious to the road rage outside. Its own version of our sordid highway reality was a little blue arrow calmly pointing forward on a clear yellow line that snaked out into infinity, unencumbered by the deranged *son et lumière* that was the truth of the world beyond my window. I scowled as I noticed there were even a few little stars to complete the idyllic calm of the night-time sky of the parallel Sat Naviverse, to which the GPS responded by flashing the outline of an empty red battery in my direction and death-rattling off into oblivion.

'Crap!'

I stabbed at the screen with a sweaty finger, performing mini-CPR on the undeserving gadget. It was no good. I glanced at my watch: time of death 8.13 pm. With at least twenty more kilometres to Nagaon, I needed directions. The road signs that appeared between bouts of visibility were all in Hindi or Marathi – two languages of which I had no inkling whatsoever – so they might as well have been hieroglyphs. I reached for my phone and poked clumsily at its tiny interface in an attempt to locate myself on its map app, a procedure that took several minutes to execute in between having to refer back to the road and having my optical nerves barbecued by fellow motorists. The signal was low and the map was irritatingly slow to load. The dot that was me flashed godforsaken against the bleak existential background of a grey grid, a little blue light lost in nameless space. I shook the phone in vain and started to perform figures of eight with it above the steering wheel, to no effect. I glanced at the little red rectangle in the top corner, which warned me that only 3% of the battery was left, and as the map struggled to download some form of cartographic image from the World Wide Web, the effort became too much for the device; it too performed a hammy death scene, swooning and shutting itself down with a histrionic twirl of its timer symbol.

'Bollocks!'

Soft anxiety now gave way to hard panic. Without the GPS or my phone, how was I supposed to know where I was going? The road signs were in Forrin, and I had absolutely no clue where I had to turn off to get to Nagaon. A strip-lit kiosk emerged by the side of the road ahead of me like a mirage, and I knew the moment had arrived. It was time to face facts, look my demons in the eye and do the hitherto unthinkable: *ask* for directions. I pulled up by the roadside just ahead of the kiosk, opening my door to the Maharashtrian night as a bus whipped within an arm's length of my ear, its horn shaking every cell down to my very core.

I approached the kiosk-wallah with caution: the look on his face when he caught sight of me implied I had appeared to him suddenly as a frightening backlit apparition. Not wanting to alarm the man too much, and working on the assumption that if the signs out here couldn't speak English then neither could he, I decided to keep things simple at the start by pronouncing only my primary intention: 'Nagaon?'

The man rocked his head from side to side and repeated 'Nagaon' in a way that suggested he wholeheartedly agreed with me. I was stumped.

'So… Nagaon?'

Again, he agreed.

'Okay, but where is it? Which way is Nagaon?'

The kiosk attendant continued to shake his head.

Impatience was kicking in and I stared into the darkness ahead of us that lay beyond the reach of the Nano's humble full beams. I pointed my finger into that darkness. 'Is Nagaon that way?'

He closed his eyes now and nodded his head. 'Aaaah. Nagaon.'

To double-check, I pointed in the opposite direction, from where I had just come.

'Is Nagaon that way?'

To my despair, he repeated the same wobble. 'Nagaon. Nagaon,' he affirmed.

'So let's get this straight: Nagaon is this way,' pointing ahead of us along the road, 'and also that way,' gesturing at the direction from which I had come. It was like asking directions from Tweedle Dum and Tweedle Dee. I was about to check that Nagaon might not also be up above us on the moon, when the kiosk-wallah's eyes opened wide in realization.

'No, no, no, no, no! Nagaon not,' he said, pointing behind us. Then gesturing ahead with a hearty, full-shouldered swing of his arm, 'Nagaon!'

His enthusiasm was convincing and I decided to take his word for it. After one final check – 'Nagaon?' – I felt the warm tingle of first success rise in my belly. Perhaps it wasn't going to be so bad after all: in the middle of this beastly morass, here we were, two people with few common signifiers and only a loose consensus on the notion of internationally agreed positive/ negative body language – a sure recipe for communicational disaster, especially given my rather irked state of mind. But a few minutes and several overblown physical gestures later, we had reached a concord, and were unified in our conviction that I was to continue driving straight on the road, all the way to Nagaon.

3

ROUND THE BEND – Defining Sanity, Osho Style

PUNE; KM 262

When people in Europe say that driving somewhere like Paris or Rome is scary, they are usually referring to hairy moments spent trying to make a circle around the Place de la Concorde or being honked at by macho moped drivers for failing to pre-empt a green light. I had always considered the French and Italian capitals stout candidates for European driving at its most volatile, but now I was beginning to wonder just how Roman or Parisian drivers would fare with their cocky Smart cars and Cinquecentos on India's roads. Here, it felt like everything was on its head: where I would normally relent, in India I had to lurch forward; where I would usually leave a chevron's distance between me and the car in front, now I was driving with my nose practically buried in someone else's exhaust pipe. Instead of heeding lights and signs, here I looked to other vehicles for tips on how to proceed.

It wasn't all bad, though: Abhilasha and I had reached Pune by what is generally thought of as the best road in India. The Yashwantrao Chavan Expressway (named after the first chief minister of Maharashtra and former deputy prime minister) is a six-lane motorway with all the trimmings I'd expect of any major artery in the world: toll booths, refreshment stops, fast and slow lanes, a smooth surface, and even a neatly manicured median. The first part of our cruise to Pune passed with little incident, feeling fairly uneventful after the previous day's assault course to Nagaon. For a brief moment, I almost found myself yearning for a rebound into the rush of chaos and I noticed the adventurer–blogger in me had deflated a little. What if all roads in India were more like this and less like the NH66 down to Alibag? What would I have to write about in my blog if driving around India only involved cruising on tranquil expressways and stopping for the odd sandwich or Styrofoam cup of chai?

No sooner had I had that unsavoury thought than fate saw fit to throw subject matter at me in the form of an obstacle. I had been overtaking a truck in the fast lane, accumulating speed on a temporarily flat stretch of road that marked a break between hills. Notching up the revs, I was parallel to the truck's front mirror when I became vaguely aware of what looked like an object in the fast lane – our lane – up ahead. At first, I didn't believe my eyes, thinking it was a mirage, but when it was still there another split second and twenty metres later, I concluded there was something in the road that Abhilasha and I were hurtling towards at high velocity. Immediate action was required. Swerving was not an option, as the truck I was overtaking was right beside me to my left, so I hit the brakes, hard. In the same moment as the truck passed me, I hauled the wheel to the left and got into the lane behind him, missing the thing ahead of me by inches.

'Holy mother of god!' I managed to spit out after the initial shock of what had just occurred sank into my rational brain. That had been extremely and most unacceptably close: hitting a large, stationary object at 80 kmph would certainly have ended in tears. And probably blood and mangled yellow metal. But we were alive and well, and as my heart regained a steady beat and the gut gremlins returned to their lair, images of the thing flashed back. I had initially perceived it from a distance as a large, rectangular piece of metal, and had assumed it was debris, perhaps something that had fallen off the back of a lorry or a garbage truck and missed by the highway maintenance crew. But on getting a better look as I screeched past, tyres burning a rubber stench into the tarmac, I realized it was in fact a sign. And not only was it a sign, it was also a sign that had been very carefully and deliberately placed in the fast lane of an expressway. And, to pop the glacé cherry atop the whipped cream tower of irony, the sign read 'Go Slow'.

I laughed out loud: I had nearly been killed by a road sign that had been put there in earnest to try to save my life. A few dozen metres down the road, a group of workers were digging up something on the central reservation, and I deduced that the sign had been put there for their benefit, most likely by their own hands. Though the well-meaning nature of their misguided intentions was plain to see, I nevertheless embarked on a ten-minute cathartic monologue, lecturing the men on why using traffic cones to gradually reduce and close off a lane was accepted and expedient practice around the world.

The expressway incident hardened my conviction that my arrival in Pune, Maharashtra's second-largest city lying 150 km east of Mumbai, hadn't come a moment too soon. I had made the decision to swing by there instead of heading straight south to Goa on the advice of a friend back home who suggested I visit the Osho International Meditation Resort. Aside from the draw of its name, which appealed to me on account of the shades of a holiday spot implied by the word 'resort', I was also curious about the reputation of the ashram's founder, Bhagwan Shree Rajneesh, aka Osho. Rajneesh, who shuffled off this mortal coil back in 1990, was more contentious than your average guru, and is popularly painted as something of a spiritual scoundrel, loved by many but also widely criticized. What interested me about Osho and his methods at this particular point in my personal development was his espousal of the principle of self-inflicted, controlled madness as an antidote to the greater lunacy of the world at large, and his concept that the key to true learning lay in the principle of unlearning our current conditioning.

After my brush with death by solicitude on the Yashwantrao Chavan, and the subsequent hullaballoo of Pune's suburban traffic, it occurred to me that Osho might be just the man to help: in order to survive (and avoid a nervous breakdown), I might need to let go and revise everything I thought I knew about driving.

'There are those to whom one must advise madness,' wrote French thinker Joseph Joubert in the nineteenth century; at that moment, while coming off the NH4 into the centre of Pune, competing with a bullock cart for a right-turning opportunity, I knew I had to be reconditioned. I was the square peg and India's roads were the round hole: I needed to take some sandpaper to my edges. For that, I decided to try the high road to psycho-spiritual liberation. It was time to hit an ashram where I could happily convene with my inner loon and prep myself for the next three months of driving like a bonkers bat fresh out of the belfry.

As soon as I arrived at the resort, a woman at the reception desk corrected my use of the term 'ashram' with indignation that might have been excessive had I suggested the place was a whorehouse. This was not an ashram, she said, but a meditation resort. I wasn't really sure of the difference until I picked up the accommodation brochure and learned that rooms there cost about five times more than at the hotel next door. With a swimming pool, tennis courts, a choice of vegetarian restaurants and a vague reputation for a bit of how's your father, this place was putting the Club Med back into meditation. Or was it trying to shoe-horn a bit of meditation into Club Med?

Even before I set foot past the entrance gate, I was inter-rogated as to my motives for coming to the resort, charged a hefty enrolment fee and subjected to a mandatory HIV test. This was followed by a trip to the boutique to buy compulsory maroon and white robes, without which I would not be permit-ted to enter the grounds. Once inside, I had to fight the urge to spend the whole day working on my tan by the side of the pool. A subsequent thirty-minute conversation with an inebri-ated Dane who cornered me with a blow-by-blow account of a gory bomb blast he'd witnessed at a nearby bakery a few days earlier was the motivation I'd been missing to remind me of the psychic deconstruction I was here for.

I consulted the resort timetable: there was a Kundalini ses-sion coming up that would involve some free dance (mortified at the prospect, I was nevertheless keen to try, figuring I'd be breaking down my conditioning by the truckload) followed by something mysterious called the 'Night Meeting'. Both ses-sions took place in a large auditorium at the heart of a giant black marble pyramid and involved working through a cycle of various forms of Osho-approved techniques: from dancing as if someone had slipped an Ecstasy pill into our veggie burgers, to playing musical statues, lying dead on the floor and running around blindfolded, screaming gibberish at high volume. The latter appealed to me the most on the grounds that it was theo-retically a lot like driving, and as hard as it was to do, I decided to give it a really good go.

'*Grarrrlllllaarrlllll!*' I roared, waving my hands frantically in the air in an attempt to awaken my inner Tasmanian Devil and have him kick up a dust storm through the rose garden of my more English inhibitions. Feeling an utter fool, I paused for a moment to catch my breath and peek through my blindfold. My fellow internees were hopping around like deranged cats, dressed in the same long maroon robes and screaming guttural nonsense. Reminiscent of a high-security nuthouse, the scene was terrifying to behold, and I was part of it. I replaced my blindfold and decided that in this case, watching the madness was more maddening than participating in it. There was nothing else for it but to jump high in the air and let out another deafening '*Ggggrrrrrraaaaaaaaaaaaaalll!*'

When the evening dancing started, the auditorium transformed. About 200 or so people, all clad in regulation white evening robes, started boogying around the hall to the repetitive strain of what sounded like a cheerful Cossack ditty mixed with a 1970s cop-show theme. The room began to resemble a cross between *One Flew Over the Cuckoo's Nest* and a Goa trance party. Gathered there were people of all ages and nationalities, and every single one appeared to be thoroughly absorbed in his or her personal dance, eyes closed and arms swinging. Their sheer number was a blessing. I could lose myself in this sea of groovers, and after a few minutes I started to feel like I was at a nightclub. I closed my eyes and let my body do what it would in time to the jaunty melodies emanating from the band. Every so often there would be a sudden break in the music and the revellers would stop mid-routine, shout '*Osho!*' at the top of their lungs, and then continue their dance. Not really sure why we were doing it, I nonetheless joined in, feeling my embarrassment dissipate with every minute.

Eventually, we were able to invoke him. Sweaty and danced out, when the music stopped, everybody in the hall plopped down on the floor and the man himself made an appearance, projected from beyond the grave onto a giant video screen at the front of the auditorium. Wearing a blue gown with Dynasty-style shoulder pads and his trademark beanie, Osho spoke slowly and precisely to the camera from somewhere in what I guess must have been the mid-1980s.

His talk impressed me. He appeared to have a focused air and a wicked sense of humour. He told a really long joke about Mikhail Gorbachev and Ronald Reagan, and I laughed out loud, as did everyone else. But when I stopped laughing, they continued. A couple of minutes passed and they were still laughing, some of them rolling around on their backs, thumping the floor in breathless mirth. Five minutes turned to ten and finally the giggles died down and transformed into something even more disturbing: gobbledegook. Hundreds of voices jabbered in unison; the sounds they made were incomprehensible, noises rising from the subconscious, but somehow they came together in a deranged harmony. It was a bit like the gibberish session, but more controlled, and with the blindfolds off.

Feeling like a daunted private among an army of demented chimps, I let my underlying fool flow out through my mouth and gave voice to all manner of nonsense. I babbled, gabbled, yabbered and yammered until I was almost drooling down my white dress. Osho thought it was necessary to walk through the fires of insanity to decompress the tensions of social living, to liberate one's soul from the frameset of rules, and I was beginning to see his point.

When I left the resort two days later, I returned to the Indian roads with a fresh outlook. I knew I had to adjust my attitude: just like in the auditorium, there was no sense in standing apart from the madness, as that only made everything seem more demented. The only way to deal with it was by gagging my inner traffic cop and entering into the fray, horns a-blazing, brakes a-braking, engine a-revving – or, at least, that was the plan.

RULE OF THE ROAD #2
Pukka Protocol

When two Indians meet as strangers, I read in an essay by Indian author Pavan K. Varma, the encounter is often a duel to ascertain the *aukaat* of the other.

Emerging wet-handed from a gas station toilet cubicle where I'd walked in on a mortified attendant taking a shower, I found Abhilasha stationed in a bumper-to-bumper standoff with a Maruti Zen. The Zen's owner, a prim-looking, mustachioed gent with henna-tinted hair and a shirt that looked as though it had spent the night pressed between two giant spring-fresh anvils, was pacing cautiously around the car, taking in her every detail. As I approached him, he shifted his gaze over to me and treated my crumpled cotton salwar kameez with the same level of critical scrutiny. Mr Fiery Redhead was apparently departing from the usual tradition of gushing sycophantic Nano-philia, possibly on account of his decision to splash out an extra couple of grand on The Other Compact Car, and was pulling no punches in checking us out. The duel had clearly begun.

'Good morning, ma'am,' he greeted me, his shoulders back, his lips tight.

'Hello there,' I responded, feeling my own eyes cast a damning glare in the direction of the Maruti, which was firing belligerent daggers into Abhilasha's headlights.

'What is your good name?' he enquired stiffly, as though it pained him to betray any hint of civility in my direction.

I told him and volleyed the question back at him.

He responded with a cascade of syllables that contained in them somewhere 'indra', 'giri', 'dhar' and 'doctor', among a torrent of other sounds that oozed authority.

Something was definitely going on here, I thought. We were walking circles around each other like two dogs going for the scrotum sniff. What did the doctor want from me?

'Did you buy this car in Mumbai?' he asked.

'Yes.'

'How much did you pay?'

'Two lakh four.'

His eyes widened and I saw a brief glint of victory flash through his retina. 'But this is the one-lakh car.'

'Yes, it is,' I sighed, 'but this one is the top model. It has air conditioning and, um, electric windows.' I was still at pains myself to figure out quite how these features doubled the vehicle's price.

'What is your fuel efficiency?'

'About 19 kilometres to the litre.'

'Oh, very good.'

The doctor fell silent. I felt obliged to continue the conversation. 'So are you, uh, planning on buying one?'

The doc shook his head. 'Oh no, I would never buy this car.'

Hang on. What was going on here? Was I in the company of a hater?

'If you have one or two lakhs to spend on a car, then you can buy a second-hand Maruti Zen, or Tata Indica. It is much more reliable than a Nano.'

I rose up like an owner scorned. 'But I've driven all the way from Mumbai in this car and I've had no problems whatsoever.'

'Maybe you have had no problems *yet*,' the man said, giving Abhilasha's back tyre a light kick with his polished chestnut-brown loafer, 'but maybe the next few thousand kilometres will not be so lucky for you.'

It was a point against which I couldn't really argue, irritated as I was at the fact his foot had just made contact with Abhilasha's wheel, a gesture that was as good as an all-out declaration of war.

'I am employed with the civil service,' the man said, thumbing his chest and moving his hand over to the right to finger the gold pen sticking out from his shirt pocket from behind a folded handkerchief. 'It is not appropriate for me to drive this Nano. It is seen as a poor man's car.'

His road *aukaat* firmly established, my red-headed friend returned to the superior fold of his Maruti and left me standing, shamed and bewildered, in his dust.

'The mentality of a stratified society is very much in evidence in everyday life,' wrote Varma.[16] I presumed he was writing about India's hierarchical caste system, which had been around for millennia and was still very much in force. I went on to read that the phenomenon of *aukaat*, which roughly translates as 'status', adds another dimension to Indian society's complex layering. As I watched the doctor pull out of the petrol station, I wondered whether his attitude was representative of the upwardly mobile middle class as a whole. Who wants to be seen driving the cheapest car on the market if you're trying to show yourself as being on the up? The Nano had proved popular with the kids of the established upper-middle class who loved its quirky design and were buying it as an addition to the existing family fleet of Beemers and Audis. But for families just entering the world of purchasing power, was it really an attractive idea to spend their precious savings on a car with unwarranted long-term prospects? And all practical considerations aside, there was also the bottom line so eloquently expressed by my civil servant friend: Who wants to be seen driving a poor man's car? I certainly didn't mind, but I was from another world.

As we pulled back onto the highway, a triad of menacing black SUVs whizzed past us in a dust cloud that left me giddy from the Doppler effect. Abhilasha shimmied slightly to the left in their wake. I sighed: two *aukaat*-fuelled drubbings in the space of five minutes. The Nano might be one of India's new industrial darlings, but when it came to the pecking order of the road, she had to take her place among the hierarchy that was dictated by one simple rule: size.

If a person has to be asked what their *aukaat* is, the question is already an insult. Varma's cautionary pointer might be perplexing if applied to social situations by a foreigner and an outsider like myself, but when I looked at his principle through the prism of highway etiquette, it was a no-brainer. On the roads it was clear who was boss: bulk and velocity ruled. If the oncoming vehicle was bigger than me, I relented; if it was smaller, I cut it up. It was that easy.

At the top of the highway power pyramid were the lumbering lorries, the articulated kind that measured about ten times the length of the Nano and moved at a majestic snail's pace, scattering all terrified objects from their path with their formidable horns that could probably be heard from space.

On the next rung down were the smaller trucks, coaches and buses. They did have a slight speed advantage over the giant lorries in that they were often driven by boy racers who handled their bulky, aging torsos as though they were featherweight Ferraris with spruced-up horns designed to present a more intimidating impression. Trucks and buses were followed by SUVs and cars, which contained many of their own subcategories, but it goes without saying that the humble low-cost Nano pretty much bookended the spectrum with the likes of a Porsche Cayenne Turbo at the other extreme (the one-lakh car versus the one-crore[17] car). Within that hundredfold price difference lay all the other Tatas, Toyotas, Mahindras and Marutis.

The next category mostly comprised a more domesticated class of machinery. The horse- and bullock-drawn carts, charming and bucolic in appearance, were straightforward farmyard transport modes that were delightfully quaint and environmentally friendly, their only downside being their speed of bullock-miles per hour. Other members of this category included *jugaads*, vehicles reconstructed from the debris and spare parts harvested from the long since deceased. A motor from here, a gear box from there, some tractor wheels found near railway tracks and the disused wooden carriage that's been rotting in the back field since the last horse died two years ago: put them all together and you have a weird hybrid tractor–cart thing that was invariably piled up with hay or people or both, and set to putter along the countryside roads in the early mornings or at dusk, taxiing its load from farms to villages and back again.

Next up were the auto-rickshaws and Tempos, three-wheelers often loaded with people that could hold anything up to an entire class of schoolchildren. In cities, rickshaws ruled the roost with their plucky moves and swift turns, but on the highways they were humbled by the sheer fact of their slowness, holding themselves rather sheepishly to the left as they let traffic hurl past them. Down another notch were the two-wheelers, a term encompassing everything from a moped to a high-speed Honda, although it usually meant a 125 cc motorbike ridden by a minimum of three to four adults with the added option of children, livestock and industrial hardware balanced at various points for optimum weight distribution. They were closely followed by bicycles, which were capable of performing similar functions but at much lower speeds. And then there were those who travelled on foot: goats, dogs, hogs and, finally, people.[18] At the bottom of the pyramid of power, pedestrians were molested the most: cars hurtled by them within inches of their elbows and honked at them angrily at road crossings where they'd let a cow pass with reverential awe.

But just as caste barriers were beginning to crumble in India with the advent of a new, modernizing wave of social structure, so too were road users trumping one another and undermining the rules of road *aukaat* by use of all manner of resources. Take cleanliness as an example: in a country rife with dust, fumes and the humidity to mix them into sticky pollution, cleanliness is very much next to godliness. Despite this, a pristine sunshine yellow coat was not something I was always able to arrange for

Abhilasha: many were the mornings I drove her out into the world looking like the Swamp Thing after a particularly bitchy mud fight.

Power in numbers was another trick for manipulating the traffic to one's will, and no road user displayed this ploy as well as humble livestock. A single sheep or goat by the side of the road was potential roadkill, but in herds they were formidable traffic stoppers who didn't differentiate between high-speed highways and back-country roads.

Speed and sprightliness were another option for blindsiding other road users into giving way. If you could outrun or even dodge the bastard, it didn't really matter how big he was. And this was the principle that I, by all rights a foreigner and an outcast, used from inside my yellow Indian avatar. When I was on form and Abhilasha in good fettle, the two of us were able to leave many a red-faced Maruti Zen or Tata Indica sprawling in our slipstream.

It seemed to me that social mobility was possible, at least as far as the roads were concerned. If I swerved, dodged and blared my horn enough in the face of my so-called superiors – leaving them in the sorry knowledge that maybe they weren't the kings of the highway after all – then there was a small orifice in the fortress of *aukaat* through which the proles and their one-lakh cars could just about squeeze.

4

THE SH11T - *Lost in Maharashtra*

KOLHAPUR to ARAMBOL; KM 500–694

woke to the sound of trance music pounding loathsomely through the wall, with beats so ferocious they were driving the metal springs under my mattress into a twangy dissonance, vibrating right into the centre of my primary auditory cortex, which also happened at that moment to be the location of my deep irritation nucleus. A vision of strangling my neighbours using their sound system's wiring took shape through the fog of semi-consciousness as my more rational brain alerted itself to the fact that there was something urgent that needed to be done this morning.

I forced open my crusted eyelids to take a day-lit peek at the quarters I had rented the night before. It was a sparse room with damp patches on the walls, cracked tiles on the floor and a fan with one broken blade that swivelled in a lopsided arc above my head. My bag had been plonked in the far corner of the room, its contents bleeding out and making a trail towards the bathroom along the murky tiles. The room resembled a detention cell, but as images from the previous day's drive began to file back onto the screen of my psyche, I remembered very clearly that the night before, I would have settled for sleeping on a morgue slab.

Yesterday had not been pretty. Best-laid plans oft do fall by the wayside, and the route from Kolhapur to Goa, a 200 km drive that should have taken just a few hours to cover, was one such disastrous scheme that ended up spanning the entire chuffing day, and had me lost in deepest rural Maharashtra entertaining the not unlikely prospect of a survival situation.

The brunt of the problem lay in the fact that, on setting out from Kolhapur – where I had decided to overnight on my way from Pune to Goa – there hadn't been anything like a best- or even an ill-laid plan on the table to begin with. The GPS having served me faithfully over the last couple of legs of the journey, I began to think I could put my trust in the technology of satellites to get us to our destination without having to exert any effort on my own part. It followed that the extent of my day's route preparation consisted of looking at a map of Goa, identifying Arambol as the northern-most popular beach, and entering the closest town, Pernem, into the GPS. I was given an estimated journey time of four-and-a-half hours, which I figured would have me swinging in a hammock by mid-afternoon, the glistening waters of the Arabian Sea providing a soothing background as I sipped coconut water and dined royally off giant pineapple slices.

I guessed the route would be fairly straightforward, assuming we continued down south on the very efficient NH4 that had brought us here from Pune. But, so trusting was I of the GPS's authoritative tones, so engrossed was I by the vision of my impending picture-perfect afternoon, that I failed to react when I realized we clearly were not headed back towards the highway. My first schoolgirl error was to assume that global positioning satellites knew more about how to get to Goa than I did after a cursory glance at the *Lonely Planet* map. The second, and even more fatal, mistake was not to verify the route that Delilah (the name I gave the GPS that day in return for her bitter betrayal) had in store for our little road trip. Forty minutes later, after trundling along an unpaved road compounded with the red dust of some very inactive roadworks (okay, it was a Sunday), it finally occurred to me to hit the 'route overview' option to see where the hell we were going.

It turned out that Delilah had no well- or ill-laid plans either, at least not for heading for the NH4. She thought it a better idea to take a little back road called the SH115 that would eventually throw us out onto the west-coast highway, the NH17. Delilah justified her decision on the grounds that it was the shortest route (a mere 180 km), and I accordingly presumed she was the expert and could be trusted with the one task that her entire being was programmed to do. After all, once we cleared the roadworks on the outskirts of Kolhapur, the landscape took a turn for the gorgeous. We were in the countryside – real thick, green Indian countryside – and it was stunning. I gave the GPS a conciliatory nod of approval; this wasn't turning out to be so bad after all.

The road was well paved and suddenly became shrouded by the curving branches of the giant trees that leaned over the tarmac, trying to touch each other halfway and making a lush arc that shaded our passage. A shepherd boy urged a goat to cross the road ahead of me, swinging a scythe over his shoulder as an old woman passed him, a bright yellow skirt rippling around her hips with a brown shawl thrown over her head. A small brick kiln in the shape of a half-built pyramid smouldered by the side of the road as we slowly overtook a man on a bicycle balancing a pile of freshly cut grass about twice his height bundled into a bow-tie shape behind him. The houses became smaller, blending better with the earth as we moved away from the city: simple, rectangular structures with terracotta-tiled rooftops, sometimes obscured by massive mounds of hay, or little outhouses that were entirely covered by dried banana leaves. We whizzed past rice fields shining saturated green and separated from neighbouring cornfields by successions of palm trees, while a couple of kilometres later I was amazed to see echoes of the Mediterranean in fields of neatly planted sunflowers. Every so often the road would open out onto a little stone bridge that spanned a river where a group of women were knee high in the water, bending down and kneading various brightly coloured fabrics before laying them out to dry in long strips on the banks of the river.

Then there were the bullocks. They paced the road in pairs, oblivious to passing trucks and buses and their perfunctory honks. I passed two of them at first, steadfastly pulling a cart with lorry-sized tyres that was carrying sticks of firewood so long they were dragging on the road behind. The driver stood upright on top of all of the wood, towering above the bullocks that he guided with a couple of fraying ropes. The beasts plodded on, their eyes fixed forward and their horns painted bright red with a couple of white horizontal stripes. We passed another pair, and another, all pulling the same kind of cart piled up with the same kind of wood. We kept passing them until it became clear they were part of some sort of procession. I presumed they were all headed for the same spot: a bullock convention, perhaps, or a giant bovine Burning Man.

Several kilometres later I realized the carts were all going to the village of Bidri, where a factory with a tall chimney pumped out smoke that blackened the blue sky. A line of bullock carts several dozen long waited to shed their loads in turn at the doors of the plant.

I had never seen so many bullocks in my life. There were around a hundred, some waiting stoically in the midday sun, while others unwound in the shadows of palm trees across the road. I parked Abhilasha in an open field near the bullocks and went out with my camera to record the sight. The animals seemed imperturbable: they were just standing, sitting, reclining and drifting off into reverie. Some of them stared into an inscrutable distance or picked at bits of grass on the ground, while others folded their legs underneath their tank-like torsos and sank down on top of them. Their drivers lay next to them on the ground or draped over their loads of wood, also drifting off into bored and careless sleep, oblivious to my picking my way between them and snapping away at their dozing forms. As road users, the bullocks' demeanour was the exact opposite of that of most of the vehicles Abhilasha and I had encountered these past few days. The bullock, cart and driver were the anti-truck: slow, steady, silent and self-assured.

I drove on, steeped in mental rhetoric eulogizing the merits of rural life. It was idyllic: people seemed so laid-back, the cattle were so unflustered. Everywhere I looked was a picture postcard and each tiny village we passed treated the Nano as a visiting hero. Children ran in our wake, waving and screaming 'Nanonanonanonanonanonano!' while men often stopped dead in their tracks and watched the car go by, keeping us in view until we were out of sight. Passengers in passing SUVs waved frantically from the back seat, while groups of women pointed in our direction, whispering, then falling into hysterical laughter. I saw the jaw of one teenage kid on a bicycle actually drop in a hammed-up expression of surprise as we overtook him with a honk. I kept him in my rear view for a few seconds more, worried he might complete his slapstick routine by losing control of his bike, veering off the road and ploughing head first into a bush.

The bucolic feel-good vibes came to an abrupt end when, an hour or so out of Kolhapur, I arrived at a fork in the road and made a spur-of-the-moment decision that would quickly change my opinion that remoteness from civilization was a thing to be desired. Having been informed by Delilah some distance back that the road would be straight for the next couple of hours, I had turned her off to save batteries, assuming there would be no major turns before we hit the NH17.

Quickly assessing the fork in the road in front of me, I failed to consult Delilah, opting instead to rely on my instincts and turning left; it was a road that looked more enticing, and anyway, the huge lorry ahead of me had gone the same way. But it was this bad error of judgement, I later reflected, that eventually rendered myself and Abhilasha hopelessly lost in a land almost entirely void of English speakers or any helpful road signs. Not to mention hammocks, coconut water or giant pineapple slices.

A few minutes after taking the ill-fated turn, the road started to narrow and a tiny pang of doubt set in. I decided to switch Delilah on anyway, just to ascertain we were still on the right track. I kept driving as she struggled to pick up a signal, but when she eventually did, the little car on the screen that represented us appeared to be driving at a steady rate about one centimetre to the right of the yellow line that was the road we were supposed to be on. I looked to my left where there was nothing but fields and trees, and was stumped at exactly how I was supposed to interpret this information. I eventually figured that since we were holding a steady course in relation to the yellow line, the one-centimetre difference could be put down to the satellite taking a little cosmic knock and registering us a few metres to the right of our actual position. Such a margin of error was permissible, I reasoned, given the distances we were dealing with and the fact we were in the proverbial butthole of nowhere.

It wasn't until about two hours later, when the road we were on had all but completely given way to a track filled with razor-sharp stones, that I stopped to think that perhaps, just maybe, Delilah might have pulled a fast one. Wary of deflating all four of my tyres in one fell swoop, I powered her up for another consult. By now her signal had completely disappeared and my phone displayed the same dumb vacancy. I cursed them both.

It had been about twenty kilometres since I had passed the last village, about twelve since the last turn, and at least three or four since I had seen another human being (an old lady aimlessly squatting by the side of the road). My situation called for drastic measures; I had to know at least if I was still heading in the direction of Goa.

Compounding my problem was the absence of an alternative. My £5.99 map wasn't even an option and, since I had entirely entrusted the trip to Delilah, I had done nothing in the way of preparing a reference list of en-route towns and villages. This meant that even if a Maharashtrian villager was to materialize, I had absolutely no idea what I would ask him anyway. And even if I did know, I'd be asking in English, a language probably as remote to my villager friend as Serbo-Croat. Not even *Beginner's Hindi* could help me now. Despite my toolbox of GPS, iPhone, large map and relatively well-functioning human brain, I had no clue where I was and even less of where I was going. It was not a proud moment.

The rumble of an approaching motorcycle crept up behind me. The driver's shock at seeing a stranded white girl in a Nano in the thick of Maharashtra was matched by my relief at encountering another person in the middle of nowhere. He pulled up before I even had the chance to hope he wasn't a crazed killer, and we sized each other up for a few seconds as I tried to decide what would be the best course of action. I chose the long shot first.

'English?'

Nothing.

'Okay... uh... Hindi?'

Nope.

It seemed I would have to revert to the international language of mime. How could I illustrate Goa manually? I started to move my hands about in a wave-like motion.

'The sea!' I exclaimed, by way of explanation. My audience betrayed no sign of recognition, sympathy or even entertainment. Undeterred, I continued, making the waves a little more exaggerated and sensational. 'The sea? You know, the sea?'

My reasoning was thus: asking the directions to Goa at this point might be tantamount to asking the way to China. It was simply too far and too general to be a destination to which this passing motorcyclist might be able to point me. And without the relevant data on towns between here and Goa, I decided the easiest thing would be to head towards the sea, where I would invariably join up with the NH17 that would take me south. And although I didn't know what the Marathi for sea was, I fancied my 'B' in GCSE Drama might finally come into its own as I enacted an impression of one of nature's most magnificent forces to the bemused motorcyclist.

He looked utterly flummoxed, but I couldn't afford to admit defeat. Maybe I wasn't putting enough fluidity into my wrists. I tried to inject them with a little more flourish, and I even began to accompany my manual demonstration with the audio effect of breaking waves, which probably sounded more like I was trying to hush the bewildered man. Whether the penny finally dropped, or whether he had just had enough and really needed me to stop the Little Mermaid show, the motorcyclist suddenly interrupted me mid-wave to motion I should just keep going over the rocky road. I was highly sceptical, but he appeared quite sure of himself. I felt certain that no one without an elephant or an SUV with platinum treads, or with half of their wits about them, should even think of attempting to cross the blades of death.

'Straight on, you say?' I asked with a grating English cadence, keeping it ridiculous with the utterly pointless question, 'And then it's the sea, you say?'

He looked puzzled.

'The sea, the sea...' I restarted the hand motion.

'Yes, yes! Ek kilometre!' I looked ahead and considered. He seemed to be telling me that the beach was but a kilometre away and that these rocks were my last trial before reaching the gleaming sands of India's western coast. Or at least, that was what I wished to believe. I badly wanted to trust that despite everything, I was still going in the right direction and it was perfectly feasible for the road to appear and disappear like this from time to time, even if it was supposed to be a state highway.

Satisfied that I'd follow his instructions, the motorcyclist puzzlingly turned his bike around and went back the way he had come. I pushed Abhilasha into first gear, gave her some gas and made our first move over Satan's own pebbled path. Despite our near-crawling speed, rocks were still flying up at the engine and the undercarriage, and I winced with every little knock and bump. This could not be good for the tyres, the paintwork, the suspension, or the low-lying undercarriage.

Ek kilometre later, I wasn't too surprised to find myself not staring out into the infinity of the Arabian Sea, but in fact looking at an impasse, as even the stony path had now disappeared and we had been ejected onto the edge of a field bordered by red sandy scrub. It was here I finally surrendered. I was lost beyond redemption. There was only one thing for it: I had to swallow my pride and start back up the road to retrace our steps.

As I winced over the rocks of death, cursing Delilah at every bump and bang, I felt the rose-tinted glasses through which I had been viewing rural India begin to steam up. I knew nothing other than the fact that we were somewhere on the 200 km stretch of land between Kolhapur and Goa. It wasn't late yet, but the afternoon was certainly ripening in a way that told me I might not make it to my hammock before sunset.

I angrily renamed the SH115 the SH11T. And to top my SH11T pie with a turd cherry, events took a turn for the even more incredible when, just after I had made my way back over the road of doom, I ran into a roadblock manned by a group of children. A long piece of cane was laid across my path at about thigh height, balanced between two rickety wooden forks. Eight or so children milled about, presumably having just been released from school and embarking on an afternoon's larks conning money out of lost people. In any other situation I might have found the wee tykes endearing and even amusing, but given the grimness of our current situation, it was all my inner Scrooge could do to press on the brakes and not shoot straight through their carefully crafted barrier.

I rolled down the window to a flock of confounded faces. I suppose that in turn, I was also the last person this little group of would-be taxmen was expecting to see that afternoon. So great was the shock at the sight of my face (I did have a quick look in the mirror to check it wasn't covered in tiny pins) that for a second no one moved. Then one boy in shorts ran to a shack to call over a taller boy in trousers, who immediately pulled up the wooden bar by use of an impressively functional pulley system. I shot them a forgiving wink and hit the gas as they remained speechless in my dust.

About an hour back down the road, I saw a white jeep and a bunch of lads clad in jeans, T-shirts and Wayfarers who had stopped to have a cigarette. Finally, city folk. I couldn't have felt more affiliation with this group of youths at that moment had they been my own brethren. I pulled up alongside, rolled down the window and took a deep breath.

'Hello there. You don't happen to know the way to Goa by any chance?'

I was met with seven blank stares suggesting the boys weren't quite sharing my overwhelming sense of sibling fellowship.

'Umm, Goa? Beach? Sea?' (Hand movements) 'Goa? Gooooooh-a?'

The light of comprehension burst behind the eyes of one of the lads. Goa! Of course. Yes, he knew, and he knew well. It wasn't straightforward, but he slowly listed for me the succession of villages I'd need to pass through in order to get back out onto the NH17, the road headed south.

Gargoti, Uttur, Aza-somewhere... I wrote them all phonetically in my notebook, thanked the chap profusely and went on my way. List in hand, I was now sure to stop at every village to yell the names in front of me to random passers-by who then pointed me on to the next stop. I was sure this flimsy method was flawed at best, but I had no choice but to follow the paper trail from one village to the next. As it turned out, the village relay method proved remarkably reliable as well as instructive. I managed to glean several navigational pointers from the experience, including being able to decipher the hand gestures that relayed the necessity of taking a right or left turning in the near to mid-term future, as well as the requisite of asking for directions three times over at each step. Every now and then my chosen oracle either stank of booze or seemed so terror-stricken at the prospect of a me-driven Nano that his instructions were hard to divine. One guy who by the angle of his stance looked as though he'd had about five beers too many thought he'd actually have a go at getting in the car with me after I slowed down at a junction to ask him the way to Uttur. I locked the door in the nick of time and motioned to him in the politest possible way that I was not at this moment taking passengers.

It was after dark when we crossed the border into Goa. Uniformed police stood amid a flood of headlights and clouds of dust to stop every car on its way into the tiny state. When it was my turn, I rolled down the window to find a beaming policeman on the other side.

'Nano!' he exclaimed, twice.

He wasn't to know that my mood had hit rock bottom, that I had been frustrated at the wheel for close to nine hours now and was in no mood for pleasantries.

'Yes, indeed it's a Nano, officer.'

The policeman sustained his smile, casting a curious eye over my lap to the junk on the passenger seat and the bags in the back.

'Very good,' he concluded. 'Goa?'

'Yes,' I replied with faux solemnity, stifling the urge to ask him where the hell else I might be going, crossing the border into Goa at 7pm.

He waved me on with official cheerfulness and Abhilasha and I finally crossed the threshold of our target state. It was another hour to Arambol, where the roads became thinner and the greenery noticeably lusher. We passed the odd church, some sweaty colonial houses and a couple of barefoot Israelis riding an Enfield at high speed and volume, before finally getting wedged into the tiny lanes of stalls selling tie-dyed fabrics, bongo drums and crystals that constitute Arambol's hippie gateway.

I settled for the first hotel I found that appeared to have some adjacent parking space down a little side street: a gap the size of a garden path between two stationary Marutis. As I sized up the space against my mental image of Abhilasha's actual width, a man knocked on my window and identified himself as the owner of one of the parked cars. He was confident, if not eager, to see me take the place next to him, and proceeded to direct me as I tried to squeeze Abhilasha into the munchkin-sized spot.

Within seconds, a small audience had gathered to monitor the manoeuvre from every angle and discuss my chances of completing the park successfully. I fancied someone might even be running a book. After several lurches backwards and forwards, I finished in triumph, sweating from the pressure of surveillance. However, with only about an inch between Abhilasha and the adjacent Marutis, the next challenge I faced was getting *out* of the car. The Maruti owner realized my predicament and beckoned me to back out again. With the engine off and the handbrake up, I watched from the sidelines as Abhilasha was gently nudged back into place under the combined effort of the bystanders until her bumper was just touching the wall behind her. Exhilarated by a job well done, the Maruti owner stepped forward and shook my hand, then informed me that I had to move from this spot by 8 am as Abhilasha was blocking the route of the daily garbage truck.

Rolling over in bed, I reached for my phone. It was 8:15 am.
'Shit!'

I jumped up, pulled on yesterday's discarded clothing from the floor and ran out of the door, expecting to find the Nano hanging from a tow-truck crane. But there she was, just as I had left her the night before. Only this time, one of the Marutis had been replaced by two rickshaws.

'Nano girl!' someone called. I turned around to see a group of four guys squatting and laughing from a doorstep behind me. I put on a weird simper to cover my true impression of 'How the hell did you know this was my car?' Feeling miserably like I was being laughed at, I nevertheless took advantage of the lads to enquire about the elusive garbage truck. My question was met with smiles.

'No problem, no problem!'

'But shouldn't I move my car?'

There was a round of shakes of the head and waves of the hands and a general consensus that Abhilasha should stay put.

The oldest looking of the bunch, a guy in his late 30s wearing a white shirt with an animal leaping across the left breast stood up and motioned me over to the car. His tone was suddenly very businesslike.

'Are you selling this car?' he asked with a concerned frown. I noticed his friends had all risen too and were making their way towards us to listen in on the conversation. I was beginning to wish I had my own entourage for such moments: a gang of girls who would pop out of nowhere and gather around me in the style of a 1990s gangsta rap video, hanging off my shoulders and shooting vaguely irascible looks at whoever it was I was talking to.

'Well, yes, eventually. But for now I'm driving it. Around India. For 10,000 kilometres.' There was a round of sage nods from his boy-gang, but my interrogator was persistent.

'When you are finished, will you come to Goa and sell it to me?'

Hang on, was he trying to cut a deal here? Seriously? He really wanted me to bring the car down to Goa after I had dragged it thousands of kilometres all the way around the country? What did he want it for, spare parts?

'Will you still want it after 10,000 kilometres? What will you do with it?' I asked suspiciously.

He brightened. 'Of course. 10,000 kilometres is like a new car!'

I made a mental note to try to start reselling negotiations when the dial was at 9,900.

'I have a Maruti Zen,' the man continued. 'But I would like to purchase this one-lakh car also.' Now it was me nodding sagely, though in reality I was bewildered. Was this guy serious? I'd never been approached by anyone wanting to perform an automobile transaction as though he were selling me a postcard. With my spine still tingling from the previous day's debacle in

Maharashtra, I almost began to take his offer seriously. I could just sell the Nano now, cut my losses, take the cash and book a train back to Mumbai, still in one piece. This complete stranger was offering me a way out, an option not to spend the next dozen or so weeks embarrassing myself by bumbling cluelessly around the Indian countryside. Should I just take the money and run?

Swimming in options, I joined Abhilasha's potential buyer and his boy-gang in turning to admire her radiant yellow sheen. I suddenly remembered the handbrake was still off and made for the passenger door to pull it up. Just as I was doing so, the man popped his head in next to me.

'Madam, will you permit me a test drive?'

I straightened up. 'I'm sorry?'

'Will you allow me to test drive this Nano?'

He might as well have asked if he could nip off with my liver for a few minutes. His request was so bold I was momentarily stunned; looking at his earnest features, I found myself flailing in a chasm of cultural relativism. I had been approached by a complete stranger who first wanted to buy my car, and now wanted to take it for a spin: was this a highly elaborate mugging or a friendly moment of village bonding? If I went with my instincts and refused him the car (and now I'd apparently agreed to sell Abhilasha to him, he considered himself as good as the owner), would I be committing an act of gross offence to a citizen of my host country? Was I about to break the last Indian taboo of not practising generosity with one's car keys? I imagined a similar situation in London that would most likely end in police intervention and decided I wasn't going to take a chance with my steed.

'Um, no. Sorry, but no.'

He didn't seem to take the rejection too much to heart. He reached into his pocket and pulled out a business card for an export company with large lettering in Couricr.

'This is my card. When you are ready to sell, you call me, okay?'

'Right you are.' I took the card and stashed it deep in my pocket next to Abhilasha's keys. I crossed my fingers as I shook his hand, satisfied I'd made the right decision to hold on to the Nano. Trauma-yoked amnesia had kicked in and yesterday's cock-up was already fast fading into a rosy pastoral narrative. The journey was young and the spectacular Maharashtran countryside had been but a warm-up, a rural test run to see what we were capable of as a team. From this point forward, we would be a terrifying pair, honed in navigation and linguistic skills, savvy to local customs, nifty with the gearstick, and most certainly *not for sale*.

5

ANARCHY ON THE NH7 – The Central Badlands

*J*ust as my and Abhilasha's union had been sealed, a new distraction appeared on the horizon in the form of an exasperatingly attractive French-American redhead, who went by the celestial name of Thor. Thor was a Doctor of Mathematics whom I'd met some months before at a wedding in France at the beginning of the terminal phase of my last relationship. The pull had been instant and painfully palpable, but the ill-timed explosion of what seemed like mutual interest was cut short by our circumstances and subsequently lost to me in the painful maelstrom of the lengthy break-up that followed.

Time passed and faintly instigated augury threw us together via social media, where our interests were reignited. In the weeks that followed, friendly messaging quickly turned into effusive e-flirting and it soon became apparent that Thor, who wrote programs for a living as a data scientist, also had an stake in India. While mine was more of the socioeconomic/motoring variety, his was purely spiritual: he'd been visiting the country annually for the last 17 years, going to an ashram in Chennai that advanced a form of Raja Yoga called Sahaj Marg and was the domicile of his guru, Shri Parthasarathi Rajagopalachari ('But you can call him Chari,' he wrote, to my relief). Quite coincidentally, it turned out that Thor was planning a trip over there fairly soon, so raising the possibility of us actually meeting up onc day.

We skitted around the subject without either of us betraying too much enthusiasm for the plan, before I upgraded the situation to code red by dropping this devastating phrase into an email: 'Why not come and travel with me for a while? Go on, it'll be fun.'

I sent the message with some degree of misgiving. Although I was always quick to advise the heartbroken that resaddling on the dating horse was the best and most efficient way to get one over on post-break-up negativity, it also felt a bit too soon to be bringing another bloke into my life. To boot, inviting another human on board the good ship *Abhilasha* was the opposite of what I was supposed to be doing at that point, namely driving, blogging and generally concentrating on some self-restoration by way of navigating the Indian subcontinent. But I hadn't the willpower to refrain; inappropriate, inconvenient, it was all far too enjoyable. So I counter-reasoned that our fling would be quick, fleeting and efficient in the single-minded goal of having a bit of no-strings-attached fun.

Thor's reply was thankfully laced with equal compunction, and the sum of our two vacillations resulted in an agreeably rough-shod plan that had him coming to India at some point in the not too distant future: he'd travel out to meet me, we'd drive around together for a while and we'd 'see what happens', which I hoped was code for we'd go our separate ways. It was a high-stakes first date, and one that gave me significant wobbles in the light of the prospective future intimacy and all the complications that would naturally follow the simple act of getting my oats.

My nerves took a further blow a few days later when Thor suddenly upped the stakes in our dalliance by actually booking his tickets and setting a schedule: he was flying into Mumbai and then taking the train down to Bangalore, where we would meet in two days' time.

Now that the potential encounter had morphed into a definite plan, I slipped into my familiar routine of rattling with the thrill of fantasy while cultivating the dread of impending reality. Doubt reared its grisly head and began to twist my thoughts into shapes of misgiving. I barely knew the guy. What if he was moody and difficult? What if he talked incessantly or never said a word? What if I realized we had absolutely nothing in common? With the realistic scenarios duly processed, I began to ponder other, more outlandish possibilities: since we had next to no mutual friends, who, if it ever came down to it, could even vouch for him? He might be deranged, psychotic, a twisted marauder of women in cars, a cannibal hungering after the flesh of a Nano-packed female. I mean, why else would he be so keen on coming out to meet me, if not to cut me into small pieces and bury me in the far-flung scrub? He couldn't possibly *like* me that much, not after a few brief conversations at a wedding and a series of, frankly, coquettish emails. There was still time, I thought, to tell him I had to bypass Bangalore, or I had far too much luggage and couldn't take on any passengers. Or that Abhilasha was allergic to men.

These anxieties began to take hold to the backdrop of the spaghetti-western starkness of Andhra Pradesh, an environment that was doing everything to nurture the ballooning notion that the further I got from Mumbai, the further down the barbed rabbit hole I was spinning. The thorny, arid landscape, giddying in its emptiness, inspired a flailing agoraphobia in me, as I took existential respite in the sceptical humanity of the listless villages at junctions, one of which must have considered itself so forsaken by the world as to have erected an unearthly, King Kong–sized statue of the monkey god Hanuman to keep vigil over the souls of its inhabitants.

The jitters had started in Hampi, a place I remembered from my student days as a quiet, laid-back travellers' sanctum replete with baggy-trousered tattooed hippie types who spent their days reading *Shantaram* in cafés and hanging themselves out to bronze over the breathtakingly large boulders scattered by the banks of the river that ran through the small town's Jurassic terrain. I had got there from Goa via the NH4a, a road that at one point receded into a dirt track so unnavigable I had to take a long, triangular diversion that shaved several thousand dendrites off my nervous system. I approached Hampi at the witching hour, expecting the effects of the long drive to be instantly soothed by a laid-back trance soundtrack infused with the scent of burning incense and weed, but was instead subject to a sequence of official procedures enforced by the town's constabulary that suggested I had entered a militarized zone. I met a set of resolutely closed gates and a guard who was reluctant to let me in before I convinced him I was indeed on the guest list by bandying about permutations of the word 'permit'.

When I finally arrived at the hotel Shanthi, where I had stayed years before during my first and second trips to the town, I was ordered to go to the local police station by the manager of my hotel. He had motioned at a sign above his head while I was filling out the guest register: 'Foreigners visiting Hampi should compulsory register their name in district police office of Bellary'.

'Seriously?'

The manager nodded gravely.

'The office is at the end of the bazaar, left side. You should go there tomorrow morning, immediately,' he said, leaning forward to intone conspiratorially, 'It is better, to avoid trouble.'

Trouble? I had always thought of Hampi as a small, unassuming tourist spot of moderate archaeological interest, but it was turning out to be more like the O.K. Corral at Tombstone, if the ongoing security measures were anything to go by. The main – and really, *only* – street of Hampi reminded me of what the frontier towns of the new America must have looked like in the early days of the settlers, minus the cool wooden buildings and a saloon. One long, straight road bordered by food stalls, shops and cheap hotels that led to – something that probably wasn't a feature of the wild west – a temple with a massive ornamental tower, a *gopuram*, and a resident elephant.

At the police station, I was obliged by the duty officer to sit and read a laminated list of fourteen commandments hanging from the wall that spelled out what might be in store for me in this dusty halfway town. Some of the rules, like 'Do not wander alone at any time with valuable things and cash', were common sense, but there were others that were a tad more unsettling. Rule number eight warned, 'No eatables or beverages given by unknown persons should be consumed'. I thought of all the times I had been offered food by strangers in India, whether on a train, bus or boat, or waiting in line for something or other when the odd puri or bhaji would suddenly be produced and offered forth amid an uncrumpling of newspaper and a shimmer of plastic bags. Could it be that the ostensibly well-meaning donors of these comestible gifts were in fact malevo-lent criminals looking to knock me out with a racehorse dose of Rohypnol and have their wicked way with my luggage?

I heard a cowbell ring somewhere in the distance as a breeze blew a few leaves over the threshold of the police station. I half expected to see a pile of tumbleweed blow down the main street. I read on: 'Strolling around the Hampi ruins after sunset is not safe. Hence return to your room before sunset.' Blimey, a curfew. No watching the sun go down by the banks of the river for me, then. The next rule that caught my eye upped the stakes somewhat: 'Do not go to interior places lonely. There is possibility of getting attacked by robbers, thieves and rapists.'

Jesus. Was this for real? The officer behind the desk, satisfied I had absorbed the information before me (I hammered the point home by taking a photo of the document, assuring him gravely that it was for revision purposes), handed me a large book in an advanced stage of decomposition and asked that I fill out my name and the information decreed by the various columns. My nationality, birthday, father's name and mother's name were all required, and, not being in a particular hurry, I filled them out with flair, curving my sticky-uppy and hangy-downy letters and putting little spirals above my *i*s.

On my way out, chuckling inwardly at the prospect of how life would look if I really were the lovechild of Dolly Parton and Cliff Richard, the policeman called me back. I turned apprehensively, suddenly terrified that this small-town pen pusher might actually be better acquainted with the celebrities of my childhood than I had given him credit for. But instead, he pointed solemnly at another poster I had missed on the way out. It was a series of mugshots of three mustachioed faces that I presumed were the local Crips and Bloods. The pictures were so fuzzy, you wouldn't be able to pick the men out in a line-up were they standing right in front of you. If you squinted your eyes a bit, one of them actually looked like the policeman himself. I thought to tell him so. He was not amused, nor did he seem flattered by the comparison. I left swiftly, stepping out with a touch of trepidation into the lawless Hampi morning.

I tried to shrug off the officer's warnings and spent the following hours suspiciously regarding the other travellers loitering by the riverside. The day passed rather uneventfully and with the exception of a hungry mobbing by a group of monkeys and a subsequent goodwill drubbing by a gang of schoolgirls that left me bereft of a banana and all the pens I was carrying, I managed to escape the town unscathed. But the psychological damage had been done: the officer's words had taken root in the caverns of my paranoia, and started to creep out with their sharp, spindly fingers as I drove out along the deserted NH67.

In contrast to so many other highways I had taken, on the road from Hampi to Gooty I went for ten or fifteen minutes at a time without seeing another vehicle. The fuzzy faces of the bandits I had poked fun at in the police station were now appearing in my mind's eye, squinting out from behind a tree or scowling at me from a rocky outcrop. I had read several stories of highway robberies in the Indian press in the last year, usually reports of gangs who had been captured along with bags of cash and a veritable arsenal of weapons, sometimes even blindsiding their victims by dressing up as women. And since it was only the mobs who had been nicked who were making the headlines, I shuddered at just how many operatives must still be out there, roaming free and lying in wait for unsuspecting small yellow cars.

The *Times of India* wrote chillingly of one particular gang who had been operating in Gujarat and focusing their game mainly on trucks: 'Their modus operandi was brutal and effective: Any truck going through a deserted stretch of highway would be overtaken with a vehicle and forced to stop. The driver and his assistant would be beaten and left bound and gagged by side of the highway while the truck and its goods would be stolen.'[19]

Keen not to be left bound and gagged by the roadside while some tranny highway(wo)man made off with Abhilasha and most of my worldly possessions, I positioned my travel-sized can of hairspray at grabbing distance on the passenger seat and worked on perfecting my John Wayne scowl. I pitied the vigilante who faced such a terrifying combo.

At Gooty, we turned south to join the NH7, which forms the gist of the country's north–south corridor, a 2,369 km-long spine from Varanasi to Kanyakumari. By all relative standards a well-heeled road still in the process of being built, the highway bore all the hallmarks of a reconstruction project in full swing, but perhaps on a public holiday: a bunch of abandoned diggers were parked at various junctions along the way and the only workers to be seen were drinking chai by the roadside. Despite the ostensible mooch speed of construction, most of the highway was already a fully functional dual carriageway, with the odd exception of several miles of tarmac here and there where one half was closed off (by use of a haphazard arrangement of rocks, traffic cones, police tape and hand-painted signs) and the road was reduced to a lane in each direction.

This frequent changing of sides clearly confused some drivers, or perhaps just encouraged reprobate opportunists. Careering in the fast lane on a completed stretch of the highway, I was – quite obnoxiously – blaring music by way of a set of battery-powered speakers with the windows down and flooring Abhilasha's revs for all she was worth. At one point we reached the shaky zenith of 95 kmph, the fastest land speed recorded by our team to date, when I saw what looked like a truck approaching from a distance, head on, in my lane.

A quick glance at the traffic moving to my right told me I hadn't gormlessly missed another diversion. To all intents and purposes it was highway business as usual, and yet there most definitely was a truck coming at us, in the fast lane, from the wrong direction. The road was mercifully devoid of many cars, so I swerved quite easily to the left and let the truck pass with an exasperated bleat of Abhilasha's horn. Our protest was met with a nonchalant expression from the driver who indignantly flashed his lights at us, as if our presence in our rightful lane had somehow inconvenienced him.

My disbelief sustained and continued to mount well after his passing. How, just how, was that possible? You can't do that. You can*not* do that. It's so plainly, utterly, painfully, blatantly, patently, flagrantly wrong to drive in the fast lane of a highway *in the wrong direction*. Where to start with the wrongness of it all? I felt my Osho conditioning begin to seep out of the window, and in this particular case I wasn't sad to see it go. After all, there was madness, which was sort of fun, and then there was consummate lunacy, which I simply couldn't condone.

The experience of a last-minute curve out of the way of an oncoming truck must have traumatized Abhilasha as much as it did her driver, as just after our life-saving swerve and my consequent stream of maligned outrage, I began to notice she kept veering towards the hard shoulder. When I straightened her out to move in a straight line, her steering wheel was crooked and pointing in the wrong direction. From the dingy recesses of my sparse mechanical knowledge, I managed to dust the cobwebs off a diagnosis: misaligned steering. That meant that a visit to the mechanic was in order – and soon – as I was also dimly aware that an unaligned steering wheel could spell all manner of problems like bald tyres and, um, other structural troubles.

Our entry into the centre of Bangalore was marked with the usual one-handed shuffling of inadequate notes and jabbing at the badly prepared maps on my iPhone while crawling in traffic and trying not to let my attention wander too far from the bumper ahead of me, lest Abhilasha end up in a compromising situation with a dirty exhaust pipe. In the confusion of this navigating–driving juggling act, I followed a car in front of me making a right turn that crossed over an empty lane at a red light.

No sooner had I executed the manoeuvre than I found myself face to face with a traffic cop holding out his hand for me to stop.

We'd been nicked.

I pulled up by the side of the road with that sinking, name-called-out-in-assembly feeling and rolled down the window. The policeman bent and surveyed the mess of bags, clothes and plastic bottles strewn over the passenger side and back seat. He muttered something illegible, of which I only caught the word 'Nano…' We were joined by a second policeman, to whom the first turned to talk in conspiratorial whispers. He came back to me and started to speak gravely.

'Madam, you have committed an offence,' he said in a weary, scum-like-you-need-to-be-weeded-out kind of tone. 'There is no turning right on this red light.'

For a second I was speechless. Had I actually found a rule to break?

'Turning right on this red light is not permitted,' the policeman repeated, in order to hammer home the fact that I had done the unthinkable.

Figuring the officer might not take too well to me laughing out loud in the face of his accusation given our current context (even as we spoke, cars coming from behind me were zigzagging like drunken moths to avoid Abhilasha and honking loudly in protest at the legal altercation blocking their route), I decided instead to adopt the look of a forlorn tourist with outrageously winsome puppy-dog eyes.

'Officer, I am terribly sorry,' I said with an overstated sincerity that made me sound like a seductive Margaret Thatcher. 'I didn't know it was illegal to turn on a red light here.'

He didn't flinch. 'Licence, please.'

I rummaged around in my bag and pulled out a slightly dog-eared States of Jersey international licence. He looked at my glued-on photo with a little suspicion before handing the document to his colleague. It was hard to tell with his back turned, but I presumed the pair were having a jolly good giggle at the Parish of Grouville crest and the shaky signature my mum had faked in a bid to expedite the licence, for which I had applied only three days before my departure to India.

Leaning back into the car, the cop did look amused. 'No problem, madam,' he said. 'Only a hundred rupees fine.'

'One hundred rupees!' I exclaimed with the well-crafted look of award-winning amazement that was one hundred per cent facetious.

The officer suddenly took on the air of an auctioneer. 'Yes madam, only one hundred rupees. Very cheap!'

Was this my cue to barter? Flummoxed by the direction our exchange was taking, I decided to opt for a different approach; an old trick I had learned from my days dodging attempted fleecing at the hands of the traffic police in Mexico City.

'All right,' I replied. 'One hundred rupees it is. Only, can I have a receipt?'

The officer's smile wavered and he squinted at me.

'A receipt,' I repeated. 'I will be requiring a ticket.'

The policeman ignored my request, reaffirming that one hundred rupees was an excellent deal. His half-outstretched hand implied it was absolutely fine with him if I just went ahead and handed it over.

'Yes. No, I agree, officer. A hundred rupees is a most, um, generous, sum. But I will need you to write me a ticket. You know, a fine. Just to keep things official and above board and all that.' My Maggie-T accent had reached such heights of clippiness I feared it might roll over into Dame Edna.

The officer referred once more to his friend.

I called to them both out of the window. 'Actually, I'm on my way to the police station right now. Foreigners' registration. Why don't you come with me and we can do all the paperwork there together?'

The smile had disappeared from his face.

'The Police Commissioner's Office is just around the corner, isn't it?' I asked, relieved I had by chance clocked the now-vital piece of information on my phone's map seconds before making the illegal turn.

My licence was thrust back through the window and into my hand.

'Okay, go, go.'

'Go? But what about the fine?'

'Okay, okay, no problem.'

'But really, it's no bother to go to the station; it's just down the road...'

The two men had already lost interest and walked away, their chai money lost to obstinacy and a yellow Nano. I was pleased with myself for having wheedled my way out of a fine, but part of me would have been happy to pay. After all, here was the law enforcement I had been looking for; here was a shadow of the rules I had been craving. That it was tainted by the pall of corruption was neither here nor there. I had finally done something I wasn't supposed to do in India – an illegal right turn on a red light – and it felt like home.

RULE OF THE ROAD #3
Horn OK Please

Many a cautionary Indian road tale attests to the imprudence of truck drivers owing to the alleged over-consumption of marijuana, booze or *doda*, an opium and betel-nut tea. Suspicious urban legends or not, further evidence of truckies' psychedelic tendencies can easily be seen in their trucks themselves and the brightly coloured paintings that adorn the exterior bodywork, often accompanied by lights or bunting. Added to this are the giant horns and long spindly antennae the drivers are wont to pimp their rides with, as well as depictions of Ganesha, Hanuman and the saintly faced Shiva, surrounded by varieties of bizarre flora and fauna. Put all together and the trucks easily come to resemble Ken Kesey and the Merry Pranksters' bus: an electric kool-aid *doda*-and-weed ride into the mind-bending Indian night.

While some drivers (or the artists they commissioned) are more imaginative than others in the picture department, the rest compensate for a lack of visual stimuli by showing instead a flair for poesy of which the beat writers would be proud. The vehicles' posteriors are most frequently inscribed with great words of wisdom: some of them read like spiritual bumper stickers, like 'God is great', 'God is one' and 'God bless you', while others carry a more nationalistic undertone – 'India is great', 'Jai Hind' and 'I love India'. A number of them bear more jovial messages like 'Welcome' and 'Good luck!' or useful driving tips like the ironic 'Use dippers at night' (as though it were an option), 'Stop!' and simply 'Relax'. The remainder are a series of mysterious non sequiturs like the very popular 'Wait for side', a riddle I've never been able to crack, and almost as ambiguous as the 'Awaaz Do' that I had started to see on more and more vehicles in the Hindi-speaking north. Roughly translated, it means something like 'Make yourself heard', which is another way of expressing the single most common phrase painted on the backs of lorries, 'Horn OK Please'.

At first, I thought I got the gist: please horn, OK? For the enormous trucks that rarely made use of their rear-view mirrors, it was essential to let them know of your desire to pass. However, I did find myself pondering, especially after several hours of chevron hypnosis, that there might in fact be more than one way of viewing this curious assemblage of words. Was 'horn' a command or a simple noun in this case? How to interpret the combination of the collaborative 'OK' with the supplicatory 'please'? The more I thought about it, the less sense the phrase made and the more the three words appeared to have accidentally collided with one another to make a vaguely baffling bumper sticker.

Senseless haiku or not, the horn is without doubt the single most important component of a car in India. The horn is not an everyday phenomenon; it's an every minute to every second occurrence. Just as English is the country's lingua franca, handy for ironing out conversational difficulties in a nation with 22 other official tongues, the horn is the major method of communication between its hundreds of millions of road users. It's a dialect, a currency, a complex system of signage and exchange that, through a gruelling process of trial and error, I was slowly beginning to fathom.

The most important preconception for me to tackle when it came to diving into the hooter game was that horns always implied hostility. During Abhilasha's maiden voyages in Mumbai, the sound of any horn within a twenty-metre proximity had me spinning around to find the perpetrator, as though every beep and parp of the road was exclusively aimed in my direction. But what I gradually came to learn – and this did wonders for my blood pressure – was that the horn covered most forms of road communication that might in other cultures be transmitted through the indicator lights, mirrors and various other subtler forms of road etiquette.

The most common application was during the overtake: I learned that in India, it's only courteous, just before passing someone – any vehicle, not just a truck – to give them a quick honk of warning. If someone is crossing lanes in front of you on a highway, a triple beep is most useful in giving them a better sense of their room to manoeuvre, while a well-timed, well-mannered parp is usually enough to gain access from an obstructive vehicle at a traffic light. Abhilasha's humble horn also turned out to be an excellent shepherding tool when faced with herds of sheep, goats, cows and bullocks strolling over highways, or making their way down country lanes, as I discovered that even India's ungulates were savvy to the parley of the road.

There were many different types of horns, from drum-shattering sirens and vuvuzela-inspired rackets to novelty musical beepers and those squeezy rubber parpy things championed by *The Great Gatsby*. On the highways at least, a good horn really sorted the wheat from the chaff as far as mobility was concerned. The drivers of trucks and buses, for example, displayed a penchant for ear-piercing musical numbers that were loud and fearsome enough to make the earth tremble. One of those coming from behind with an alarming intensity of Doppler shift was extremely efficient at making me move, as I learned quickly that the sound would be emanating from a large and unusually speedy lorry on a suicide mission. Such vehicles were wont to drive remarkably long distances with the horn in a state of constant depression, a tactic I can't say I didn't admire just a tad.

I often thought the Nano's horn was not quite as powerful as it could have been. Later on in the trip, it even started to give off little quivers and shakes like a soprano in a bad state of training and after three chain-smoked packs of Lucky Strikes. I began to think that other drivers who couldn't see the source of its wee hoot thought they were dealing with a two-wheeler, as that was often the amount of space they allotted for passing. Or sometimes they didn't move at all, a flagrant defiance of my newly discovered road lexicon that invariably brought out in me what came to be known as The Spirit of *Braveheart*.

The *Braveheart* Tactic involved emulating at least the attitude (if not the terrifying volume) of a cross between a fearless, war-mongering William Wallace leading his armies into battle, and the king-of-the-road stratagem employed by the previously mentioned monster trucks who drove with their horns on perma-blare. If the vehicle ahead of us gave me so much as a few centimetres to work with, I would go postal with the blasts, shooting them out in rapid fire so the vehicle in question could know exactly what kind of psycho they were dealing with. As I passed in bloodthirsty mode, I kept the horn going all the way till the end of the over-take. If Abhilasha had a face, it would have been red by this point.

All of this was hugely satisfying, and once I began to enjoy myself, the horn was all mine and trigger happiness set in. Old lady crossing the street ahead: 'BEEEEEEEEPPPPPPP!' Dog saunter-ing happily in the fast lane of the highway: 'BEEEEEEEPPPP!' Cow about to lay itself at perpendicular angles to the oncoming Nano: 'BBBBBEEEEEPPPPPPP bloody BEEEEEPPPPPPPPP!!!'

Horn please? Okay, and then some.

6

MISTER THOR – Girl Meets Boy

The machinations of gastro-intestinal upheaval in India are rarely worth going into. To me, puzzling over the causes of near-perpetual Delhi belly is about as useful an activity as debating the existence of beings in the metaphysical realm: whether they're there or not, shit will invariably keep on happening. So in the same way, no matter which school of thought I subscribed to – be it the eat-anything-you-can-get-your-hands-on creed or the treat-all-food-with-high-suspicion doctrine – I always eventually ended up with an incendiary sphincter. For every several portions of street food I'd apprehensively eaten – uttering a silent prayer as I nervously ingested lunch from a dubious banana-leaf bowl – it seemed I was just as likely to be sent running to the loo after dining at an air-conditioned restaurant with tablecloths, proper menus and waiters with name badges. My best guess was the pithy excuse that I had a sensitive stomach and needed to be fed tasteless, starchy comfort food (read toast and eggs) at every available opportunity to balance out the spicy, oily fare that sustained me the rest of the time.

It was a dietary supplication that staff at the Ashley Inn, a family-run pension in Bangalore, were happy to accommodate on my first morning. Come day two, however, after an evening at a downtown restaurant gorging on what might have been the best spiced and barbequed chicken I had ever tasted, I was a no-show, locked in my loo, my belly carping and contracting at various intervals, while I flipped mournfully through a copy of *India Today* to distract myself from thinking just how inappropriate a situation this was to usher a new romance into my life.

My timing was horrible. Thor was due to reach the Ashley Inn in a few hours, possibly hoping to find me reclining seductively on the bed in my Ann Summers' finest and a black feather boa, while the reality of our first encounter here in India was more likely to involve outings for loo roll and Immodium, me trying to disguise my intestinal noises with well-timed coughs. I brooded as I studied the foot of the bathroom door with fresh intensity. This was not quite how I imagined us igniting the flames of passion.

The demons of uncertainty tainted with pre-date nerves slithered into the toilet bowl from out of the sewer and began to whisper again in my ear; perhaps the universe was trying to tell me that kindling a new interest was a terrible idea. Here I was, on the journey of a lifetime, in my own uninterrupted heaven of selfish existence. The last thing I needed was another person and the inevitable necessity of compromise to encroach on that hard-won and highly enjoyable space, as well as to distract me from the work at hand.

And anyway, where was he going to sleep? Here? In the heady rush of pseudo-tentative emails exchanged about how he'd accompany me from Bangalore all the way through to Chennai (via Kanyakumari in the south and back up again; it was a roundabout route, but, both of us drunk with sexually charged romantic anticipation, we'd agreed it'd be *fun*), we had neglected to touch on the embarrassing practicalities of the instant intimacy that would be thrust on us, sharing a small car and numerous hotel rooms together over the coming fortnight.

Just as I was thinking about getting in the shower, the phone rang. I waddled into the bedroom with my pants still around my ankles.

'Hello?'

'Hello, madam, I am calling to inform you that your husband has arrived.'

'My husband?'

'Yes, madam, your husband,' the woman said. 'Mister Thor. He is on his way up to your room now.'

'But, I'm not…'

There was a knock at the door. I slammed down the phone, froze by the unmade bed and pulled my pants up to their rightful position. Seconds passed as the room spun around me and I scoured the back rooms of my creative imagination for a way of fishing this situation out of the gutter.

Another knock.

'Um, hello?' I squeaked, despite my best attempt to deepen my voice to Dietrich-like standards of sexiness.

'Hi, it's Thor,' came his voice, which I had to admit, despite all events conspiring to the contrary, turned some deep-set part of me to jelly.

'Oh! Er, hello! You're here,' I grunted from the other side of the closed door.

'Yes. My train got in early, would you believe? Or I screwed up the timetables. In any case, can I come in?'

'Oh, of course. Of course!' I exclaimed with a forced cheeriness that must have had him already regretting not taking the train straight to Chennai. 'Just bear with me for a couple of minutes, will you?'

I ran into the bathroom to try to make myself presentable in under thirty seconds, then back into the bedroom where I rummaged through a mound of dirty T-shirts and some crumpled salwar kameez I'd bought the previous day in FabIndia[20] as an act of concession to local fashion, comfort and climatic necessity. As far as I was concerned, the optimal thing to wear at that moment would have been a large paper bag to cover my body from head to foot. Instead, I settled on a conceptually similar billowy dress that concealed as much of me as possible. I blitzed the air around me with deodorant and tidied my hair into a bun. Then I took it down again; too matronly.

Thor was in all probability reconsidering his options by the time I came round to opening the door. When I finally did, I washed over with a goosefleshy species of fairy dust at the sight of the figure who was looking no more glamorous or date-worthy than myself, clad in a coffee-stained white T-shirt and road-worn drawstring linen trousers, and clutching a green holdall about the size of my cosmetics bag that oozed the miasma of overnight train journey. He was a picture, I conceded almost jealously. How was it that a guy could look like he'd just had a fight with a tipsy tea urn after not bathing for a week and still be a candidate for a *GQ* fashion shoot? Unlike me, who probably looked mildly traumatized, Thor was grinning, clearly oblivious to either of our appearances, or the pit of infirmity that lay beyond the door. I exhaled.

'Hi. I believe you're my husband?'

'Sorry about that,' he smiled. 'Just keeping up appearances, you know. We don't want to cause any scandals, do we?'

'Certainly not, Mister Thor. What would the neighbours think?'

He stepped into the room, dropped his bag and threw himself onto the bed, to my horror right on top of an overlooked bra and some discarded pants.

'God, I feel terrible,' he moaned, squeezing the bridge of his nose. 'Sinuses. This fucking country always screws with my sinuses. Have you got any toilet paper? I need to blow my nose.'

So our first date in India did indeed consist of a loo roll mission. Not that I couldn't have asked the guesthouse for more, but frankly I thought three top-ups in 24 hours would have been borderline cringeworthy. We made it about 100 metres to the nearest kiosk before the effort became too much: my malady had drained all the energy from my limbs and I was obliged to take Thor, who was intensively perusing the vendor's cigarette selection, under the arm for support. I confessed I might need to spend the day in bed, a proposal to which he initially reacted with some excitement until I explained that it was, sadly, necessary convalescence due to a malfunctioning gut.

What followed was an afternoon and evening a world away from the ignominious hell I'd dreamed up prior to Thor's arrival. After he saw me tucked up in bed with enough water and mango juice to quench a foreign legion, he went out to the nearby Coffee Day to answer my feeble, bed-ridden request for a cheese sandwich. The afternoon passed as we lay in bed and held hands and talked and studied each other's faces with the rapturous curiosity of rediscovering something long forgotten. We were both in an invalid state, me intermittently dashing to the loo, Thor blowing his nose every twenty minutes and executing a bizarre procedure in the bathroom that involved siphoning half a litre of salt water up his nostrils, through his nasal passage and back down his throat and out of his mouth. It looked and sounded like some sort of unpleasant, choking form of brain irrigation, but it seemed to help him breathe easier. In the same way that he insisted my belly bedlam made me no less desirable in his eyes, for me he was still god of thunder-like, bent over the sink, hacking and rasping as he emptied the contents of his nasal passages. The issue of where he was going to sleep didn't even arise, as he got into bed next to me in his coffee-stained T-shirt and drawstring linens and we spent the evening watching *The Hurt Locker* on my laptop. I fell asleep before the film finished and was vaguely aware of the room turning dark at the click of a light switch before a warm arm curled around my waist and I drifted off, feeling thoroughly cared for.

By the following morning I had made a good enough recovery to be able to ingest half a pack of Good Day almond biscuits while watching doe-eyed from the bed as Thor sat with his freckled back to me, jabbing at the keys of his laptop on a table in the corner next to a pile of tissues. He had an easy presence, one that left the air light and open, even if we had just spent close to 24 hours locked in a room together. All of my previous misgivings had dissipated in the mellow intimacy that already hung between us. He seemed in no way disconcerted or thwarted by our sequestration, and in some ways was quite pleased by it.

Thor was in the fortunate and rare position of having a non-artistic job with a bohemian's schedule. As a mathematician, he worked as a consultant to clients from the US to France, Germany and Italy. As such, he only ever needed to be at dashing distance from an internet connection, and could maintain flexible work hours as well as locations. The downside of this, as I slowly began to uncover and relate to myself as a lifelong freelancer, is that there is never really a defined point where the effort starts and ends. He was in a constant state of guilt over not doing enough work, and was consequently wary of any activity that wasn't maths related.

That was why he welcomed our convalescence: it gave him the opportunity to sit at his laptop, graft equations and write thoroughly illegible programming code for hours without having to succumb to the nagging necessity of sightseeing or other non-mathematical pursuits. And as the act of tourism was frequently my own bread and butter, we were brought to a minor impasse that morning when, after checking my emails for the first time in two days, I read an invitation for paid professional sightseeing. It was a commission for a travel piece on Bangalore from the Mexican newspaper *Reforma*, to which I was a sporadic contributor. It would mean staying in the city for a few days and having a reason to explore its more travel-newsworthy side. I figured this was an excellent opportunity to amp up my appeal in Thor's eyes through the veneer of plausible professionalism (or at least, marginally more plausible, if driving a car around India could even be considered a job). I accepted the task.

Bangalore, or Bengaluru – its pre-colonial name that was reinstated in 2007 and subsequently ignored by just about everyone I spoke to, I assume because of the phonetic hassle and the fact that it actually means something like 'City of Boiled Beans' – is famously the hotbed of India's info-tech revolution. One of the fastest-growing cities in the country, it was also at the time of my arrival home to the greatest number of rupee millionaires, which basically translates as people with expendable income. As such, it was the perfect place to go in search of that grail of India's upward mobility that had eluded me since I left Mumbai (mostly because I had been putting the majority of my energy and focus into the act of driving, with the residue occupied with minor activities like eating, blogging and finding places to sleep). Bangalore was a city ripe to accommodate the dozens of foreign multinational companies that had opened offices there, as well as newbies on the start-up circuit. I saw stories in the press about PIOs[21] who had returned from their comfortable lives in the US in order to profit from the boom, as well as fully fledged foreigners who were coming in a tentative trickle to milk the burgeoning economy. Bangalore's reputation in the international press, combined with the assertions in various bits of travel literature that it was India's greenest city due to its large number of parks, primed me for a sort of high-tech Shangri-La.

So I was a bit disappointed when, on entering the metropolitan area and dodging my first traffic cop, I found that Bangalore looked quite similar to the rest of the country, at least on the surface. There was the same traffic, the same chaos, the same smoky pollution hanging in the air and the same sense that life was in leisurely overdrive, if there was such a thing. Between entering the city from the north via Bellary Road and reaching the Ashley Inn, it was imposing government buildings like Karnataka's High Court and its state legislation HQ, the Vidhana Soudha – not, as I expected, Google, Microsoft or IBM megaplexes – that dominated the architectural landscape. It turned out that most of the big company headquarters and IT parks were located in the city's suburbs, while the centre was undergoing a very involved facelift. From Mahatma Gandhi Road, I could see cranes and construction in every direction. The road itself was a giant building site, where a half-finished overpass was throwing the street below into shadow and covering everything within sprinkling distance in a film of concrete dust.

Not far from there, finishing touches were being put to a luxury shopping centre called UB City that was the kind of place only heiresses and rap stars could possibly want to shop. Thor and I made it past the mustachioed guard at the front door to enter a world of Ab-Fab brands the likes of Vuitton, Zegna and Versace. We went up to the roof of the complex for some air and discovered a piazza that had been engineered to resemble – according to the brochure – 'an easy, street side ambience' of a high-end international food court. From there we could see, framed by a set of fountains in the foreground, an uncanny *trompe l'oeil* city skyline that was attempting to create the effect of being in the midst of a clutch of flashy skyscrapers; think movie-set rendition of downtown Philadelphia. Drawn in by the smell of baking bread and a waft of garlic, Thor and I did a round of the restaurant menus, me dizzy with the glamour of it all and salivating at the prospect of European-style food; Thor, a bit disgruntled for having been wrenched away from programming, rolling his eyes at the European-style prices.

'I could feed myself for a week on this money,' he sighed, to my disappointment. But he was right: it was a world away from the wholesome and inexpensive Indian food I'd come to know, and the prices were, relatively speaking, extortionate. But hypnotized by the veneer of cool, I pressed for more.

'Let's just go take a look in there,' I suggested, eyeing up a huge glass-fronted structure with what looked like a giant Buddha's head surveying its hiply lit interior. The place was called Shiro, and the concept was a pan-Asian restaurant-stroke-terrace-stroke-club, heavily influenced by the Buddha Bar. We walked in to find the manager and staff engaged in a photo session, clustered around a framed certificate of a food award from the *Times of India*. Eastern ambient music filled the cooled air and stragglers from the late-lunch crowd tweaked morsels of food into their mouths with chopsticks, large shopping bags leaning casually against the table legs.

I looked down at my feet cased in plastic flip-flops: they had acquired a semi-permanent layer of dirt from the sum of all the streets they had passed through since Mumbai, and the once-glossy nail varnish on my toenails had chipped back like a peeling inner-city wall. The bottoms of my trousers were caked in a mysterious mud of whose origin I had no idea, but whose presence I had grown used to as an inevitability of circulating in India; in the discerning light of Shiro, what I'd thought a couple of days ago to be groovy local attire looked more like lame FabIndia dowd. We had fallen down the rabbit hole, which was to say we had crossed the line between the world outside – the cacophony of life that jostled through the day to the soundtrack of jackhammers, caterwauls, car horns and human voices – into the sterilized world of designer labels and meze plates that was the domain of a tiny minority.

I found myself staring at a woman with impeccably tressed hair and a trouser suit that was pressed to match. How did she keep so *clean*? I looked to Thor, who appeared to be experiencing the same level of disorientation. His annual visits to the ashram in Chennai were pretty much the extent of his experience in the country. He had never felt the urge – or he simply hadn't had the time – to travel around, and had certainly never come across places like UB City. For Thor, India was where street vendors provided thimbles of chai and fresh coconut for only a few pennies, and where one ate rice and dal daily at the ashram canteen. Everything else was excess. The idea that I was on the verge of ordering a cocktail that would cost him several days' living budget was visibly vexing him. I took pity.

'Subway?'

'Oh yes, yes. Let's get a sandwich. Thank god.'

Indeed, Subway was a welcome sanctuary of mass consumerism (albeit still quite high end by relative standards) in the bizarre realm of exclusivity we had discovered. From the discomfort of the fast-food seating there, we gained space for reflection, trying to find a speck of meaning where really there wasn't any. UB City didn't reveal anything too interesting beyond the fact that there was obviously a significant number of people with the cash to blow on keeping Salvatore Ferragamo and his haute-couture colleagues in business. For sure, the number of super-rich in India has gone up in tune with the economy in general since the early 1990s, but they still only count for about 1% of the population. Leagues more interesting is the new economic bubble towards whom the Nano was ostensibly aimed – the emerging middle class. They were the new generation of consumers carving out their own niches in the gaping territory between UB City and the slums, and it was their backs on which the hopes of the new Indian dream were pinned.

That night, we followed up our Subway subs with veg fried rice in the company of an IBM software engineer called Arunsai, whom Thor had met on the train. Thor showed me the piece of paper with his phone number, shaky from the seismographic effects of the railroad, and I insisted we call him straight away – I was eager to hear at first hand about the life of an IT worker here at Ground Zero. After the disorienting extremes of UB City, I wanted to discover more about the people in the middle.

Arunsai suggested we meet in a Chinese restaurant somewhere on the outskirts of town, an air-conditioned family joint with little embellishment other than the odd hint of Chineseness in the form of a lucky cat or a goldfish. Arunsai ordered chicken fried rice and launched straight into bemoaning the fact he might soon need to forgo his meat-eating ways. He was about to be engaged, he explained, to a girl from Chennai, and she was a vegetarian. Her family were intractable on the issue that she was to remain so, and that she would never have to cook meat for her husband. Arunsai looked downcast.

'I don't know how I can never eat meat again,' he sighed, before remembering something clse that made him reach for his phone with a sly grin. 'You want to see her picture?' He pulled up a muggy, pixelated image of a young, plumpish girl dressed in a sari and adorned with all manner of golden trinkets, hanging from any part of her head that would support it.

'Our engagement is next month and the wedding is in May,' he beamed. 'You must come.'

I had yet to get used to the Indian tradition of inviting any random stranger to a wedding, and was thrown a bit off kilter by his good-natured proposal.

'She seems nice. What's she like?'

'I don't know; we haven't really spoken yet. But I think she will be a good wife.' He forgot to add, *if only she could whip me up a weekly roast lamb*, though it was written all over his face.

Arunsai had come to Bangalore from his home in Thanjavur, Tamil Nadu in 2005 to claim his own stake in the IT gold rush. At first, it had been hard to find his feet: after many weeks of applying for jobs and sifting through rejections, he was offered an internship at Compuserve, though he had to pay the company for the privilege. He subsisted on the meagre Rs 5,000 (£60) his father was able to send him each month. Clearly a savvy worker, Arunsai managed to scale up the chain in a snakes-and-ladders motion that saw him transferring to Pune for a while to work for IBM, before being duped into travelling to the US in search of work that never materialized.

'I dreamed of America and a Honda Civic,' he confided with a self-deprecating grin. 'Everyone in India does.' But that dream didn't come true and after a few months of fruitless job hunting, he returned home.

After dinner, Arunsai insisted we go to visit his home. It was about a five-minute drive from the restaurant, in a brand new apartment building with its own parking garage where, having driven ahead of us on his motorbike, he showed us proudly to his very own parking spot. His flat was sizeable, with three bedrooms, two balconies and a security system, but not a scrap of furniture. His bed was a mat on the tiled floor and his kitchen was a single gas cylinder with a pot perched on top. He was clearly a man in need of a woman, and living in anticipation of his impending wedding and the gifts that would follow and furnish his house. In the meantime, as far as he was concerned, he'd done the right thing by his future wife by finding them their first family home, and that was all that mattered.

Driving back to the city centre that evening, I became aware again of Abhilasha's errant steering, which I was sure had grown worse since I'd first noticed it on the way to Bangalore a few days earlier. It called for immediate action; she had to go to a mechanic. A quick Google search informed me that a nearby Tata garage by the name of Prerana Motors was at my service, and I called them to make an outpatient appointment for Abhilasha the next day. That night Thor had the opportunity to see me at my obsessive-compulsive worst as I went online to ensure I was as informed as I could be prior to handing her over to any potentially unscrupulous mechanics.

My online research had done little to shed light on her disorder, which I learned was referred to in the trade as a 'steering pull'. Ploughing through a cascade of search results, I was forced to battle with an impenetrable mechanic's lexicon of the various causes of a crooked steering wheel. An authoritative-looking website called aa1car.com ('Automotive Diagnostic and Repair Help for Cars and Trucks', if you're interested) listed no fewer than 31 possibilities for why Abhilasha was out of joint, from binding in the upper strut mounts to an uneven parallelogram steering linkage. The page continued with dense passages written in small fonts that showed no consideration for the notion that there might be anyone other than a doctor of auto-mechanics reading the text.

'Too much cross-camber can make a vehicle pull or lead towards the side that has the most (positive) camber or away from the side that has the least (negative) camber; the under-lying cause may be a bent strut or mislocated strut tower, a bent spindle, collapsed control arm bushing, weak or broken spring, or a shifted cross member or engine cradle.'

This was not going to be a straightforward deal, not now that spindles, strut towers and arm bushings were involved. I needed to go to the best garage in town in a bid to stem the tide of the what-ifs that had started flooding the flittery membranes of my subconscious. What if we had to wait for spare parts? And what if those spare parts could only be sourced from a mine in the deepest Himalayas? And what if they could only travel here on the backs of lame mules? In my pessimistic mind's eye, the future didn't look too bright.

Still, lady luck hadn't entirely jumped ship: we were after all in Bangalore, home to some of the best cerebral matter the subcontinent had to offer. What better place than this city full of geeks and engineers to search for a cure to Abhilasha's condition?

The photographs on Prerana Motors' website spoke of an impressively large workshop filled with state-of-the-art machin-ery, lots of colourful balloons and a very shiny floor. It was an image that bore little resemblance to its real, rather more makeshift appearance. The actual entrance was a sign painted onto the brick wall of an enclosure off a dusty back road. As Thor and I stood looking confused in the parking lot, we were approached by a man in a pressed white shirt whose eyes lit up at the sight of Abhilasha.

He walked straight to Thor. 'Can I help you, sir?'

'Yes, actually you can,' I cut in. Irritatingly enough, my hard-learned engineer lingo jumped out of the window before you could say mislocated strut. 'It seems that the steering wheel is a bit, erm, wonky.'

'The problem is your Nano has a wonky wheel?' the man asked with genuine concern, still looking directly at Thor. I nodded. He gave the tyres a sage once-over before adjusting his glasses and straightening back up to face Thor. 'Please, give me the key and I will take it for a test drive.'

Thor turned to me and I hesitated. The man insisted with an almost impatient gesture of his hand.

'Please, wait in the visitors' room, backside,' he said, pointing towards the building behind the wall. Against my better judgement and every screaming maternal instinct, I gave the man my keys. He and Abhilasha disappeared in a white cloud out onto the Old Madras Road.

Thor sensed my concern. 'Don't worry, she'll be fine. Come on, let's go check out the visitors' room *backside*.'

The visitors' room was a hot and poky little space with nothing in the way of shiny floors or balloons. Instead there were a few plastic chairs, a copy of the previous day's *Deccan Herald*, another paper in the local Kannada script (which looked like an alphabet constructed during a particularly creative night spent with a couple of joints and a baroque love-heart stencil) and a water cooler proffering about an inch of liquid and two suspiciously recycled-looking plastic cups. We waited for half an hour with no news and began to wonder whether our white-shirted friend hadn't already reached Madras by way of its namesake road. I decided to take matters into my own hands and went outside. There was Abhilasha, surrounded by a formidable pit-stop crew who were washing and polishing her bodywork with urgency, commanded by the man in the white shirt standing in their midst and conducting the service symphony in a hoedown of waved gestures.

I approached him apprehensively with the air of someone meeting a surgeon who'd just performed a triple bypass on their next of kin. So, was everything all right?

'Yes, yes, everything is done,' he beamed.

'You, uh, fixed the steering?' I asked, incredulous that there appeared to be no need for any inpatient treatment, nor for new binding for the upper strut mounts to be ordered from up north.

The steering, I was assured, was fixed, and he had personally checked over the whole car himself. Oil and water had been topped up and now Abhilasha was getting a good clean on the inside and out.

It was all too easy...

'Well, I'll just go over and pay while you finish off here then,' I said, stepping towards the garage office, mentally totting up the price of the list of jobs he had reeled off, but white-shirted man stopped me in my tracks.

'No, madam, please, no money!'

'No money?' What was this, a TV show set-up?

'No, free service, madam.'

'What? Why?' Surely this was a ruse. I didn't really believe him until he handed me Abhilasha's keys ten minutes later, my little yellow companion gleaming like the Koh-i-Noor diamond. The man didn't stick around for a palm of baksheesh or even a mild show of gratitude; he simply turned on his heel and marched back towards the garage.

'Thank you,' I called out after him, a bit choked. He looked around, surprised, so I tried to think of a good follow-up.

'I'm very, very... satisfied.'

The man smiled and continued walking. I sat down in the newly vacuumed driver's seat to find the steering wheel perfectly aligned and the floor covered with large pieces of brown paper that wished us 'Happy Motoring'.

7

PEDAL TO THE METAL – The Hills of the Nilgiris

MYSORE to FORT KOCHI; KM 1,709–2,105

The drive south began in the regal city of Mysore, a place we opted to overlook entirely in the name of clocking up some decent kilometres after a week's hiatus in Bangalore. This was in spite of the *Lonely Planet*'s claim that it was 'one Indian city that deserves a slower pace'. The pace Thor and I opted for resulted in a total of twelve hours in its vicinity: seven asleep, two eating, one cursing the hotel's slow internet, and a further two hours stuck in traffic on the way in and out. A cheeky ten-minute peek at the Maharaja's floodlit palace through the crack in its closed gates before dinner was the closest we got to any appreciation of the architecture there, a fleeting encounter that was a symptom of my diminishing urge for cultural edification in the face of the growing compulsion just to keep on driving.

It was while we were leaving Mysore for Fort Kochi, the old colonial fishing port on Kerala's coast, that Thor finally dropped the question that gave air to a Pandora's box of worms.

'Would you like me to drive at all?'

The tone of his voice betrayed the prospect that getting behind the wheel of the Nano was about the last thing he had any desire to do. But perhaps he felt compelled, after a week of having me taxi him around Bangalore, to offer to pitch in with the driving. For my part, I had absolutely no intention of even offering Thor the wheel. The primary reason was that despite the emotional-physical gumption his presence was inspiring in me, I was still harbouring traces of guilt in view of the fact that I had originally intended to make this journey alone. Taking a lover had been an unforeseen development and infringed a little on my single-girl-hero self-image. To compensate, I decided that at least I would ensure that I planned and drove the entire route. Up to now, this had seemed a situation that suited Thor well, since he hadn't exhibited any special flair for map reading, nor a vocalized preference for any particular style of driving.

'I was hoping to drive the whole route myself,' I said. 'It's important to me. Like a sort of a challenge, you know.'

Thor brightened. He was visibly relieved as he lowered the backrest of the passenger seat.

'Great. You be the boss, then.'

And so I was, at least as far as the roads were concerned. I was route planner, executor and chauffeur all in one, and occasionally it went to my head, in as far as I found myself commanding my companion to double-check a particular road or run out to ask directions from a savvy-looking passer-by. Still, my bossiness seemed to roll off his back: Thor was my happy partner who controlled the music, passed me the water, fed cookies into my mouth as I drove and lowered the window from time to time to stick his head out to smoke.

After Mysore, our route towards the coastal town of Kochi followed the NH212 down to the national parks of Bandipur and Mudumalai that mark the intersection of the three big southern states, Karnataka, Tamil Nadu and Kerala, and form part of a much larger highland area called the Nilgiri Biosphere Reserve. Thor and I were particularly excited by the website's inventory of fauna that suggested a safari might be on the cards: tigers, leopards, elephants, pythons and hyenas all inhabited these parklands in the company of more fantastical-sounding animals like four-horned antelopes, giant flying squirrels and mugger crocodiles.

As our path through Bandipur progressed along a road that wound through dense, leafy scrub, however, I had the sinking sensation that the closest we would get to any of the afore-mentioned beasts would be through the pictures of tigers and elephants that hung from the trees and carried sombre warnings not to disturb the wild animals or make any sudden noises to alarm them. Within seconds of spotting the first such sign, we were overtaken by a rickshaw parping his horn with gusto. Another passed us a few minutes later with similar pomp, as did another, then another. Deeply peeved by the prospect of their horns scaring off potential wildlife, I secretly supplicated the tigers and elephants to take traffic matters into their own hands, if they found the sound of the horns half as irritating as I did.

By the time we passed through Bandipur and crossed into Mudumalai, we spotted a couple of wild elephants between the branches of roadside bushes. Thor bade me pull an emergency stop and he jumped out with a camera to get a closer look at one that was bathing in the stream below. It was a spectacular sight, and strangely intimate. As soon as he sensed our presence, however, the elephant turned to the opposite bank and made up its steep slope with a sprightliness I had never before witnessed in an animal larger than a Labrador. It seemed we had made some kind of incursion on his modesty.

The tigers, leopards and giant flying squirrels were nowhere to be seen, but one group of animals we couldn't avoid were the langur monkeys who roamed in tribes and hung out menacingly by the side of the road as though daring us to slow down enough to warrant nicking a wiper. As we drove by one particularly large group of the animals, Thor had me stop the car again. He tore the side of the packet of digestive biscuits we'd been eating and emptied the remaining few into my hands.

'You want to see a cool trick?'

'Wait, you're not giving these to the monkeys, are you? They'll lynch us for them. We'll die of rabies before we even get to Kerala.'

'No, we're going to feed them from the safety of the car,' Thor assured me, grinning.

He opened the passenger window about an inch, to the curiosity of the monkeys who were closing in on us at an unsettlingly fast speed.

'Hang on. You can't feed monkeys biscuits, can you? We're in a national park. Isn't there some law against that?'

'It's just a few digestives,' he answered, taking one of them from my hand and holding it through the gap in the window. The largest of the attendant group of langurs saw his opportunity and lunged at the biscuit, grabbing it out of Thor's hand. Almost instantly, two of his companions jumped onto the windscreen, while I could hear from the patter of feet that there were at least another two on the roof. Four or five tiny clawed hands were grasping at the air through the open window. We were under attack: it was like being in a monkey car wash. I went for the button and pushed the glass back up as the simians withdrew their mitts just in time.

'They'll kill us,' I squealed.

Thor was laughing. 'And just how do you think they're going to push themselves through such a tiny gap in the window? What are they, David Blaine monkeys?'

After my heart rate normalized, I conceded that actually it had been quite something to be set on by a cluster of langurs.

'OK, I'm going to try.' I prodded my window button until the glass had lowered just enough to allow for a biscuit to be posted through the slit. It was grabbed out of my hand before

I even had the chance to clock the approaching beast, who appeared from nowhere and had most likely been lying in wait on the roof. I kept pushing the digestives through the gap in the window, and they kept being snatched from my hand. When they were all finished, the monkeys disappointingly showed no gratitude; they simply scarpered off into the trees, sugared up and satisfied.

Once we were out of the national parks, the highland landscape of the Western Ghats opened to swathes of gleaming green tea plantations and teak forests in an area called Nilambur, whose smaller roads and absence of noisy traffic gave it the air of the Swiss Alps. We pulled over at a village where a group of kids were playing in the river, screaming at the top of their lungs as they flung themselves from a wooden jetty into the water below. When we parked, delight with the water quickly transformed into fascination with us and the Nano, which after a few minutes became a preoccupation with my camera and a series of increasingly dangerous diving stunts exuberantly performed for the benefit of a photo.

Thor, egged on by the kids' enthusiasm, came very close to ripping off his own shirt and jumping into the water, before I warned him of the combined dangers of water-borne parasites, freak river currents and wet clothing on nice clean Nano upholstery.

The jumps finally exhausted, Thor turned to magic and riled the boys with a series of disappearing coin tricks that elevated us to a low-level celebrity status among the children, a situation that was spiralling into chaos as I found myself surrounded by a dozen or so wet little bodies requesting pens and my country coins. We got back into the safety of the car and locked the doors.

'All right, I'll admit it just once that I'm glad you came,' I told Thor.

'Not bad, is it, our little road trip?'

No, it wasn't, not bad at all – even though it was never supposed to be *our* little trip, it was supposed to be *my* brave mission. But things were different with two of us. Playing with kids and inciting monkeys to attack the car for biscuits were things I'd never think to do if I was on my own, or just wouldn't dare. This whole co-pilot thing was working out – for now.

We rejoined the NH67 and slowly descended back to the coast via the town of Malappuram, finally hooking up with the trusty NH17 that had been skirting the seashore all the way from Goa and beyond. Back at sea level, the road straightened out and Abhilasha was once again immersed in the black mist of trucks, buses, three-wheelers, motorbikes and the rest of the increasingly familiar, eclectic cast of the Indian traffic palaver. I was back to swerving, overtaking, honking my horn, flashing my lights and swearing at oncoming vehicles encroaching on my lane.

A rude awakening after the peace of the Nilgiris, the situation was soon compounded by yet another opportunity for self-annihilation courtesy of the local road authorities, in the form of a series of speed barriers set out to control the flow of the traffic headed south. The system involved placing two large metal gates within a couple of metres of one another on either side of the road and at right angles to oncoming traffic, in a way that tended to bring vehicles (okay, maybe just my vehicle) to a panic-stricken halt rather than a slow stop.

I noticed the first barrier only a few seconds before I nearly ploughed Abhilasha into it. I slammed on the brakes and swerved around it in time, thanking Ganesha there hadn't been another car in the opposite direction to break my speed once and for all.

Then began the usual post-close-call flood of expletives. You can't – I began to lecture whoever had put the barrier there, using Thor as my medium – you simply *cannot* put a big metal gate right across a highway with no prior warning, lights or traffic cones. It was plain dangerous, ridiculous, stupid… And who the hell were they trying to slow down anyway? The vast majority of vehicles hauling themselves along this sorry excuse for a road (as it had now become in my enraged eyes) were surely in themselves speed-control measures enough: overweight flatulent lorries, bullock carts, decrepit buses, rickshaws or bicycles, all of which were tootling along at an irritating 40 kmph, usually right in front of me.

There was another speed-control feature on most national highways: villages and towns. Every ten minutes or so, by the time we had overtaken a long line of trucks headed by a tractor pulling an enormous trailer piled with earth and were cruising at a happy 60 kmph, we'd find ourselves in the thick of a village and its resident herds of goats and wandering dogs, buses in the middle of the road, markets whose stallholders you could high-five as you drove by, cows crossing the road and the mandatory group of school children who would run after us shouting their enthusiasm: 'Nanonanonano!' All these factors contributed to keeping our average speed maddeningly slow with so much ground to cover.

By the time the second set of speed breakers rolled around, I was ready for them. I slowed down in time to avoid hitting the first barrier and even managed to read the text printed on a sign attached to it that advised, 'Kill your speed; life is only once.'

'Wait a minute: life is only once?' I consulted Thor, who, despite not being an expert in Hindu cosmology, was still more clued up than I. 'I thought life here in India stretched on and on through endless rebirth cycles and, what are they called, *kalpas*?'

It was a belief system I had thought could go a long way in explaining the laissez-faire approach to motorcycle safety, for example. The absence of helmets and protective clothing as well as the proliferation of riders on a standard two-wheeler appeared to speak tomes about the travellers' innate faith in fate and detachment from their current human forms. And I never had to look very far to see drivers hell-bent on cata-pulting themselves into the next life as soon and as creatively as possible: right ahead of me was a barefoot youth on a TVS scooter with a television set wedged between his knees and a bundle of iron rods at least a couple of metres long balanc-ing behind him perpendicular to the road, while just in front of him was a three-wheeler van holding about three times its capacity of passengers, guys perched on tiptoe along the min-ute wooden ledges attached to the outside of the bodywork, holding onto the roof (home to another five or so passengers) for not-so-dear life.

But on the NH47 at least, the traffic authorities were very much at odds with the road users. By denying drivers and roof-riding passengers the prospect of rebirth, they were flying in the face of Hindu values and a philosophical system that had been millennia in the making. Maybe this was done in the hope that by presenting life as a unique phenomenon rather than one chapter in an infinite series of returns, they might be able to instil a keener sense of caution and self-preservation in road users.

Then Thor said, 'Kerala's a Communist state, isn't it?'

Of course! Kerala had been the first place in the world to elect a Communist government back in 1957, and since then various regroupings of Marxist parties had held power, always endorsed by the ballot. Currently in government was the Left Democratic Front, which had ruled in intermittent terms since 1982. Was it possible that the road authorities here – in a state modelled on Soviet and Chinese forms of government – were appealing to motorists on a very humanist level not to let their belief in infinite future incarnations get in the way of a little prudence in this one?

According to a 2009 report by the National Crime Records Bureau, despite having a fairly high accident rate, Kerala had the second lowest rate of deaths in road accidents in any state after Goa, with less than 10.8% of accidents ending in a fatality. Compared with Arunachal Pradesh's 48% or Bihar's chilling 52%,[22] that's a fairly good figure and implies that though accidents do happen in Kerala, they tend to be of the milder, scratchy bumper variety.[23] I began to think that the Marxists might be onto something after all, until I noted in the same report that Kerala sadly also held the record for the highest suicide rates in all of India.

'Well, that's a cautionary tale about godlessness, don't you think?' Thor remarked.

I gave the dashboard Ganesha a little tap. 'What do you reckon we get a little Lenin or a Che to keep him company? Make sure our bases are covered?'

'Not daunting enough. I reckon, up the stakes and make it a Stalin or a Mao. Or even a Kim Jong Il. Let's see fate fuck with us then.'

RULE OF THE ROAD #4
Full Beams or Bust

Most rural highways are hardly lit – if at all. After sunset, drivers are usually swallowed into an all-encompassing obscurity that finds no relief in any form of street lamp, cat's eye or even white chevron to guide the way and show up the divisions of the road. Inventing them mentally (as per the advice of the Delhi Traffic Police) is one thing, but making up the actual edges of the highway in the absence of any illumination whatsoever is another. Therefore, full beams are required, and in their glow, the boundaries of the grey tarmac become sufficiently apparent.

This works well enough until the gloom beyond the scope of one's own headlights begins to brighten and a pair of lights shining at about as many hypergiant lumens as the Dog Star appears from over the horizon. Full beams meet full beams. Here, I would shield my eyes and automatically dim Abhilasha's headlights in anticipation of the oncoming vehicle doing the same. But one of the first lessons I learned on the road after just hours in India was that it never did. The Other Vehicle invariably kept its lights on Absolute Wither until we had passed one another and the car/ truck/bus (whatever it was; I had no chance of being able to make out the form lurking behind the glare) had disappeared behind us, out of sight of my rear-view mirror.

The same thing kept on happening: a pair of scorching white headlights approached us from the opposite direction, Abhilasha lowered her full beams as she believed was customary, and the approaching vehicle ignored her gesture, refusing to reciprocate, and carried on, its blinding lights blasting through the darkness, bathing every object within reach of its rays in a miasmic white mist – which was all well and good except for the blindness bit. A lifelong night-time opener of cracks in curtains and ardent aficionado of the bathroom nightlight, I've never been a big fan of all-out murk. However, in fighting deep blackness with unbridled dazzle, I realized that the drivers I was encountering were serially blinding other road users: while we were scrambling about in the glare of fully charged headlights, the sides of the road disappeared from view, so if there was something up ahead like a bend, an ox cart, a cyclist, a rickshaw with gammy rear lights, even a pedestrian, I was none the wiser. The only way to remedy this temporary blindness – and I think you know where I'm going with this – was to switch on our own full beams in turn. This was a vicious circle, a snake eating its own brightly lit tail; a negative feedback loop that, as Gandhi almost certainly didn't say, left the world blind.

I decided to employ a little reproachful reasoning. When the next car approached us, instead of deferentially lowering Abhilasha's headlights, I flashed them, in order to try to bring attention to the fact that someone was behaving like a total road jerk. The first car completely ignored the gesture, as did the second and third. They probably presumed Abhilasha was suffering from some kind of electrical malfunction. The fourth vehicle to pass us flashed us back, as though we were chums sharing a jolly greeting from across the road. The strobe method was also proving dishearteningly ineffective.

I was at pains to understand the logic behind this insistence on using full beams. Surely it made sense that if everyone lowered their beams, we'd all be able to see the road we could not see by this ridiculous, suicidal *lex talionis* that was rendering an entire country of drivers visually impaired.

I realized with a heavy heart that there was no choice in the matter. I reverted to the old maxim: when in doubt, switch your headlights to full and frazzle the retina of anyone within flashing distance. Right or wrong, it was the only way.

8

SOUTHERN COMFORT – A Swami's Words of Wisdom

KANYAKUMARI to TIRUCHIRAPPALI; KM 2,442–2,819

For a brief but seminal ten minutes, Abhilasha was the southernmost car in all of India, parked as she was in a no-parking zone by a wall at the lowest point on the Indian subcontinent: Kanyakumari. It was a photo op worth risking a fine for: the giant statue of Tamil poet-saint Thiruvalluvar towered stoically on a rock among the waves in the background, and as Abhilasha posed, she attracted the attention of a couple of souvenir merchants, a candy-floss salesman and a Polaroid photographer, who were far more impressed by her fuel-to-mileage ratio than they were by the fact that our team had reached a veritable landmark in our journey that day.

Touching 2,442 km on the odometer meant that a quarter of the trip was pretty much in the bag, and I thought Kanyakumari, the town at the extreme end of the whole country, was an appropriate place to mark the achievement of the first quarter. From where we were, looking out over Cape Comorin, the spot where the Indian, Arabian and Mannur seas all came together, we had nowhere to go but back up again. And we had arrived, Thor told me, in the footsteps of Swami Vivekananda, the famous Indian sage who had stood on this exact spot back in 1892 after an epic journey of pilgrimage to discover his homeland.

A geographical coincidence separated by nearly 120 years was, however, where the resemblance between the Swami and myself ended. Vivekananda, a mendicant monk at the time, was armed with nothing but a staff, a bowl and a couple of books (rest assured that neither of them was the *Lonely Planet*) as he spent four years cheerfully traversing India on foot and occasionally by train. Despite all the modern comforts of an air-conditioned car, guidebooks, GPS and a thermos flask, I, on the other hand, still found copious occasion to grumble about my travelling conditions. Exalted to have reached the end of India, the Swami plunged himself into the waves and swam out to a large rock a few dozen metres off the mainland, where he sat for three days in divine contemplation. I bought a chai in a paper thimble off a man on a bicycle and tried to think of a convincing excuse for not taking the small ferry across the choppy sea to Vivekananda's Rock, where a memorial now stood to the great Indian sage. The best reason I could come up with was the most obvious one, namely that my tummy didn't like the look of it.

Thor tried to tempt me into the sea via the beach at the end of town, where fully clothed Indian tourists were tentatively taking on the waves up to their thighs, but frankly, my impulse to follow Vivekenanda's lead and throw myself into the water in a life-affirming gesture of merriment was soured by a succession of churlish torrents of irritation. The trifling reason for my annoyance was a combination of the plodding journey times (the drive from the beach resort of Varkala, where Thor and I had snuck in a couple of nights, had taken double Delilah's predicted time of three-and-a-half hours) and various physio-neurological consequences that were beginning to manifest as a result of my dogged refusal to let Thor drive.

I christened them Accelerator Foot Strain, Clutch Foot Strain and Right Wrist Strain: three conditions of irksome discomfort that had befallen me after excessive pedal pumping and one too many emergency turns of the wheel. There was also Speed Bump Hallucination Syndrome, or SBHS, the result of repeated ordeals incurred by hidden speed bumps, potholes, rocks and other features of the road surface that involved steep inclines, declines or outright drops, culminating in skull-rattling jolts and some worrying thumps from Abhilasha's undercarriage. So tortured had I been by the continuous bombshell appearance of these demons, which were often extremely well camouflaged into the road surface, that I naturally became more adept at spotting them. Such unremitting concentration on the shapes and forms of the tarmac passing under Abhilasha's front wheels gave rise to the aforementioned syndrome. This tended to manifest after several hours on the road: my SBHS-riddled brain would spy some kind of obstruction up ahead and before I knew it, a subconscious process took place where my aching, AFS-afflicted right foot went for the brake, while the CFS-plagued left calf stretched towards the clutch and the RWS-addled hand tried to curve the wheel. It was the teamwork of a pitiful company of invalids that often saw me slowing down in the middle of the road, only to realize sheepishly that I had just come to a stop before the shadow of a tree, or a patch of grit fallen off the back of a passing lorry.

Looking out at Vivekananda's rock among the white horse–tipped waves, my legs, back and right wrist throbbing from the day's drive, I had a feeling I could learn something from the sage about the levels of endurance necessary for travelling in India. From under a ceiling fan in a room at his ashram – we decided that since we couldn't (be arsed to) visit the Swami's rock, we could at least spend the night at his digs – I came across an inspiring quote of his: 'What I want is muscles of iron and nerves of steel, inside which dwells a mind of the same material as that of which the thunderbolt is made.'

'Blimey, he wasn't aiming low, was he?'

Thor, who was a fan of the Swami's, concurred. 'I think he's sending you a message from beyond the grave to pull yourself together and put a sock in it.'

I growled at him from the bed while rubbing my calves.

'Since you won't let me drive, I mean. That's what you're going to get.'

And so all talk of my driving gripes was henceforth banished. There were people out there walking, cycling, riding camel-back the length and breadth of the country, and I was moaning because sitting in a comfortable air-conditioned seat was getting a bit too much for me. Out, out with the malingering mardy grouser, I resolved, and in with the thunderbolt mind. I concluded that with the dawn there would rise from Kanyakumari a transformed, refreshed Nano driver, and it would be the first day of the rest of our trip.

Kanyakumari gave Thunderbolt and Thor a VIP's send-off via a quiet, smooth road that cut through miles of wind farms whose blades spun silently and unwitnessed. So filled was I with fresh resolve for the trip, I had announced to Thor after a few minutes studying the map that morning that we would make Pondicherry, a former French union territory on the east coast that we had marked as our next destination, in one shot; all 600 km of it. Thor was sceptical, but humoured me for the sake of preserving my newfound reservoir of welly. Plus it meant going through a town called Tiruchirappali, which gave us hefty mileage in terms of pronunciation yucks.

An hour later we were on the NH7, which turned out to be the dual carriageway of my dreams, or at least the road I would have given Abhilasha's spare tyre for during our journeys on the national highways in Kerala. It was driving bliss. After hours plodding down the west coast, cursing rural roads and all the obstacles in their many manifestations, Abhilasha was finally in her element, cruising at a euphoric 90 kmph on newly laid tarmac where vehicles were in their correct lanes and moving in the direction they were supposed to be. We were set to cover 300 km in four hours, a distance that would take at least double that time on the auxiliary roads. I eulogized to Thor the wonders of modern highways and their innate civility, and began to wonder if this marvel of a road wasn't a gift from the gods, mediated by Vivekananda himself as a reward for my new stoic resolve. My AFS, CFS, RHWS and SBHS were already fading into the past.

There was little argument in my mind: a few well-placed highways between strategic locations and cities in India would do wonders to alleviate congestion on the smaller roads and in the villages, which themselves acted as complex speed breakers to hordes of long-distance traffic. As if to affirm my feeling, every few kilometres, Congress President Sonia Gandhi and Prime Minister Manmohan Singh beamed down from information banners posted by the National Highways Authority of India. I presumed whatever was written on the lengthy signs was a manifesto of the same progressive ideals of twenty-first-century transport that I was busy expounding to my increasingly bored companion.

After all, the NHAI was one branch of the Indian government that really had its work cut out: although India could boast the same road density as, say, the United States, around half of those roads were an unpaved, dusty, rocky affair more suitable to gritty off-roading than transporting freight and passengers from one place to the next. I had read (not without a heavy sense of foreboding) that it could take truck drivers anything up to 65 hours to drive the 1,375 km from Mumbai to Delhi[24] (a mind-bending average of about 13 kmph), and that the delays cost businesses millions of rupees in revenue. The cause was simple to diagnose but hard to fix: bad roads, horrible traffic. Thousands of villages were sometimes cut off from their neighbours due to dirt tracks that disintegrated during the monsoon. And even along the routes where concrete had once been laid, maintenance was so poor that the roads often ended up with enough craters to pass for the surface of the moon.

'Our roads don't have a few potholes. Our potholes have a few roads' was the famous remark by Prime Minister Atal Behari Vajpayee in the late 1990s when the NHAI – by then a decade old and with little to show for its ten years of existence – decided to get ambitious and put into action a plan for a modern highway to connect India's major cities: Mumbai, Chennai, Kolkata and Delhi. It was a much called-for undertaking in a country that had seen nothing in the way of major road building in the five decades since the Brits had shipped their last cement mixer back to London. The project was called the Golden Quadrilateral, and once it was completed, the NHAI began to set its targets much higher.

Under the leadership of Congress minister Kamal Nath, the Authority headed for the stratosphere in 2009 by declaring a target of 35,000 km of highways to be built in the next five years. With the government coffers not even marginally primed for such an enterprise, it was decided that India's roads would be opened up to private investment, both foreign and domestic. The idea was that independent companies would be invited to build the roads – a significant policy change – and be allowed to operate them, earning revenues through toll booths. It was a bright idea that was unfortunately coming at a time of global economic crisis when it was tough enough to get a company CEO to invest in so much as a bus ticket, let alone a high-risk, low-return road-construction project in India. And although Nath did manage to attract some investors, his ambitious targets couldn't be met, as banks soon reached their lending limits for the enormous amounts of cash the project required.[25] An extra spanner was also thrown into the works over the sticky issue of land-acquisition rights. Mr Nath's task was unenviable.

All too soon, our dream road began to show signs of fallibility. At one point Thor and I realized that all the other traffic had petered out and Abhilasha was the only car on the road. Why this had happened was a mystery, but we figured we must have been talking and missed the sign for a diversion.

'What shall we do? Should I turn around?'

'Hell, no! This is amazing, our own private road. I actually organized this especially. It was a surprise, just for you. Tell me you like it.'

'Actually, it's my every fantasy come true. It's like being in a school or a museum after hours. I feel the urge to do something extremely naughty like a wheel spin in the fast lane, or driving all curly-wurly-like.'

Just as I was about to start tracing ribbons across the road, a massive pile of rubble appeared in our path and brought Abhilasha to a grinding and rather pensive halt.

'Hmmm.'

'Indeed.'

'What do you reckon?'

'I reckon let's keep going. I mean, it might not be perfectly paved all the way, but at least there's no traffic. Think of all those suckers who took the diversion and are most probably labouring in a jam on a tiny road all the way to Tiruchiru-whatsitcalled right now.'

I edged forward. Although the empty road was beginning to inspire in me some rather eerie feelings of postapocalyptic isolation and fear, I didn't want Thor to think I was soft. After all, it was Thunderbolt at the helm today. I was Nanogrrrl.

But another few hundred metres further ahead we encountered a very final and entirely non-negotiable impediment; quite simply, there was no more *road*. I'm not talking a gradual fade-out or tarmac that blended into rocks and dust. I mean that the road came to an end, followed by a long and terrifying drop, like in *Road Runner*. A trusty highway that had delivered us safely under the smiles of Sonia Gandhi (who, now that I thought about it, I hadn't seen in a good while) just cut out, ceased and disappeared. I slammed on Abhilasha's brakes and we skidded to a standstill a few metres before the precipice, to the mild interest of a group of female labourers who were taking their lunch by the side of the road.

The smell of burning rubber wafted through Abhilasha's AC vent. I stopped to catch my breath and turned to Thor, who was rubbing the arm he had thrown across my chest as we lurched forward.

'Is this actually happening?' I asked him feebly.

'Well,' he said, checking the state of the cigarettes in his chest pocket, 'that's definitely the end of the road.'

The road had finished, but only for a few metres. There was a half-constructed bridge up ahead that would one day continue the trajectory of the NH7, presumably all the way to Madurai. One day; just not today. I felt misled, betrayed, downright stupid. We hadn't clocked on to what all the other vehicles obviously knew: that the unbroken NH7 was still a dream, one still under construction, stone by stone, by the team of four skinny women who were heading towards us with a small child in tow.

I presumed they were coming to check that we were all right after nearly meeting a *Looney Tunes* end off a half-built flyover. Instead, they surrounded the car with shady smiles, put their hands out and pointed to their mouths.

They were petitioning the wrong potential benefactor. If ever I was in a generous mood, it was not right now and it was not towards what had been a most passive audience in the face of our near-annihilation; the only humans, in fact, privy to one of Abhilasha's most traumatic and humiliating moments. We locked the car doors, spun a dust-raising U-turn and headed back along the deserted motorway in search of the elusive diversion we had neglected to follow that would inevitably be a speed bump–filled, pothole-laden route of a thousand villages. But there was no choice. And of course, I could call on my new-found inspiration, the travelling monk Vivekananda, to furnish me with all the equanimity I'd need to get over the demise of what had been the best road ever, and the accompanying trans-port dream it had shattered.

Disenchanted by the failure of the NH7, I began to execute a revision of my previous highway-exalting rhetoric. Motorways sucked, I told Thor. They were enormous and merciless in the way they sliced through villages, leaving nothing but a big con-crete obstruction for farmers who were plagued with the task of getting their herds of goats and cows from one side to the other. Just as I was clearing my throat to move on to pollu-tion and our modern-day obsession with speed, an elephant with a brightly painted face lumbered into view, galumphing from side to side with a man balancing sleepily on its back. On spotting Abhilasha, the elephant was visibly moved; on

spotting the elephant, Abhilasha slowed down to a mesmer-
ized stop. What were they doing on the deserted highway? The
elephant stepped up its pace and came lurching towards us at
what seemed from the nervous recesses of the driver's seat to
be stampede speed. Thor flung open the passenger door and
jumped outside, at first I thought out of sheer cowardice, until
I realized he was filming the beast as it attempted to destroy the
Nano. If we were going down, at least Thor would have some
gruesome footage to leave behind, for the news networks and
any future documentarians to play with. The elephant saw his
opportunity in the window that Thor left open, and pushed in
his trunk as far as it would go from the passenger side of the
car.

Now, if you've never had an elephant's trunk groping blindly
around your dashboard while you sit and quiver only inches
away like Sigourney Weaver in *Alien*, I can assure you it's an
unsettling experience. I was sure there was an outside chance
it would end in my own dismemberment. After a few moments,
however, I realized that the elephant's bristly grey trunk was
actually looking for something specific, and on reaching my
handbag, it seemed it had hit the jackpot. Concerned I may be
on the brink of a most unorthodox stick-up, I gave it a tap on
the trunk hard enough to communicate my displeasure, but
still light enough not to ignite elephant rage.

At the top of the long list of things I never knew about elephants (next to the fact that they can swim) is the truth of
their disturbing proboscises; namely, that they are, or can be,
extremely runny. Either this particular elephant had a cold, or it
was the practice of all these oversized mammals to leave a trail
of pungent mucoid slime in the wake of their nasal gropings.
In any case, I soon had a very slimy car interior. As I searched
around for something with which to wipe its runny nose, the
elephant's trunk reached for my hand, having given up on

lifting anything from my bag. I gave it another little pat before deciding that was about as much cross-species intimacy as I was comfortable with, and hit the button to nudge up the electric window. Nelly got the message and the trunk beat a hasty retreat. Meanwhile, its owner had dismounted and I got out of the car to greet him, hoping to quiz him on the practical challenges of travelling in India by elephant. But this guy was not here for small talk. He simply held out his hand for a spot of payback.

I was irked. 'Are you serious? Your frigging elephant just covered the inside of my car with stinking trunk slobber and now you want *me* to give *you* some cash?'

The man managed to maintain his hopeful expression. I turned around to see his steed fondling Abhilasha's exhaust pipe in a way that made me feel uncomfortable. Thor pulled me back in the car before my temper bubbled over, and I started the engine with a humph. Abhilasha stank; there were massive goblets of slime dripping from the dashboard, the passenger seat and even bits around my handbag. I swore revenge on elephantkind while Thor cleaned up the fusty trail of slime with a packet of wet wipes.

We were barely a hundred metres closer to the exit road when we were animal-ambushed once again. An old man who was attempting to manoeuvre a flock of about sixty sheep across the road was succinctly illustrating my earlier point about the inconvenience of motorways for livestock-herding shepherds. The scene was risible. Abhilasha was rendered immobile as sheep swarmed around her bodywork from all sides, bleating acquiescently and tripping over one another. With the Nano jammed in the middle of a sea of *Ovis aries* on a half-built deserted motorway, I had no option but to turn off the engine and surrender my will to heaven. What surprised me most was that the shepherd seemed unfazed by the prospect of any other car approaching, of which I knew there was a fair chance. He stood upright and dignified, a greying scarf around his head and a checked dhoti wrapped around his waist and brought up between his legs, brandishing a long stick with which he knocked at the tarmac as he slowly picked his way through his flock and continued as though he were leading the animals through the fires of hell to the promised land.

My vision of arriving in Pondicherry before sundown was, of course, a pipe dream. We made it as far as Tiruchirappali (whose name we finally discovered is commonly and quite sensibly shortened to Trichy) when it was starting to get dark and I reluctantly called it a day. We'd been on the road for almost ten hours and I was exhausted, between almost driving off the edge of a motorway overrun with vicious beasts and the hours of bumpy rural roads that had followed.

That night we lay in bed under an air-conditioning unit, a premium perk that Thor had sweetly insisted on as reward for the day's travails, at the appropriately named Breeze Hotel, which had a view over a deserted car park. I was worn out and a tad peeved.

'You think I'm a loser,' I mumbled.

'Why on earth would I think that?'

''Cos we didn't make it to Pondicherry.'

'600 kilometres was one hell of a goal, little Thunderbolt.'

'We could have done it, if it wasn't for that pesky break in the motorway. And the elephant. And all those sheep.'

'You know, you'd do well to lower the bar on your driving ambitions, just a tad. You'll make yourself crazy.'

'Hmph.'

'Cut yourself a little slack.' He took my hand. 'You wouldn't be trying to prove something, would you?'

'Hmph.'

'Hmph?'

'Hmph.'

The other elephant, the one that had been with us inside the Nano all day, had been duly addressed.

9

DIVINE (CAR) INSURANCE – Consecration and Catastrophe

PONDICHERRY; KM 3,041

If you're going to be colonized, I mused as I tucked into a ham and cheese pancake while Thor and I debated the idea of an evening of jazz and surrealist poetry at the Alliance Française, be colonized by the French. After all, they're the one nation with a god-given knack for bringing the chic into the wilds of the developing world due to their staunch refusal to leave their cultural and culinary foibles at home. Climate, geography, local economy and distance from Paris have never been factors in discouraging the French from carrying on as though they were in the thick of the Champs-Elysées. From lobster and foie gras luxury on Caribbean islands like St Barths and the twee-latticed wooden porches of New Orleans to the flouncy neoclassical flourish of the Opéra de Hanoi, there's a tangible thread that runs through the former French colonies that would read something like: 'Well, if we're stuck out in this *trou du cul du monde*, we might as well make the most of it. Châteauneuf du Pape, anyone?'

Pondicherry was governed by the Tricolore until 1954, which was a good few years after the British left India. Its moulding at the hands of various Franco–Tamil architects over the centuries left a genuinely pretty town replete with churches, cultural centres and big mansions surrounded by court-yards and beautiful walled gardens worthy of filling several issues of *World of Interiors*. Compare the cutesy, picturesque, bougainvillea-adorned streets of Pondicherry with Lutyens' monumental brick and mortar–fest around Delhi, and you'll get a fair idea of the difference in Franco- and Anglo-colonial styles.

More than half a century after the administration packed their Louis Vuittons and left, Pondicherry is still fragrant with the essence of Gaul: the gridded streets of the old French Quarter (today referred to rather uncomfortably as White Town, which I had to presume was a reference to the skin colour of its former inhabitants rather than the few remaining whitewashed walls) were named after notable Frenchmen with Indian connections, like author and philosopher Romain Rolland, Admiral Pierre André de Suffren de Saint Tropez and François Martin, Pondicherry's first governor-general. Many former colonial houses had been converted into fancy hotels, restaurants, internet cafés and boutiques; menus around town boasted relatively impressive wine lists to go with their Steak Frites and Croque Monsieurs; and the *boulangerie* Baker Street seemed to be frequently filled with homesick Frenchies munching on croissants and pains au chocolat that were a fair replica of the ones they'd be buying back home. In short, there seemed no better place to spend a romantic few days prior to leaving Thor at his ashram – which was only three hours away in Chennai – than in India's own Little France.

In addition to the French accent, Pondicherry had other merits: it was the kind of town where Christians, Muslims and Hindus appeared to live quite contentedly side by side in their respective quarters; mosques, churches and temples stood within streets of one another and were often subject to varying degrees of stylistic overlap. Not far from the Alliance Française was a bright turquoise building I had presumed was a Hindu temple until its caretaker spied us and pulled us inside for a gander. He asked Thor hopefully if he was a devotee of St

Anthony before showing us the interior of a Christian hall with a thatched leaf ceiling held up by bamboo poles. There was a pink altar at one end containing a small statue of the saint surrounded by flowers and cherubs in a vibrant, cacophonous style that would have been more at home among the colours of Holi than the usual sober décor of a Christian church.

We emerged after a lengthy chinwag with the custodian (who was disappointed by my scant knowledge of St Anthony and all his good deeds) to find Abhilasha relaxing on Suffren Street with the insipid obedience of a well-trained hound at a dog show. Her jovial, upwardly pointed headlights demonstrated blissful indifference to what lay outside the phlegmatic streets of the French Quarter, as well as what seemed like a lightly flirtatious bearing directed towards a rather handsome Hyundai that was parked right in front of her, bumper to bumper in an Eskimo kiss. The car was sparkling grey, its bonnet draped with a garland of marigolds and its headlights daubed with large dots of red powder. I imagined it was these decorative details that had attracted Abhilasha to the dishy vehicle in the first place, though I doubted she knew that in fact they were tell-tale signs that this particular jalopy had come fresh from the car showroom via a Brahmin's benediction.

When a new car is purchased in India, barely does the ink dry on the registration papers than the owner makes a beeline to the local temple, where a priest marks it with a sign of divine insurance. Even for the non-religious, a car's spiritual servicing is considered as important as checking its brakes and testing its horn; having it blessed before taking it out on the road greatly increases one's chances of not being pulverized under the wheels of an articulated lorry.

I had also read about the Ayudh Puja ceremony (a festival to mark the worship of implements, especially cars and other motor vehicles) and thought it to be an excellent idea. And yet I couldn't help but wonder whether the respect afforded under the sanctimony of a Brahmin was some form of guilty and superstitious compensation for the extreme lack of consideration that seemed to kick in once the car was safely out of the temple and on the roads. Was it basically okay to drive like a maniac before going into a temple and begging your god for forgiveness for all the heinous traffic sins you'd just committed? Was this obeisance to one's car in a whirlwind of incense and a sprinkling of powder a bit like wiping clean one's weekly sins at Sunday confession? And did such attention to a car's spiritual wellbeing mean that one was then covered by the ultimate divine insurance company?

Contemplating the flashily garlanded Hyundai that looked like it was trying to get its leg over Abhilasha, I began to wonder whether I had such godly protection. Had Mr Shah of Mumbai thought to have the Nano blessed before selling it on so quickly? And even if he had, did the blessing only apply to the current owner or to the car's future proprietors as well? The issue seemed laden with complications, and I was beginning to think that Abhilasha and I might be at a disadvantage. How could we possibly compete with all the other cars on the road, the ones with swastikas (of the Hindu variety, the holy symbol that embodies a great spiritual thumbs up, and not, I presumed, of some local Nazi drivers' movement) dangling from the rear-view mirror and little framed pictures of Shiva and Lakshmi next to the ignition? Looking around at the other cars parked on the street, I realized that all of them carried some sort of talismanic trinket, ranging from the religious as far as the political. My favourite was an arrangement of stickers on the back of a Mahindra Verito that displayed the petition 'Jesus Save Me'. The stencilling was detailed and intricate and looked like it had taken someone the best part of a week. Whether it had occurred to them that they had paradoxically also reduced their chances of earthly salvation by almost entirely blocking all visibility from their rear window was another matter.

I decided nothing would be left to chance. Our dashboard-bound three-inch plastic Ganesha did not necessarily guarantee adequate divine protection. I wanted more; I wanted the full monty. Exactly how to have Abhilasha properly consecrated became the next big question. Did it matter that my name wasn't on the registration papers? Should I wait until Dussehra, the Hindu festival celebrating the victory of good over evil? Could a non-Hindu feasibly waltz into a place of worship and demand that her car be blessed?

I decided to consult Radhika. She was a professor of media studies at Pondicherry University to whom I'd been introduced by a fan of the Nano Diaries blog, a Mumbai professor by the name of Mangesh Karandikar, who contacted me when he saw we were passing through town. He insisted I meet his colleague, a ballsy Delhi-born educational crusader, who, it took me under a minute to realize, was also a most frenetic soul.

'Excuse my appearance,' she said breathlessly, as I followed her striding lead through the corridors of Pondicherry University's Communications Department. 'It's just that I haven't been home for ten days now…'

'Where have you been?' I asked, thinking she looked just fine and trying to keep up.

'Here at the department!' she exclaimed, turning round to face me, her eyes fizzing. 'I have no problem with sleeping on the floor of my office. We've been so busy…' she started, before her attention was pulled away by a lad hauling a large cardboard box in our direction.

'Bagalavan!' she cried out.

'Yes, ma'am?' came a voice from behind the box.

'Bagalavan, do you have all the recording equipment in there?'

'Yes, ma'am.'

'Well, fine, then take it to my office and make sure you lock the door behind you.' She turned to me. 'We have so many problems with this recording equipment, it's driving me crazy. Last week one student lost a microphone from the department's store, and two days later a tripod went missing.' Radhika put her hand to her temple and grinned. 'Every day I have migraines from this job. My nerves are all wrecked, you know…'

We came to an abrupt stop outside a large door in the department. I was puzzled, as I thought Radhika and I were meeting for coffee. I had left Thor blissfully programming in a café in order to come out for a bit of girl bonding, but instead of lounging in the university canteen, Radhika and I seemed poised to enter a lecture theatre. She put one hand on the door and looked at me with academy-award-grade supplication. 'Can I ask you for a favour?'

I began to cringe in anticipation of what she might be about to say.

'Would you talk to my Year One Media Studies group about your project?'

'You mean… give a lecture?' I stammered. Public speaking came somewhere near sticking my head in a basket of irate cobras on the list of things I'd rather not do if that's all right, thanks.

Radhika threw her hands up in exaggerated astonishment. '*Noooo*! Nothing like that; nothing so *formal*!' She leaned in towards me and lowered her voice to a conspiratorial whisper. 'I think these students could learn a lot from listening to you. About your journey, your blog, your process… There are some girls in there who are frightened even to take a bus on their own. I want them to be inspired. Can you do that?'

Inspired? How on earth could I inspire a group of late teens into anything but a pre-lunch nap? I was flummoxed. What was there to say? I had bought the world's cheapest car, mostly because I didn't have the cash for that coveted Toyota Innova, and had decided to come to India on the back of a failed relationship while chasing after some lost nostalgic notion of the Indian dream that these students would probably think was utterly cheesy. In addition, I'd spent the last two weeks fawning over the ginger-haired French American in my passenger seat; I was a living breathing soft-focus road romance, who spent most of my time planning routes, cursing Delilah and complaining about pain in my legs and lumbar region. What on earth could I pull out of my backside to galvanize a class of media studies kids?

'But... but I haven't prepared anything...'

She grabbed my arm and smiled in a way that was both placatory and expertly guileful. I realized I wasn't getting out of this one. The lecture hall doors swung open and not one single student looked up.

'Can I please have everybody's attention?' Radhika commanded with a zeal I knew I couldn't come close to emulating. Most of the class eventually hauled their gazes from their laptops and phones. I wished for a moment I could be as uninteresting to the rest of India as I was to the first-year Communications students of Pondicherry University, who clearly saw me as some irritating interlude in their lesson break. Radhika gestured towards me. 'This is Vanessa. She is a journalist from the UK who is doing a very interesting project here that she has come to talk to you about today. Dileep! Where is Dileep?'

A hand went up at the back of the lecture hall.

'Dileep, will you please turn on the fans?'

Dileep shot up and sprinted over to the fan controls. Five sets of blades overhead started whirring, necessitating that all conversation be held in tones very close to yelling.

'So I will leave Vanessa to tell her story. Please ask her questions at the end. Anything you like. Anupama, Deepa, make sure you take notes; you can write an article about this for *The Inquirer*.'

The Inquirer? This was escalating out of control. What I was about to say was to be set in stone in the student rag. Every word would be immortalized, unretractable, howled at over beers at the student union. And in the face of such pressure, who emerged but my stuttering Hugh Grant alter ego?

'Right. Well, um… hello. Nice to be here. Um… (bugger).'

It was painstaking, but it seemed I had no choice and I launched into my story. An hour later, all the students were still sitting upright and looking earnestly in my direction. They appeared curious, a fact that shocked and terrified me at the same time. Until this point, Abhilasha had been my little bubble in which I was sailing untouched through a sea of adventure, doubt, frustration and repetitive strain injuries. It was true that I had been writing missives to the outside world via my blog, but every time I went to publish a new post, it didn't occur to me that someone, somewhere would actually end up reading it.

To my amazement, the Nano Diaries Facebook page had by then accrued a thousand or so followers, most of whom were people I didn't know, and of these the large majority were young Indian men. On top of that, our journey was starting to reap a bit of press interest. A woman, coincidentally called Janelle Nanos, had contacted me for an interview for *National Geographic*'s 'Intelligent Travel' blog (a title I thought in my case could be construed as wildly ironic), which then led to emails from *CNN Go*, *Budget Travel* magazine, *Asian Correspondent* and a Mumbai tabloid called *Mid Day*. We eventually even got a radio interview with *Voice of America* and a mention in the *Washington Post*. Abhilasha and I were garnering celebrity status and – quite surprisingly – people seemed genuinely interested in what we were doing. Perhaps this wasn't the world's worst idea after all.

'I think it's great to see a woman do what you are,' Radhika told me, smiling over her glasses as we tucked into fried rice in the university canteen after my stutterthon. 'It's so brave.'

I told her I quite honestly didn't think my gender mattered either way. A woman was just as capable of driving a car as a man, after all. Some studies even showed females to be better drivers. Surely the fact that I was a girl didn't make much difference.

Radhika didn't agree. A bit of an idiosyncrasy of Indian society, she was a mum who loved travelling alone with her daughter. She told me stories of when her little one was a baby and she would strap the child to her chest and a rucksack on her back and hop on a bus or a train from Delhi up north to the mountains or south to Goa and Kerala. 'A lot of people would approach me and tell me what I was doing was wrong. They said, "Alone! Where is your husband? You should be with your family,"' she revealed very matter-of-factly.

I was amazed. In the time I had been driving alone, I had encountered nothing of the sort. Was it Abhilasha's charm that was too distracting for people to see that she actually contained a single, husband-less female, or was it the colour of my skin that prevented the people I met along the way from airing their real opinions and instead led them to pump me for information about the Nano's fuel-to-performance ratio? However, I told Radhika, there was one thing she could do to help stack the fates a little better on my side…

Radhika assured me that consecrating Abhilasha would not be a problem; she suggested I have the blessing performed right there in Pondicherry and immediately dispatched the ever-acquiescent Bagalavan to follow me on his motorbike to the Manakula Vinayagar temple in the centre of town. Particularly appropriate in that it was dedicated to none other than Ganesha himself, the temple came complete with its very own elephant, who went by the name of Lakshmi, and who stood obediently outside the main entrance. Lakshmi's main job appeared to be taking coins and bananas from faithful devotees and nervous tourists and in return imparting *darshan*, a blessing, in the form of a light pat on the head that made most recipients quiver and screech.

Following Abhilasha's recent manhandling on our way from Kanyakumari to Tiruchirappali, I was very wary of the lumbering, runny-nosed proboscidea. However, Lakshmi appeared to be a different class of elephant altogether: elegant, polite and decked out in some rather attractive ankle bracelets. She seemed quite happy to dole out blessings to anyone who tossed her a prize, and I eventually succumbed to her charms and flipped her a ten-rupee coin. I figured garnering a bit of goodwill with a real-life Ganesha could only further my cause of maximizing favour with the gods.

Bright-faced and businesslike, Bagalavan wasted no time in rushing me towards a kiosk inside the temple, where he pushed some rupees over the counter in exchange for a couple of flimsy tickets. We took these around the corner where a Brahmin appeared, ready with his assortment of materials for the ceremony. Wearing a dhoti and a thread looped diagonally across his bare chest and over his shoulder, he was balancing four limes and a pot of deep red sindoor on an aluminium tray with a burning oil lamp soldered onto the end of it.

Bagalavan disappeared somewhere and I was left grinning at the Brahmin over the smoke of his oil burner. I pointed towards Abhilasha and his expression became grave as he nodded his head in a gesture of acknowledgement. Bagalavan returned with a garland of marigolds, which we hung from Abhilasha's rear-view mirror, as well as a line of jasmine for my own hair.

And so the ceremony began. The Brahmin started by standing in front of the Nano's bonnet and applying dots of sindoor on her headlights, number plate and a spot on the windscreen that fell roughly where her forehead should be. Then he circulated his burning oil lamp around to the driver's door, where he got in (my maternal gut clenched at the sight of an uncovered, smoking oil lamp thrust deep inside her delicate and presumably flammable interior) and proceeded to dab bits of sindoor powder around the steering wheel and dashboard. He then placed a lime underneath the front and back tyres, before moving around to her posterior, where he applied more sindoor dots to her rear lights and number plate. The remaining limes were duly placed under Abhilasha's left tyres and all that remained was for me, my own forehead now also sindoored, to get in and slowly drive forward, thus making limeade with Abhilasha's treads.

As quickly as it started, it was over. Abhilasha, smoky and powdered, had now officially been blessed and sanctified. As far as the gods were concerned, she was all right and well worth keeping a divine eye on. Ganesha beamed up at me from the dashboard as the Brahmin hovered by my open window.

'Ma'am, you must give him a little baksheesh,' Bagalavan informed me from over the holy man's shoulder. I gave him a fifty-rupee note and he went on his way.

'So is that it?' I asked Bagalavan, incredulous that this all-important act of karmic insurance had been so fleeting, simple and, er, cheap.

'Yes, ma'am. That is all. Now you are safe to drive and you will be protected from all accidents.'

Excellent, I thought. Pricey insurance policies be damned, I now had a much more powerful source of indemnity on my side. I thanked Bagalavan – who seemed eager to be dismissed, as I guessed Radhika had piled him high with jobs for the day – and set off with Abhilasha for a celebratory croissant.

Later that afternoon, I was taking the Nano through the narrow lanes of Pondicherry's Muslim quarter looking for the front porch of the man with whom Thor and I had left a bundle of our washing hours earlier. As I rounded a corner, I had a weird rush of uncoordination and took the turn too tight. The laundry man's ironing table hove into view as I felt an almighty scrape on the right-hand side of the car. I stopped dead with a stomach-churning wince of recognition as I turned to see that I had rubbed Abhilasha against a concrete lamppost; a bit like how a cat would rub up against your leg, only to the teeth-clenching sound of grazed metal.

'Shit. Shit, shit, shit!'

The laundry man stood on his porch watching me with the curious inertia of a doctor sloth.

'Shit!' What to do now? I figured that if I kept moving forwards, I would inevitably draw out the scratch even further. Going backwards seemed a much more sensible option, so I put Abhilasha in reverse and tried to extricate her from her concrete clinch.

Another hideous rasping noise. It seemed that my attempts at retracting my imbecilic action had piled stupidity on foolishness. We were back where we started, except that Abhilasha now had two enormous scrapes along her right rear haunch.

I looked down at Ganesha, who was as indifferent as the laundry man. He gave me no clues where to go next. Why had this happened? Weren't we supposed to be protected? Irony didn't begin to describe the situation. The heat-withered marigolds still hung from the rear-view mirror, the sindoor clung to the steering wheel and bits of lime remained freshly wedged between the rubber grooves of Abhilasha's tyres. Here we were, four hours after our blessing (our fifty-blimming-rupee blessing, I inwardly snapped) and we were in the midst of our first accident of the whole trip.

And what an accident. This was not one to regale audiences with; it was hardly the stuff Hollywood car crashes were made of. There had been no errant rickshaws crossing my path; no buses swerving ferociously into my lane; no drunken lorry drivers falling asleep at the wheel and taking the Nano head on. It was a bright and sunny day, I had been driving on an empty road at 10 kmph, and the only extenuating factor in the entire incident was my own stupidity. I had scraped the lamppost with all the composure and grace of a pissed vagrant falling against a wall. And then I had reversed for more.

The laundry guy was still staring at me. He hadn't moved a muscle. I mentally willed him to get back to his ironing, as his proximity to the accident and the fact that he was the sole human witness of my injudicious manoeuvre put him first in line for unfair retribution.

I swung Abhilasha's wheel hard to the left and managed with only a small additional scrape to free her from the lamppost's clutches. I pulled her up outside the laundry man's porch and got out to inspect the damage. It was as bad as I imagined: there was a series of thin, wavy lines stretching from the tail light all the way to the hinge of the passenger door that had scraped away the paintwork and exposed the grey metal underneath.

'Shit!'

I turned to face the laundry man, who continued in his wordless contemplation of the scene. I put my best anger-management skills into action as every ounce of my being was channelled into the act of politely asking him for my washing back, not for the chance to furnish him with a knuckle sandwich. He reached for a pile of familiar folded clothes that had been placed on a stack of newspapers behind his ironing table. He then quoted a price that was Rs 30 more than I had agreed with his wife that morning. My blood pressure rose to mass-murder levels, and the man seemed to instantly recognize the killer instinct in my eyes. I handed over the agreed price and he accepted without a word. Not looking twice at Abhilasha's mangled haunch, I got back in the driver's seat, ripped the marigolds from the mirror and sped away from the laundry-wallah's house.

RULE OF THE ROAD #5
Learn at Every Turn

I might be giving the impression I found Indian people to be bad drivers. In fact, it's quite the opposite: I think Indians might be the best drivers in the world. The more miles I clocked up with Abhilasha, the more I realized that, contrary to the impression of utter chaos when I first landed in Mumbai, traffic in India did move to an impressive kind of algorithm, albeit one that was hard to discern at first. It was a bit like crowd theory at a rave or during rush hour at a busy train station: lots of humans crammed into a small space, each of them freestyling in their own particular direction, but somehow avoiding mashing into one another through the tiny instinctual corrections of movement.

With my mounting hours of experience, I began to realize that the trick was to treat it like a dance and get into the groove – not to think too much, but instead to act on intuition. I learned as much as I could from the drivers around me, and when one day in Pondicherry I saw a car passing on the street with a rectangular roof rack that read Super Star Driving School, I knew what I had to do.

It occurred to me as I entered the school, just opposite the train station, that I might not exactly fit the profile of Super Star's average pupil. Frantic exchanges were passed between the six or so men who were manning the office and whose relaxing afternoon I had clearly shattered with the sledgehammer of my presence. My Parish of Grouville licence was studied with the usual mix of curiosity and ridicule while I feebly piped up that I also had an international one, though I feared that the laughable, now dog-eared document might incite even further mirth on their part. India has been converting to smart-card driving licences for several years now, using state-of-the-art embedded chips that store information about drivers, their safety records, history of chronicled offences, past car ownerships and so on. It was an efficient, high-tech system way ahead of many first-world countries, which seemed tremendously at odds with the grimy, anarchic reality of the roads outside.

The general gist of the commotion fuelled by our linguistic shortcomings appeared to revolve around the question that since I already had a driver's licence, why did I need another one? I explained as articulately as I could using only bare-bones sentence structure and mime: 'India – driving – very – chaos.' I rapped on my chest bone. 'I – need – help.'

A round of consensual nods Mexican-waved its way around the room before one guy eventually stepped forward and introduced himself as Kathi. He would, by the looks of it, take a chance on me. He led me outside to a Tata Indica parked next to a huddle of motorcycles and a loitering cow.

Kathi's detailed introduction to the basics of ignition location, handbrake kinetics and horn functionality implied that he for one didn't take my Parish of Grouville credentials seriously at all, and was bent on treating me with the kid gloves he believed I deserved. When he finally allowed me to turn on the engine after a protracted period of foot-pedal explanations that were carefully monitored by three of his colleagues who held vigil from the pavement, I wasn't sure if I was capable of driving any more. Predictably, I stalled, lunging the car forwards and sending the adjacent cow galloping down the road.

Our first encounter while trundling down the street at a speed that would make a sloth blush was a man in a shortened dhoti cycling a home-made cart with long steel rods hanging off the back in an arc that meant their end trailed along the road surface. Kathi gestured that I should overtake the vehicle, adding that a mid-manoeuvre parp of my horn was very much 'compulsory'. From then on, at just about every obstacle, junction and overtake, Kathi shouted out 'make ha-ran!' with life-and-death zeal. A motorbike stopped in the middle of the road ahead of us and on Kathi's imperative I held down the Indica's ha-ran in a deliberately exaggerated and hammy misinterpretation of his instruction.

It was as though, due to Kathi's insistence on treating me like a dumb wench behind the wheel, I actually became one. I felt plain naughty, and in the mood to vex Kathi to his limits. A few seconds passed and I was still holding down the horn. Kathi lurched towards me and pushed my hand from the button.

'Okay, okay, okay, long ha-ran not necessary.' But it was a fraction of a moment too late for the dismounting motorcyclist, who was clearly and rightly enraged by my extended show of (apparent) aggression towards him. For his part, Kathi was exasperated and couldn't bring himself to answer my simple query, 'Do you think I just made that man angry?'

Besides driving slowly past the police station, not using my horn in front of ashrams and other religious institutions, and not driving over the yellow line at the side of the road (which Kathi dubbed the 'danger line'), the driving tips I was getting from my Super Star instructor were pretty slim pickings. I tried to up the stakes by suggesting we drive over to a busier road. Kathi was disinclined. No, no and no; absolutely not. This was my first lesson and I needed to get used to driving on the small roads before I could graduate to mixing in with the main street traffic. The fact that I had already driven thousands of kilometres from Mumbai seemed to have little effect on his decision.

The driving lesson was not producing the desired result. I had signed up to tap into some local knowledge about how to handle Indian roads better, but Kathi's lack of faith in my skills was proving to have the very undesirable effect of actually making me a worse driver. I could feel my confidence ebbing further with every junction where Kathi saw fit to slam down the instructor's brake in his own footwell ahead of my own better-timed intention to do so a split second later.

The final straw came as we were pulling out onto a main road near the end of the lesson. An old man wobbled towards us from our right on a wiry bicycle. 'Go, go!' Kathi egged me to pull out in front of the man.

'But there's a cyclist coming,' I protested.

'Vehicle is always coming,' Kathi reasoned. 'You don't stop here.'

I could see his point. If I stopped to give way to every bike, car, cow and truck that crossed my path, I'd still be somewhere near the McDonald's in Navi Mumbai. But much to Kathi's growing irritation, I was not able to cut up an elderly gent on a bike. Call it spinelessness, call it stupidity, call it the genetic backwash of most noble Chaucerian *gentillesse*, I just couldn't be so damn rude. I might be a deferential, bumble-arsed Englishwoman, but if that meant having good manners towards the elderly, then I would stick to my guns and uphold my values.

Back at HQ, his feet on solid ground and in the presence of his boss who'd just arrived, Kathi's tone changed from disparaging to reasonably encouraging. I asked for a rating on a scale of one to ten and he gave me a six after some consideration. Was I good enough to take the Tata Nano up to Delhi? Kathi fell silent and knotted his brow.

'Okay, okay, okay! But still you need four or five more classes.'

I whined in protest and insisted he give me one good reason. He held up an instructive finger. 'Because in India, road is very traffic is.'

10

PARADISE BEACH – Finding Eden in Little France

our blessing was very luck,' the spray-paint technician at Manakular Motors – Pondicherry's certified Tata garage – assured me, sucking his teeth and running his fingers along Abhilasha's newly sprayed backside after I'd rattled off to him the previous day's sequence of events. 'With no blessing, accident is very bad,' he stated with certainty. I couldn't argue with his reasoning, but it did little to lessen my rage over the fact that Abhilasha's perfect yellow complexion had been tarnished with scratches of karma gone askew, and that putting right the damage was now costing me ten times what I'd paid at the temple.

Still, she was back to fine fettle, sparkling clean and her graze erased, which in turn put me in good spirits as I drove back to rescue Thor, who was passing the morning programming from the terrace of our hotel. We had decided to spend one more day there before heading up to Chennai, where our journey as a couple would come to an end. Though Thor was visibly eager to get back to his ashram and I was growing impatient to head up north, the impending separation lingered like the threat of a distant storm; prone to horrible bouts of amorous wistfulness, I tried not to think too much about what life on the road would be like post-Thor, vaguely reasoning that since things had been just fine before he joined me in

Bangalore, they would surely continue to be just fine after he left.

Two weeks of travellers' intimacy with my redheaded mathematician had pretty much sealed my conviction on what had been an uncanny hunch the first moment I clapped eyes on him: providence was somehow heavily invested in our union. I had always been easily seduced by the veneer of romance, and as such had an awful track record for making myself scarce before the first-date roses had started to wilt. When affairs did develop into relationships and the question of ramping up commitment floated to the surface, my enthusiasm had always turned into emotional paralysis. I concluded I was an awful stickler, exasperated by every tiny flaw and painfully aware that the perfection I thought I was looking for was unlikely to exist beyond the realm of romantic fiction. It was a maddening realization that I dragged away from the last break-up I initiated – which I swore would be my very last – and hung around my neck for the few short months before Thor came to Bangalore and restarted the cogs of affection. In a flash, I went from the conviction that I was destined to stew in a state of perennial dissatisfaction to the sunny thought that there might be hope of salvation after all.

This time is always different; but this time really was. In a rush of ardour, I went a bridge too far by uttering the fateful words: 'Might you like to drive?'

Thor scanned my face for evidence of a ruse. 'Really?'

I handed him the keys.

'Wait a minute. What happened to Little Miss Control Freak? Where'd she go?'

'I just, you know, thought you might like to give it a go. Just from here to the market. It's not far.'

'Well, if you're sure.'

I wasn't sure. You can never be sure. You can only jump in the right direction and hope you don't hit a rock, or a bit of scaffolding. The ten-minute drive from the Swades Guest House over to where Mission Street crossed Nehru Street saw me white-knuckled in the passenger street, straining myself to the point of internal rupture not to play back-seat driver and exclaim on each occasion (about every five seconds) Thor came heart-stoppingly close to knocking over a cyclist or not braking in time to let a cow cross the road. His horn technique was aggressive and his relationship with the gearstick shaky, by the evidence of no fewer than four stalls in the first third of the journey – each of which was accompanied by a torrent of impressive curses.

When it came to parking in one of the streets that surrounded the market, whose edges were already replete with motorbikes, rickshaws and cars, Thor's quick reverse produced a dull crunch as Abhilasha's rear bumper ploughed into some scaffolding behind us. He turned to me with a look of sheepish panic.

'Shit, what was that?'

'I'd say that was probably you reversing the car into the scaffolding behind us.'

'Shit! I'm so sorry. Do you think it's bad?'

'I daren't look.'

We got out of the car and went around reluctantly to inspect the rear. It wasn't so bad. The bumper had taken a minor hit in the form of a scratch on the left side, and apart from now being cocked at a subtly rakish angle, there was little evidence of the collision. That was more than could be said for the wooden panel at the base of the scaffolding the Nano had reversed into. There was a long crack stretching belligerently from one edge of the wood to the other in an accusing grimace that suggested we get the hell out before anyone caught wind of our accidental vandalism.

'Maybe I'll take it over to another spot,' I suggested gently, aware that I was far less irked by Abhilasha's disfigurement at Thor's hands than I had been at my own, and yet the rubber blades of passive aggression were nonetheless sharpening against my guts.

'Yeah, I can't get used to these stick-shift cars,' he admitted, a bit defeated.

As I sat back down in the driver's seat, I felt bad for him and indignantly stroppy at the same time. 'They're *hideously* difficult to manoeuvre,' I lied. 'And on top of that, you're driving on the wrong side of the road here. This is piss easy for me; I was brought up driving on the left. But it must be a complete *nightmare* for you.'

'Well, it would be had I managed to go further than ten minutes without writing off the bumper.'

I put my hand on his knee and likely irritated the lifeblood out of him with condescending kindness. 'It's alright. You know, you'll have another opportunity. We'll try again tomorrow.'

This was also a lie. I had already decided that after that initial display of driving dexterity – or lack thereof – there was no way I'd let Thor near the driver's seat again. I knew it was one of those points early on in a relationship when little episodes give a sense of the bigger dynamics that lie in wait. The die had been cast: from the moment Abhilasha's bumper hit the scaffold under Thor's supervision, the roles had been apportioned – I was the driver, the authority, the wearer of gloves, hat and driving pants. Any future attempt of Thor's to get behind the wheel would invariably result in a distrusting nervousness on my part that would be so formidable as to completely incapacitate the poor guy, preventing him from being able to drive with any degree of unselfconsciousness and so bringing the situation tragically full circle.

Probably out of loving-kindness and possibly out of fear of further recrimination for his negligent reverse, Thor refrained from addressing the palpable psycho-bitch atmosphere that had expanded to occupy the Nano. I felt the hairy scrub of its backside as I remembered my father manifesting similar behaviour during the road trips of my childhood, when one small motorway skirmish forever banished my mother from sharing the driving on long-distance journeys.

In search of another parking space, we rounded a corner on the edge of the market and came to a standstill on a small road lined with open-fronted shops and zigzagged by deliverymen zipping in every direction hauling boxes, crates and sacks on their shoulders. It was a picture of industry, save for a large lorry standing idle three cars ahead of us that was the opposite of industry and ostensibly the cause of the choke-up. We strained to see from our seats exactly what was going on, but were egged on by the chorus of horns around us to join in and add our parp to the fray.

Minutes later, the game was becoming tiresome. Thor was getting impatient, and without warning he swung open Abhilasha's door and strode towards the offending lorry. A minute later, he was back in the car.

'This crap drives me crazy.'

'What's going on up there?'

'There's like five guys supposed to be unloading that lorry. It's full of massive sacks of flour or rice or something. But they're not unloading it, they're just standing there, shooting the shit, *waiting*.'

'What are they waiting for?'

He turned to face me and executed a perfect Indian head wobble. Then he opened and closed the fingers of his hand to imitate the gesture that was the national symbol for five minutes. I giggled.

'Pfive minutes only.'

In my experience so far, 'pfive minutes' had usually been employed to excuse a task that would take longer than was acceptable or comfortable for any of the parties involved. It was as much a sign of appeasement as it was any accurate prediction of timing, and I soon came to learn that the actual time it was referring to could represent anything from three minutes to an hour. Five minutes later, we hadn't moved an inch. I turned the engine off, though I still enjoyed giving a little toot on the horn to coincide with the sporadic eruptions of noise from the cars in front and behind us.

'See, everyone's sitting in their cars beeping their horns, but no one's actually doing anything,' Thor protested. 'I swear, if they don't move their arses in the next sixty seconds, I'm going to get up there and move those sacks for them.'

I was appalled. 'You wouldn't. Would you?'

Indeed, another minute and he was out of the car and striding with purpose towards the men around the stationary truck. Through the muted glass of the windscreen, I saw him gesticulating at the guys, who didn't seem moved to respond. Seemingly frustrated by their lack of reaction, Thor took it on himself to open the door of the truck and climb in. The quick illumination of the vehicle's rear lights implied the engine had been started. Abruptly, all of the men who had been standing around not moving the sacks jumped in unison and sped over to the driver's door. One of them, presumably the driver from the look of mortal panic on his face, opened the door and started shouting and gesticulating into the cabin, while I closed my eyes and tried to reconcile myself to the fact that week two of my new romance could well end in a public lynching.

I half expected to see Thor crawl out of the driver's seat of the truck, wilting from the anger of the gathering crowd, but instead he bounced out, apparently undeterred and grinning from ear to ear, and made his way to the back of the truck. Some more conversation was exchanged, before he jumped into the back, on top of the pile of sacks, and began to haul one up into his arms. It looked spectacularly heavy, but he didn't flinch, instead completing his gesture by passing the sack down into the arms of one of the men waiting on the road, who in turn passed it to another, who piled it by the side of the road. Two other men jumped up on top of the sacks to join Thor and soon there was a chain of sacks making its way out of the back of the lorry and onto the side of the road. I noticed the beeps of the cars around me had stopped and I wondered if everyone was as beguiled – and a tiny bit excited – by the spectacle as I was.

When Thor returned to the Nano, he was panting, sweating and covered in flour. I wondered to what extent I was to blame for the episode by having previously undermined his road mas-culinity. I could think of little to say but, 'Wow. You showed them.'

He patted down his pockets in search of his cigarettes, try-ing to get his breath back. 'Yeah. That guy got really pissed when I started up his engine.'

'I thought they were going to kill you.'

He laughed. 'Did you?'

'Well, yeah. They thought you were about to nick their lorry.' I nearly added, thank god you didn't try to reverse it.

'And would you have run out to try and fight for my life?'

'What, and leave Abhilasha here, alone and vulnerable?'

Thor frowned. 'I feel bad, though. I think I burst one of their sacks. I was just so angry that I grabbed it wrong and ripped it a bit.' He slapped his hand down over his T-shirt and a cloud of flour dust rose into the air. 'I must have lost them quite a bit of flour.'

The truck finally empty, it started to move forward down the street as all the cars that had been stuck behind it restarted their engines and rolled forward. The flour now floating around the Nano settled like a tiny snowfall over the jagged peaks of our previous conversation. Where we had hardened, I began to feel us softening towards one another once more. Perhaps, I thought, our idiosyncrasies could eventually be fine-tuned to a form of good teamwork.

'What the hell were they waiting for in the end?'

'Fuck knows.'

The market was putting up too much resistance, so we decided to forgo it in favour of a trip to the sea. We headed north to a beach called Serenity, which had already been invaded by a mob of Euro-hippies dressed in varying styles of tie-dyed sarongs wrapped around their heads and hips. Some bikini-clad girls were dousing themselves in the ocean in a way that might have looked incredibly tempting were it not for the audience of fishermen their antics had gathered to the shore-line. They sat on the edge of their brightly coloured grounded boats, fiddling with nets and shooting side glances at every shrieked 'Putain!' coming from the water. I badly wanted to swim, but I wanted to do it unobserved. We met an American woman who lived on the beach called Kasha, who gave us directions to head south for more complete serenity at a place called Paradise Beach.

At Paradise, we found Eden. It was a low promontory of sand separating the Indian Ocean from a quiet inlet that was actually the mouth of the Sangarabarani river. The light of late afternoon had already smoothed the landscape down to deep-baked putty and we arrived just in time to feel the day slowly exhale around us. With not a fisherman in sight, we left our clothes in a heap on the sand and waded into the ocean, which was tepid and foamy.

Thor ran straight for the waves while I remained stationed at knee level, frightened as I always have been of currents and the undertow of big breakers. I'd heard that many people had drowned on this coastline (outside of the 2004 tsunami, which devastated the area) and, given how well my odds were coming through on a daily basis as far as driving was concerned, I didn't much fancy challenging the fates at sea as well as on land.

So for the second time that day, I sat back and watched Thor from a distance, doing things that I couldn't. He was lit by the sun that was setting behind us and shining out over the inlet, as he bounced in and out of the waves that intermittently consumed him, then spat him back out. At intervals, he emerged with his eyes red, his nose streaming snot and his hair stuck to his face, spouting a mini-fountain of water from his mouth. A seagull took a break from its business to join me on the water's edge until its attention was snatched by a dead, inflated blowfish that bobbed slowly by. I felt like Thor, the seagull, the blowfish and I had been here for centuries.

We dried off on the sand. The ocean was behind us, rough and raging, though settling into an evening murmur, while the river ahead of us was smooth as a lake of glass. The world turned pink as the sun eased itself down.

'Do you forgive me for crashing your car?' Thor asked.

'You didn't *crash* it. You just rearranged the bumper a tad. It was nothing compared with what I did to it the other day.'

'Put that way, I suppose it was quite a skilled manoeuvre.'

'For sure.' I scuffed about in the sand to lie with my head on his belly, a bony-flesh pillow that tightened to cradle the weight of my skull. 'Do you forgive me for being horribly aggressive? In the passive sense?'

'Only if you promise to chill out a bit and stop trying to steer everything past your impossible goals.'

He kissed my head. We had emerged from a tunnel of weirdness and things were better than before we went in. Thor had a way of turning conflict into something constructive, so that instead of bashing one another down with the dead blowfish of recrimination, we were instead tending to one another's sore spots. It was an answer to a yearning I never knew I'd had.

'Do you think that if we're good driving long distances in India in a small car in the blistering heat, that we'll be as good back in the real world?' Thor asked.

I had been wondering the same. Back in Europe, or wherever we were destined to see one another again, would I slip back into my old habits of finding fault in every nook and cranny of the relationship? Were we just drunk on India and looking at one another through Kingfisher goggles? And yet, when I thought about it more soberly, there seemed to be nothing discernible in our current togetherness that in any way relied on India, driving, Abhilasha or the outside temperature. Instead, there was an effortless fellowship that seemed to override any anxiety I might have had about what lay ahead. There seemed to be no question about what would follow, since it was quite clear to both of us that *we* came next.

Although Chennai is undoubtedly loved by many, to me the city formerly known as Madras was a featureless urban sprawl and one long traffic jam, punctuated with transvestite panhandlers at traffic lights and islands of irritable traffic police. It was the only place in India where I was indignantly cajoled into paying an official Rs 100 fine (that means I got a receipt and the cash presumably didn't go into the officers' holiday coffers) for running a red light,[26] and where I met with the fury of one very angry cop who stopped me for talking on my phone while driving. It was a grave offence that I managed to neutralize through a combination of Jedi mind powers and my increasingly refined Margaret Thatcher impression. I told the cop, in assured, low-pitched tones, that I had in fact been consulting the device for directions and could he possibly tell me how to get to that damn elusive Mount Poonamallee High Road? In a spectacular turnaround of temper, he stopped yelling and quite helpfully pointed me in the direction I knew I had been going all along.

The district of Manapakkam that was home to Thor's ashram was a suburban neighbourhood defined by a strange and uncomfortable mixture of ramshackle housing and residential comfort, set in the shadow of the growing skyscrapers and cranes that lined its periphery. Middle-class pillbox houses, whose rough cement walls looked like they had been freshly popped out of a rubber mould, stood streets away from a slummy bog whose mountains of noxious debris steamed a stinking slow burn as goats, hogs and dogs spent their days picking through the junk that humans left behind. Nearby were the gates to the ashram, called the Sri Ram Chandra Mission. A security checkpoint waved us onto a palm tree–lined pathway that led to a large covered pavilion that was the centre's main meditation hall. Chipmunks scampered between the branches of trees as birdsong filled the air and men and women strolled the grounds with looks of happy intention. It was a sunny bell jar of a sanctuary within a world that was developing at breakneck speed, and when the gates closed behind us, they shut off the noise and bedlam outside. I could see why, once Thor had arrived here, he was loath to go anywhere else.

Our digs were situated just around the corner of the ashram's back gate in the homely outbuilding of a house belonging to a French couple, Marion and Hénoc Marceau. It was an arrangement for which I was very grateful after I spied the communal dorms in the ashram, which would have meant sharing a large concrete floor with hundreds of other devotees and, I feared, the odd rodent.

A friend of Thor's for almost twenty years, Hénoc had moved to India as a boy with his family, and decided to stay when his parents and brother eventually returned to France. Despite his decades spent in the country and the kerfuffle endured in the name of acquiring Indian nationality, I had the feeling that Hénoc and his wife were, like me, still having trouble nailing Chennai's redeeming features. Caught in the overlap between an international spiritual centre, an IT park and the developing world, the slightly surreal realm within their four outer walls contained a red-brick house and a smaller cottage with a garden occupied by a cat called Kiri, a pair of Lhasa Apsos, a stray pup called Leia and a domesticated squirrel called Lilu, who had befriended a thus-far nameless gecko. With the exception of outings to the ashram and Marion's job as a schoolteacher in the city, the pair appeared to prefer bedding down at home, blessed as they were with plenty of greenery, household appliances and a DVD collection primed for a decade of Siberian banishment. Any mention of having to venture beyond the limits of Manapakkam inspired in them both pained expressions of reluctance.

Nevertheless, this didn't mean they could keep India from their door: their garden attracted an endless stream of visitors, Europeans from the ashram as well as the local neighbours, who appeared quite taken with the floral and faunal abundance of their abode. And the Marceaus were exemplary in their capacity for hospitality, accepting the incursions on their privacy with admirably cheery compliance and greeting everyone who dropped by with a drink and the offer of a seat on the garden swing.

Happily nested on said swing, it was all I could do to drag myself up and plan the next section of my route. I had decided to head north and inland towards Hyderabad, a city of stunning historical architecture that I had visited once before and remembered for its unfathomable draw. Hyderabad was 700 km away, which I figured would require at least one overnight stop along the route. The choices weren't abundant: an agitated search through the *Lonely Planet*'s Andhra Pradesh chapter had informed me I was about to enter a large swathe of the country where guidebook-endorsed hotels were few and far between. After some deliberation, I settled on a government hotel in Nellore – a large town on the east coast, north of Chennai.

Whether I was succumbing to a wave of road weariness, or whether my impending departure from Thor was taking its toll, I noticed that my resolve to continue the journey had begun to slide. Since the afternoon at Paradise Beach, there had occurred a shift in my psyche that no longer required me to sit in a car for the next two months, urgently burning rubber and clocking up miles. If I was honest with myself, all I really wanted to do right then was stay in Manapakkam with Thor, the Marceaus and their menagerie. Thor was due to spend another week there before heading back out to Berlin, where we agreed we'd meet when all of this was over. Eager not to cake the situation in too much nostalgic crud, I exercised great willpower in not falling to my knees and begging Thor to take me to Germany with him. Instead, I tried to sound cool and optimistic when he asked me where I'd be staying that night. Oh, in a place called Nellore, I piped.

'I've never heard of Nellore.'

'Oh really? That's strange. It's not far from here and it's so well known for its, er, mica.'

'Its what?'

'Never mind. I'll be just fine.'

'Of course you will, little Thunderbolt. Just take it easy.'

Given that Nellore was relatively close, I tried to delay my departure from Chennai as long as possible. It was 4 pm when Abhilasha and I trundled off (not daring to look at Thor waving in my rear-view mirror), which was just the right time to meet the rush-hour traffic coming to a complete standstill. Two hours and enough creative cursing to fill an Eminem lyric book later, we began to move around the northern outskirts of the city.

Crossing the border from Tamil Nadu to Andhra Pradesh, the landscape flattened out and we finally picked up speed. As the massive Pulicat Lake passed unseen somewhere to our right, the sky began to fall through several shades of crimson. It was a picture worth freezing – an open and now relatively unimpeded road, a vast surrounding panorama, a sky slowly sinking into darkness and a few tungsten beacons blinking here and there on the horizon. I felt like the lonesome cowboy, riding off alone into the sunset with a throbbing heart and a fistful of rupees. So I had left my lover behind: what did I care? The road was mine once more. I had over 6,500 km left to drive over India's feral topography, and the journey started right here. I gave Abhilasha a jolly good cuff around the wheel to celebrate.

11

SMART CAR – More for Less for More

As far as I could see, the Nano's popularity was showing no signs of recession. Passing through towns and villages, we were treated to the kind of reception more appropriate to a troupe of touring, puppy-dispensing tycoons. The enthusiasm was unremitting, and surprising to me. It was only a car, after all. How exciting could it be? I tried to imagine similar levels of adulation poured on, say, a Mini driving through an Oxfordshire village: kids dropping their games to run in its wake, screaming its name like they were trying to draw out the spirits from its frame; adults stopping dead in their tracks for a gander, knocking on the windscreen at traffic lights to ascertain the exact fuel-to-distance ratio – it wasn't probable. I mean, I liked the Nano – and in some ways I was even beginning to *love* Abhilasha – but I wasn't about to start sprinting down the road after one.

Nevertheless, the sustained hype did make me wonder. Was it the Nano's elusiveness that made it so appealing to the masses? Once it went on general sale, how would the market reflect its popular celebrity? Were people ready to put their cash down on what might be a passing fad?

Before arriving in Hyderabad, I'd been introduced to a professor at the Indian School of Business there called Reuben Abraham. He'd been recommended to me for his expertise in emerging markets, and as such I hoped he might be able to shed some light on the behaviour of the Indian consumer.

'You should come down to ISB to see what the future of education in India looks like,' Reuben wrote to me after I sent him the awkward 'you don't know me, but...' email. They were bold words that duly perked my interest. Besides, I didn't have much choice: the 450 km round-trip detour I'd taken to see Hyderabad had been rendered futile by the fact that most of the city centre was currently out of bounds. On arriving at the Taj Mahal hotel, an establishment whose appearance fell a few tacky architectural flourishes and luminescent signs short of tallying with its name, I learned from a Mr R. Janardhan at reception that a series of local Hindu–Muslim skirmishes had closed off most areas of note in the city, where the police had cracked down on residents and enforced a curfew.

The nature of the unrest and the reasons for it were unclear to me. Even after time spent quizzing R. and scouring the front page of *The Hindu* (a businessman had been beaten to death by a mob, a teenager had suffered rubber bullet injuries, more than two dozen people had been hit by stones), I was still at a loss as to *why* it was all happening. And when it would end.

R. remained taciturn but chipper, waving off my anxious queries and trying to change the subject. Keen that age-old inter-religious rivalries should not diminish my enjoyment of his city, he suggested I take a trip out of town to visit Ramoji Film City, Hyderabad's own Bollywood. Having been underwhelmed by a Wild West show there a decade earlier, I politely skipped over the proposition, asking R. what he thought instead of Hi-Tech City, the suburban home of the ISB and a place whose name inspired in me *Bladerunner* visions of interlocking monorail flyovers and airborne jet skis. R. was less enthused, shrugging off its appeal as if my intention to go there was a personal snub, though our exchange did eventually finish with his blessing by way of a room upgrade.

As I divined the route to Reuben's office through the corridors of the ISB – after a five-minute face-off with security that was precipitated by Abhilasha's lack of discernable trunk – I was growing nervous at the prospect of meeting the man who, according to my research, was a stalwart of his field. Executive Director of the Centre for Emerging Market Solutions, he had a host of accolades under his belt, including the position of Young Global Leader at the World Economic Forum, board member of the Soros Economic Development Fund, a TED Global Fellow and a member of the Clinton Global Initiative. What, apart from a short chat about the Nano, would I have to talk about with this superbrain economist?

Instead of the nerdy professor I'd been expecting, Reuben was a sprightly man of my own age with a penchant for parties and electronic music. He shot up from his desk to shake my hand eagerly and introduced me to anyone who'd listen as the girl who was driving around India in a Nano, before whisking me around the college to ascertain the veracity of his conviction that the ISB was a blueprint for education in tomorrow's India. He took me through the building, which looked like a modern desert fortress with a huge inner atrium and a library that spiralled up like New York's Guggenheim Museum. He showed me a system of natural air conditioning that harnessed the cooling power of the wind to blow around the bridges and walkways, and introduced me to a girl who had started her own fresh juice business within the college. Pricey artworks adorned the corridor walls while outside, the manicured grounds stretched for acres of green lawns, and the waft of frangipani trees floated among the campus housing as far as the on-site hotel. Reuben left the final cherry for the last part of our tour: the swimming pool, surrounded by sunbeds where weary, overworked students could take a break and catch some rays.

It was clear that Reuben was proud of the campus and he had reason to be; it was a stimulating training ground for the businesspeople of a future global superpower that made my list of attended academic institutions look like dingy 1960s throwbacks, and not just because of its arresting architecture. In 2010, the *Financial Times* ranked the ISB's MBA programme as the twelfth best in the world, way above the likes of Yale and Cambridge. Graduates from the school came ninth in the world in terms of average starter salaries, which range from £20,000 to over £100,000.

I had by chance met a recent alumnus the day before who told me how painful leaving the college had been. Students were furnished with top-notch serviced spaces and enjoyed such high standards of living that post-college life was invariably a bit of a let-down. 'It was tough having to go back to cleaning my own apartment,' complained the graduate, who was now working at a microfinance agency.

An enthused speaker on the subject of free markets, Reuben could whip even the most clueless and under-informed subject (i.e. me) into a raging debate within minutes. Some of his assertions instinctively set my teeth on edge, like his conviction that India needed to be more urbanized and that village life was something to be abandoned and not subsidized by the state.

'But... but... villages are... nice,' I protested weakly. 'Aren't they?'

'That's urban bourgeois romanticism!' he exclaimed, smacking my comment clean out of the ring. 'Would you want to live in an Indian village? With no running water or electricity or phone connection?'

I shook my head.

'With an active and discriminating caste system?'

I kept on shaking.

'The single greatest remover of poverty in the world has been the economic growth of China and, to a lesser extent, India,' Reuben continued. 'In the last 30 years, over 700 million people have been lifted out of absolute poverty, and this is almost entirely due to the functioning of free markets and liberal economic policies.'

My knowledge of Indian economics was shaky to say the least, but I did have some facts knocking about in the recesses of my noggin that helped me put some of what Reuben was saying into perspective. It seemed that as far as the country's financial system was concerned, there were two landmark years in the last century: 1947 and 1991.

The former was when the British packed their bags and retreated to Blighty, taking with them the Raj and all its exploitive failings. India declared itself an independent republic and, with Jawaharlal Nehru at its helm, went on to construct an economic infrastructure that was primarily socialist with some traces of capitalism. The idea was that it would invigorate its economy independently, that its land would provide everything its people needed – from agriculture to manufacturing and industry – without any interference from the international market, and with no need for imports or exports. The drive to self-sufficiency was an understandable sentiment, given the two centuries of colonial manipulation the country had suffered, but the system itself turned out to be slow, unproductive and above all a fertile breeding ground for misbehaviour and corruption; thoughts of reform only started to bubble in the 1970s and nothing really changed for the Indian economy until the fateful summer of 1991.

That was the year of Rajiv Gandhi's assassination, shortly after which the economy went into a crushing nosedive. It was a calamity of huge proportions: India was on the verge of bankruptcy and needed a bailout plan, fast. The newly elected PM called on his minister of finance, Manmohan Singh,[27] to figure out a master stratagem. What Singh came up with, within a matter of days, turned upside down a great deal of what Nehru had implemented and the Congress party had upheld for the past half-century. His idea was that the government free up the market, both for domestic businesses and for international ones. The reforms were pushed through quickly, and suddenly India was a much freer, much less regulated place. Indians wanting to start their own businesses no longer had to jump through dozens of hoops before ringing up their first transactions,[28] and international companies were now at liberty to deal in India, by importing or exporting their goods and by investing in Indian companies.

The fruits of the reforms succeeded in bailing the country out of its short-term crisis, and before long the enriching effects of the reforms became apparent. India's GDP began to rise steadily, along with household incomes. The percentage of people living under the poverty line has fallen from a staggering 90% in 1985 to under 29% today, so it's difficult to argue that India's economic liberalization efforts have not been largely responsible for lifting millions out of deprivation.

I asked Reuben if the Nano was a direct product of the country's economic growth.

'Absolutely. It's a sign of industrial power to the extent that you've got a large corporation that has money to put into research and development,' he explained. 'If you have money to put into R&D, then you've crossed a hump.'

Coincidentally, Reuben was working on a similar project from within the Centre for Emerging Market Solutions: the Nano principle transferred to housing. His team was in the midst of a scheme to build low-cost, high-quality housing for low-income industrial workers in small towns who might otherwise be living in slums. The houses they were building were set to cost between $6,000 and $10,000, but were by no means a form of charity; this mission was also very much focused on profit. Capitalism, Reuben argued, could be reshaped to include and even benefit the poor, as long as business models were well thought out. The key was frugal innovation or, as he put it, the principle of more for less for more.

Whereas the Nano encapsulated this within engineering, other entrepreneurs around the country were exercising the same principle in different arenas. He cited the example of Dr Devi Shetty, who was performing open-heart surgery in Bengaluru for less than $2,000. 'That's a classic case of the you-do-not-have-an-option principle,' Reuben said. 'You can price it at $100,000, but there aren't going to be any patients. You have to price it at something that people can afford. So you are forced to innovate.'

Frugal engineering is currently quite a buzzword in India. It seemed to make sense, the way the country's economy was developing, that industries would be focusing on bringing down the costs of manufacturing and services in order to target the millions of households who were emerging into the arena of expendable incomes and aspirations. Most of the hype surrounding the Nano in the run-up to its launch wasn't centred on the fact that it was set to be the cheapest car in the world, but rather that its price had been fixed *impossibly* cheap. How could a car be sold for £1,000 and still leave its producers in profit?

The story goes that the price itself was a bit of an accident. It emerged at a press conference with Ratan Tata back in 2002 when he announced plans for a new low-cost car. Journalists pressed the CEO for a figure, which he declined to disclose, given that the project had hardly entered the first phase. Determined to fix a price, one journalist asked whether one lakh rupees would be a viable target, to which Mr Tata responded guardedly that yes, it might be possible. The story that hit the headlines the next day was that Tata was set to launch the one-lakh car, a fact that hadn't been confirmed. But instead of calling the papers to correct the error, Ratan Tata decided to go with it and set one lakh rupees as the price target for his new car.

All around India, those headlines must have been read with gasps of incredulity. How could it be possible to manufacture a car for so little? The Maruti 800, at the time India's most affordable car, was priced at more than double that. Would this new car be half a Maruti? And what would that look like?

At Tata HQ, the team that had been assembled to realize this seemingly impossible task started off by thinking quite laterally. They referred to the auto-rickshaw. A brand new Bajaj three-wheeler cost about three-quarters of a lakh; it seemed that with the remaining budget they might just be able to tack on an extra wheel and carve out a bit more storage space. In fact, the first drafts of the Nano did indeed resemble a four-wheel tuk-tuk. The golf-cart concept slowly evolved into a more glorified version, which eventually developed into something that looked like a car, pushed at every step by Ratan Tata, who had a very personal stake in creating the vehicle. His vision was that the Nano be a bona fide car with competitive specs that met national safety requirements, not some comedy buggy to be ridiculed on the roads.

The Nano's exterior came to resemble a car. Its architects – a group of engineers that eventually swelled to 500 in number, led by promising young engineer Girish Wagh – dispensed with the original roll-down plastic curtains and rickshaw-style tarpaulin roofing, and instead gave it a steel finish and glass windows. All through the process, the Maruti 800 was used as the benchmark for the minimum standards of performance that the Nano had to live up to, and preferably exceed. Size was one aspect in which the team excelled: the Nano turned out to be a few centimetres shorter than its competitor, but with 21% more space on the inside.[29] The story goes that the drive for increased interior space was largely fuelled by Ratan Tata's own considerable size: the six-foot chairman was keen that tall people should not feel cramped inside the small car and that he himself would be able to emerge nimbly from the vehicle at the time of its launch.[30] The fact that the team had decided to place the engine at the back also proved a big saver – when an engine is located at the rear, the drive shafts do not need as many joints and so are much simpler and cheaper to produce – while the tubeless tyres made the car lighter and perkier on the roads.[31]

However, the engine still left a lot to be desired. Designers had been experimenting with low-cost motors sourced externally, but since not one engine fitted the stringently tight bill, it was concluded that Tata would make its own one using only a few third-party components. This brought the price down considerably, and along with various other alterations to individual parts, the car was finally able to go on the market for the promised one lakh. The gamble had paid off hugely for Ratan Tata, who marked his own massive boldness at the car's launch with the tagline 'A promise is a promise'.

'Fancy a shot?' Reuben raised an inquisitive eyebrow as he flashed me a glance of the vodka bottle he had stowed in a messenger bag. He had to shout to make himself heard over the twangy beats of the music that was wafting across the lawns in celebration of the latest wave of graduations. It turned out I had hit the college at an auspicious time, two days before the class of 2010 would get its round of diplomas and be unleashed on a country ripe for the well-trained entrepreneurial minds this institution had nurtured. The Future of Education in India was on the brink of becoming the Future of India, and it would not be long before it was India's reality. These happy few were set to be the ones to push their country's economy further onto the global stage to new heights, and I had little doubt they would succeed – but how would they do it? Social responsibilities like the eradication of poverty were high on their professor's agenda, if not also their own, but at what cost would these changes take place? Would Reuben and his students really have the villages bulldozed and cities megapolized in the name of progress and economic expansion? With what degree of sensitivity would the new economic order handle the remains of centuries of tradition, undesirable as they sometimes might have been? I guess what I was really getting at was, were these guys the goodies or the baddies?

'Hey, Reuben,' I asked, over our third shot of Absolut Ruby Red, 'so you like the Nano, right?'

'Damn right, it's pretty cool.'

'So, would you ever think about actually buying one for yourself?'

'No way, man!' he cackled rakishly in a way that made it hard to know if he was serious or not. 'I don't own a car! I'm pretending to be carbon neutral.'

RULE OF THE ROAD #6
Stay Safe

On a dark, moonless night, the day after I had left Hyderabad, I pulled into what I hoped – but had no means of proving – was the deserted, locked-up and turned-in-for-the-night village of Nagarjuna Sagar.

An hour and a half before midnight is a relatively chipper time in India's larger cities, with vendors, rickshaws and late-night diners still going about their business under the yellow glow of halogen streetlights. But nights in rural India are a different situation altogether. It's hands down the darkest darkness I've seen: a menacing blackness; an empty, closed-down, boarded-up void. I drove up and down several roads emanating from the main square and could see nothing in the way of the hotel the guidebook assured me should be there. Was I even in the right place? I consulted Delilah, the sum of whose visual information on this area was a thick yellow line on a white background that gave no quarter to the surrounding side streets or even the name of the village. I checked my phone, but there was no signal. The only person available for directions was an inebriated lorry driver contemplating the stars from a curious position underneath his steering wheel.

My options were limited, and for the first time since setting out from Mumbai, I realized that bedding down with Abhilasha might be my only choice that night, a thought tinged a deep shade of dread. Although my direct experience so far had been entirely to the contrary, most people I encountered seemed to be of the unshakeable opinion that a single female on a solo road trip was a brutal assault and murder waiting to happen. It was by no means an outrageous perspective: women on India's roads do face some very real dangers. Kidnappings and carjackings are more likely to happen to female targets, as are the risks of falling prey to police impersonators and sexual predators. General advice ran along the lines of keeping a can of pepper spray to hand and practising general good sense, like not stopping to withdraw thousands of rupees from a deserted ATM in the middle of the night.

My own attitude to safety was light prudence (I opted for hair-spray rather than pepper spray and made sure I always had at least a vague idea of where I'd be staying the following night) combined with pragmatism based on statistical likelihood. It was a stance that allowed me to breathe easy most of the time. But plans would oft go awry, journeys would take significantly longer than anticipated, and before I knew it I was a potential victim in my own Hammer Horror scenario – like this night in Nagarjuna Sagar.

Courage, Thunderbolt: if the truck driver could sleep at the wheel, then so could I (my lack of a quart of Bagpiper notwithstanding). I pulled up at the side of the road and switched off Abhilasha's lights to test the situation. We were thrown into darkness. I forced a yawn to simulate relaxing, then pushed back the seat and wound down the backrest to see just how peaceful a position this could be. I curled up on my side and tried to extend my legs over to the passenger seat without impaling them on the gearstick. About a minute of murky discomfort passed before my imagination began to twitch. It started with an eerie feeling that someone was watching me through the window, and very quickly amplified to a roll call of the cast of every horror movie I had ever watched. Opening my eyes, I saw nothing but a profusion of shadows, one of which I was convinced belonged to that dwarf from *Twin Peaks* who has been a regular fixture of my more wobbly moments since I first encountered him in my early teens. I winced and turned the lights back on, full beam this time, in order to dispel the last of the demons.

Sleeping in the car was not going to be an option. I reached for my phone to dial Thor's number, but there was still no signal. Besides, I reasoned with myself, what could he really have done for me right now, except maybe stay on the phone until sunrise?

All that remained, I thought as tears welled up in my eyes and a childish despair gripped my throat, was to be brutally murdered by the sleeping truck driver who was bound to wake up at any moment.

This disagreeable thought coincided with the sudden appearance of an actual face at my window. I shrieked as I saw a pair of dark eyes looking in, framed by copious dreadlocks and bundles of beads, and it took me a few seconds to register that I was looking at a tall, half-naked sadhu – a wandering mendicant. I exhaled and wound down the window an inch, praying he was a good and true sadhu and not one of the fake ones I'd heard about who would spike tourists' tea with opium and then rob them for every penny they had. The man, who I now noticed was also sporting an impressive collection of homemade tattoos that with any luck were not occult symbols of bloodlust, was quickly joined by a group of five ladies so intricately adorned with beads, piercings and coloured headgear that I concluded they had to be tribal women.

Hilarity ensued as I rolled the window down further and enquired whether anyone spoke English. Piled on top of the wave of insecurity that had gripped me, the women's feral laughter deepened my fear and triggered irrational thoughts of cannibalistic tribes roaming the barren lands of Andhra Pradesh at night in search of fresh meat for the village pot.

'Um... hotel?' I blathered, trying to banish images of myself on a slowly rotating spit.

More laughter. Cackles, even. The sadhu stepped forward and held up his hands in a gesture of surrender.

'No English!'

What did he mean by that? Was he trying to communicate his ineptitude with the British tongue, or was he expressing some morose local prohibition of my nationality? The women kept on laughing as I hastily rolled up the window and launched Abhilasha forward around a corner from where, incredibly, partially obscured by a large set of gates and some trees, I spied the celestial words 'Nagarjuna Resort'.

The resort was a drab concrete block, but never had drab concrete appeared so beautiful in my eyes. As I pulled into the car park, a light came on from inside the building and a couple of guys emerged bleary-eyed from the entrance with a small dog called Puppy in tow. I wanted to embrace them all, restraining myself at the last minute out of a sense of social decorum and a desire not to contract fleas from the persistently scratching Puppy.

One of the lads proudly showed me to a room that was unequivocally the least-inviting accommodation I had witnessed on the trip so far. I spotted a few ant-like bugs crawling over the off-white sheet on the bed; mysterious clumps of black hair lay like dead rats on the bathroom floor. The constant sound of running water from an unseen source could be heard from every corner of the room, while the curtains and other random bits of upholstery around the place bore stains suggestive of bodily fluids gone a-scatter. Worst of all was the apple of the hotel guy's eye, the fridge-sized air-conditioning unit wedged into the far wall, which contained enough black dusty *Legionella pneumophila*-infested crud along its ventilation panel to wipe out an entire foreign regiment. My stomach turned in anguish, but my brain stepped to the fore: this was a one-village lake and a one-hotel village, and my choice was to spend a night in the company of bed bugs and bloodstains or to sleep in the bottomless darkness of a sweltering car with one hand on my keys and the other around my can of hairspray.

The twin joys of shelter and company were a godsend, no matter how gag inducing and itchy. I recriminated myself for my shambolic performance that evening and promised it wouldn't happen again: behind the cocky Thunderbolt exterior lay a girl who was just as vulnerable and assailable as the next, should the misfortune of predatory intentions befall her. These fates were not to be messed with.

12

O-R-I-S-S-A – *Pastoral Paradise and X-rated Architecture*

BHUBANESWAR to KONARK; KM 5,217–5,389

The NH5 that ran the length of India's east coast was a swift highway, unencumbered by too many delays or diversions. It was primed for carefree cruising and only occasionally punctuated by the odd fleet of lorries, herd of goats or roadwork diversions that bottlenecked all the highway traffic through a single tiny village. Thor called me on the road and found an unusually calm and composed Thunderbolt on the line.

'You're not supposed to be talking while you're driving.'

'Uh-huh. I'm willing to risk the fine. Besides, I'm on a straight-shot road right now.'

'Wow, really?'

'Yeah, it's like the highway of our dreams. I'm holding a steady 85 and I haven't seen an animal in like twenty minutes.'

'You sure you didn't cross over to China by mistake?'

'Yep. I'm pretty sure the trucks in China aren't this colourful.'

'You missing your passenger?'

'Eh, maybe. I could do with some company. In fact, I've got a confession to make.'

'What's that?'

'I'm a bit bored.'

'Bored? How is that possible?'

'It's the road's fault.'

'It's always the road's fault. A bad driver always blames...'

'Nothing's *happening*.'

'I thought you wanted stuff to *stop* happening. Like highways ending abruptly and elephants attacking the car. Like potholes and diversions and...'

'Yeah, but not like this. I keep falling asleep.'

'Asleep? I can't begin to imagine anyone getting sleepy behind the wheel in that traffic.'

'Blame the Golden Quadrilateral.'

Thor was back in Berlin, but continued to call me every couple of days. He phoned during times he knew I was on the road for long stretches and needed some company, and we talked like he was back in the passenger seat.

'Fuck me, you should see the size of the balls of this horse I'm tracking. They're like coconuts, I swear.'

'Take a photo, take a photo.'

'I can't, they won't fit in the lens.'

'Aw, I wish I was there.'

My spirits were high: the roads were good and we were moving fast, which was just the combo I needed after a stocktake in the town of Vijayawada, which had been my stop after Nagarjuna Sagar. There I had spread out the long-neglected Stanford's map on my king-sized bed at the budget-busting Quality Inn (my only choice since I discovered too late that wedding season had descended on Vijayawada and spare rooms in the city were very hard to come by) and scrutinized our current position with a pencil and a calculator app. We were just under halfway up the east coast from Kanyakumari to Kolkata, which was a bit disheartening since I had marked Kolkata as our next major destination. It had been two and a half weeks since Vivekananda's ashram, which – not taking into account the Hyderabad diversion – was around 1,250 km and nine days behind us. Kolkata was the same distance ahead, and the prospect of taking a further week and a half to get there was about as appealing as another night feeding microscopic buddies my epidermis at a lakeside hotel. With a little over five weeks remaining to reach our 10,000 km target, I realized we needed to get our groove on.

A peek at my bank balance sealed my conviction. Another nine days to reach Kolkata was not an option; the clock was ticking and the coffers were draining. I had already completed six weeks and only covered 4,000 km, a pace that was not going to suffice unless I wanted to be greeted back in London by a bankruptcy suit. And the Playboy Mansion nights at the likes of the Quality Inn were only aggravating the situation. I needed to step up and reach Kolkata within three days, which meant travelling at three times the current pace. I felt my chicken biryani dinner do an uncomfortable turn somewhere in my duodenum at the prospect of the impending hours at the wheel.

But if there was a bright side, it was that the NHAI had our back; on its online project map, the NH5 was coloured in glorious, victorious, fait accompli red. According to the key, this meant it had already been lovingly fondled by the restorative fingers of the roadwork team, which potentially meant an uninterrupted stretch of two-lane highway with an average speed of at least 70 kmph all the way up to Kolkata. At that rate, 400 km a day would be a cakewalk.

And they were; but this particular piece of cake was laced with something eminently soporific. Between slugs of energy drinks and hyperventilation exercises designed to shake away the looming sleepiness and send blood back to my brain, I reflected on this easy road I had spent the last seven weeks wishing for. It was smooth, it was fast and it seemed relatively safe. My close encounters had been fewer and further between and not quite as butt-clenchingly terrifying as those before. Here, as Thor rightly pointed out, was the infrastructure I'd been harping on about, the progress the multitudes were calling for; well oiled and effective, it was nonetheless as dull as monsoon ditchwater, and as sleep inducing as a tank of chloroform.

The erratic pendulum of my desires set itself back in the opposite direction and began to hanker after something more colourful, more exciting than mere efficient plod. After a night spent among the easy-wash linoleum floors, sparse pine-veneer furniture and the kind of bathroom you might expect to find in a space-age mental asylum at the Tata-branded Ginger Hotel in Bhubaneswar, my impulse had upgraded to a yearning, and by morning, my resolve to keep pounding relentlessly on to Kolkata had dissipated in favour of a burn around rural Orissa. The final straw might have been waking up to the austere Swedish-prison interior of my room, or it could have been the glyco-synthetic qualities of the Coffee Day Iced Eskimo and chocolate doughnut I'd gorged on for breakfast, or even the uncanny smell of ginger that lingered through the hotel's corridors, but the prospect of another day watching chevrons disappear under my dashboard at a steady speed, unimpeded by livestock or holes in the road, could not be tolerated. Abhilasha and I needed to return to rural roads, get back to nature.

Consulting the guidebook, I came across a strong recommendation for the beach resort of Puri, only 75 km away, which apparently attracted two types of visitors: the 'spiritual' and those after 'worldly pleasures'. Having a penchant for a bit of each, I thought this would be just the place to break the monotony of modern progress: a small coastal settlement and a favourite with hippies in the 1970s. I imagined a less-developed Goa from which full English breakfasts and even the likes of Café Coffee Day would be mercifully absent, and where an evening could be spent contemplating the gently cascading tide from the terrace of a converted Maharaja's palace. Screw the time limit, the devil take the budget – I was not a driving machine, and Abhilasha was not just a means of slogging from one business hotel to the next in order to chug coffeeccinos and battle with uncooperative wireless networks.

The Orissan countryside was an eyeful. Lush feral fields bordered by palm trees and criss-crossed by pathways and bicycle tracks the colour of the terracotta earth were plentiful grazing grounds for cattle, who lowed serenely between mouthfuls of grass alongside their companions, the white storks, who looked on quizzically. Sporadic temple ruins punctuated the landscape, their pyramidal shapes echoed by the outlines of the loosely stacked bales of hay, scenes worthy of a subcontinental Constable painting. Grass huts that looked like they were about to melt into the ground were surrounded by swamplands blanketed by a profusion of untamed lilac flowers.

I watched as a line of women in bright saris waded through the rice fields, while a gang of teenagers whizzed past, howling from a trio of overloaded bikes. A man holding a large black umbrella squatted in the corner of a field; another hacked away at the ground for all he was worth with what resembled a highly ineffective wooden machete. Across the road from him, a driver in a pressed beige uniform pulled a rag over the headlights of a parked Ambassador with the leisurely air of someone passing an abundance of excess time. The cattle mooed behind him, snazzy new Hyundais and Suzukis occasionally whizzed by in front: three ages of Indian transport condensed into a single snapshot.

Aside from invoking a pang of guilt that Abhilasha and I had never shared such an intimate moment of personal hygiene (the only washes she had ever received had been at the hands of the odd-job boys and parking attendants at the hotels where we'd stayed), the image also ignited in me a curious nostalgia. It was a given that the luscious bucolic terrain that surrounded us was a world in decline as agriculture and village life dwindled in India. But I was also aware that the Ambassador – the graceful, old-fashioned Ambi, as people affectionately called it, with its curvilinear bodywork and the enduring robustness of a reliable old mare – was also on the edge of obsolescence.

I had loved the car since I'd seen it in Delhi the first time I came to India, but I was perplexed about its origins, mistakenly believing for a long time that it was a remnant of the Raj, left in India by departing Brits in the 1940s. I was very wrong: it turned out the Ambassador was an Indian car, first put out by Hindustan Motors a decade after independence. Its blueprint was taken directly from an English jalopy, the Morris Oxford, devised by Sir Alec Issigonis, the Greek-British car designer who was better known for drafting the Mini. I was amazed to discover that India's Ambassadors were still in production in a form quite similar to the original 1957 model. But all this was set to change: that very month, the government passed a new set of emission standards that spelled the beginning of the end for antiquated cars not running on greener engines. Within a year, sales of the car for use as taxis in India's cities would be phased out altogether.

For decades the Ambassador had been one of the only two cars available in the country, along with the Fiat 1100D Padmini, made by India's other car manufacturer, Premier. The Padmini ceased production in 2001, but is still famous for being Mumbai's yellow-and-black taxi of choice. The Ambassador and the Padmini basically ruled the roads until the early 1980s, when the cogs of economic liberalization began to turn and other car manufacturers arrived on the scene, including Maruti Suzuki, which produced India's own Tin Lizzie prior to the Nano, the Maruti 800 (now rebranded the Alto).

Tata Motors put out its first passenger vehicle in 1991, the same year Ratan Tata was appointed chairman of the group. Its foray into the world of private cars came at the perfect time: India's economy was starting to expand and individual purchasing power was on the verge of rising. Since then, India has seen the influx of international car brands the likes of Hyundai, General Motors, Ford and Honda, so it makes sense that relics like the Ambassador have already been pushed to the back burner, and will soon be shoved out of the market altogether. There's little room for old uncles in this rapidly changing family picture in which a younger generation of cute, cheap, fuel-efficient little yellow cars have become the new point of focus. For now, at least.

My escape from the ho-hum turned out to be a bit more tumte-tum, as it dawned on me just how ambivalent I was towards homogenized progress on the one hand and barmy bits of rural life on the other. Drawing closer to Puri, I began to deck out my fantasies with increasingly elaborate images of sandy white beaches and golden sunsets, a vision that, in retrospect, was only doomed to disappointment. The slippery slope to disenchantment began on the outskirts of town when Delilah was scuppered in her attempts to get us to the centre by a number of road closures and diversions. Disoriented at a forlorn train junction somewhere that seemed miles from my vision of a Bay of Bengal *Baywatch*, I decided to wind down the window and let the world – and its road directions – in.

I waved down a nearby motorcyclist wearing an enormous padded white leather jacket. Having furnished me with excellent directions to Chakratirtha Road, the man proceeded to cross the hospitable local–psychopathic stalker divide by tailing Abhilasha and sticking to us like Velcro for the next few kilometres. Whenever the road afforded him the opportunity, the motorcyclist sped up to come level with my face and actually rapped on the window for my attention. The first couple of times I thought he might be trying to alert me to the fact that a flock of man-eating seagulls had nested on the car's roof, or that one of her tyres could do with a puff of air, but his intentions were far more amicable.

'Where are you from?' he screamed with urgency against the wind, which was carrying his voice back down the road at 30 kmph.

Perplexed at the high-speed small talk, I mouthed back through the glass, 'Uh, England.'

Spurred on by my participation in the curious dialogue, and not even fractionally letting up on his speed, the motorcyclist continued his line of questioning in earnest.

'What is your good name?'

Before I had the chance to answer, a rickshaw van piled up with wooden crates that was coming in the opposite direction forced my friend to swerve and slow down to take his place behind me and let the vehicle pass. Within less than a minute, his knuckles were at the window again.

'Which hotel are you staying at?' he asked with an interrogator's seriousness that consigned him once and for all to the nutters' wing of my estimations. I declined to answer and instead scowled at him from the driver's seat, baring my teeth. His was a friendliness that gave me goosebumps and I had no intention of encouraging his attentions further. Several thumps of the window later and even a disrespectful slap of Abhilasha's posterior, my eager escort went on his way, ostensibly bored by my indifference and definitely terrified by my well-honed vitriolic growl.

We finally pulled up on Chakratirtha Road, home to the main run of small hotels in Puri, to be treated to a sight somewhere between the scene of a recent natural disaster, a horror movie set and a building site. The trinity was a painful one, spiked with the thorns of my own broken dreams of a night at a beach paradise. The surrounding streets were lined with boxy concrete buildings, all of which bore an eerie air of emptiness. A thick cloud of dust rose from the unpaved ground under Abhilasha's wheels as we drove around the grid of streets lined with scattered building debris and hog-wild weeds. I found my hotel, the so-called Maharaja's Palace, only to see that it was walled in and shut up and looked as appealing a venue for a night's dreamy sea-watching as the deck of a sinking ship. In fact, where *was* the sea? According to the map, it was only three blocks away, so I tried steering Abhilasha in the right direction. Maybe after a lungful of fresh Bay of Bengal air and a paddle in its waters, I might have a renewed, more positive perspective on this town that, to all current intents and purposes, seemed a bit of a dump.

But every time I thought we were close to seeing the sea, the street would be blocked off by a wall of rubble or a pile of sandbags, to the point where getting to it seemed so difficult, I finally gave up the ghost. It was hardly St Tropez, and no sooner had I had that thought than a French-looking lad with an expression that suggested he was dealing with a very bad smell passed by. We made momentary eye contact and looked away immediately as though any kind of camaraderie in this place would amount to lesser chances of saving oneself. We appeared to be embroiled in a game of escape and survival, and as far as that went, the four wheels under my posterior were my advantage.

That day, in Puri, all the pains of driving a car in India paid off in one happy reimbursement: unlike the suffering back-packers who arrived by long and agonizing bus or train journeys, I was mobile and free as a bird. With only 75 km back to Bhubaneswar and the simple pleasures of the Ginger Hotel (once again coloured sunny and appealing in my fickle memory banks), I was under no obligation to stay in this two-bit excuse for a resort.

'This place has bad juju, Abs,' I obliged myself to say out loud, in case there were any doubt cast over my awesome coolness. 'Let's get the hell out.' As we sped out of town, I allowed Puri one last concession: that it was off season, which was probably the reason for its construction sites, sandbags and uncanny lack of people. Or was it just my increasing boredom with all things developed or developing and the homogenous sludge they exuded?

I decided to take one last detour: nearby was Konark, the famous Temple of the Sun, ostensibly Orissa's most fascinating archaeological site and largest tourist draw. Given that Puri went under the guidebook designation 'undiscovered', I figured mass consensus might work in my favour for once in this rapidly disintegrating day of adventure and sightseeing.

I pulled Abhilasha into a space at the end of a row of cars just outside a gated entrance to a long bazaar that led up to the temple. Our arrival immediately attracted the attention of a group of loitering youths, one of whom stepped forward and – much to my surprise – took the liberty of opening the driver's door after I had barely cut the engine. What I first took to be a charming gesture of chivalry turned out to be a means of giving the Nano's interior a thorough and quite unsolicited inspection. I nudged the impudent adolescent out of the way and, hauling myself out of the seat, made an exaggerated show of locking all the doors and giving Abhilasha a proprietary pat on the roof before walking away. Was it me, or were the young men of Orissa more roguish than their counterparts in the rest of the country?

At the bazaar entrance, I was set upon by a throng of guides, from which I settled for a man called Suryamani, the only person who claimed to guarantee the Nano's safety in addition to showing me the sights, and who tried to appease me regarding the fact that Abhilasha had now become a leaning post for the young guys who had propped themselves up against her with an air of entitlement that made me plain uncomfortable.

'Don't worry,' Suryamani said with a dismissive, boys-will-be-boys laugh, 'they don't want to take the car, only to touch it and look. Is very new and exciting, you know.'

Yeah, I knew, but my inner maternal jackal was roused at seeing such flippant manhandling of her bodywork.

Suryamani turned out to be tour-guide gold. After fifteen years on the job at the Sun Temple, he had the spiel down to a fine art. The building was a truly impressive and magnificently preserved temple that dated back to the thirteenth century and was dedicated to Surya, the sun god (a nominal coincidence that appeared to tickle Suryamani pink). The temple was aligned along perfect coordinates for solstice and equinox wow factors and the structure was a chariot, with twelve pairs of stone wheels adorning the outside and seven bucking horses pulling it from the front, towards the sunrise.

We started with an introductory stroll around the pillared remains of a dance hall, where Suryamani pointed out various animal carvings in the stone. 'This is sheep – S-H-E-E-P; and this one is bull – B-U-L-L; over there is cow – C-O-W' and so on.

With Farmyard Spelling 101 in the bag, Suryamani, who had appeared distracted for the last five minutes as though something was on his mind, finally cut to the chase. 'Madam, can I talk about the *Kama Sutra*?' he asked in a conspiratorial whisper, to which I cautiously answered in the affirmative. If I hadn't, our tour would have stopped right there, because almost the entire perimeter of the main temple building was covered with sexually explicit carvings of a highly imaginative variety.

'This,' said Suryamani, adopting a very business-like tone while pointing at a twelve-inch man in a compromising position with two members of the fairer sex, 'is bigamy. B-I-G-A-M-Y. Two women and one man.'

'Gosh,' I said, not knowing how else to react.

'Yes!' Suryamani exclaimed triumphantly. 'They are having intercourse together.'

I nodded sagely and we moved on.

'Three women together,' he continued, gesturing at the relevant carving. 'One woman giving one man oral sex. O-R-A-L S-E-X.'

I went closer and squinted. 'Good lord!'

We kept walking and the sculptures became increasingly X-rated. At one point, Suryamani threw a furtive glance over his shoulder. 'This,' he said in a hushed voice, 'is doggy style. And these are two elephants doing doggy style. Look!'

I looked and can confirm that indeed they were.

We turned a corner and something in Suryamani's excited demeanour told me we had reached his favourite part. 'Look you!' he signalled at the figure of a woman riding an unidentified animal. 'One woman with dog. D-O-G!'

I thought it only polite to match Suryamani's enthusiasm with incredulity, but as I widened my eyes in overacted shock, I realized I was genuinely stunned. What from the onset had seemed like an 800-year-old temple constructed by the very regal-sounding King Narasimhadeva the First, head of the Eastern Ganga Dynasty, was actually an array of chiselled hardcore pornography, from girl-on-girl scenarios to threesomes and even a bit of bestiality, put on by some ancient-day Hugh Hefner. If the artistic evidence of this temple was anything to go by, it was a wonder empires were built at all, given all the hanky-panky with which thirteenth-century Indians ostensibly passed their time. Or perhaps it was all fantasy: the men who were drafted to work on the temple were, Suryamani told me, often separated from their womenfolk for months at a time. So is it any wonder their imaginations might have started to run wild?

Whatever the reason, I had to admit that in principle at least, thirteenth-century Indian cheesecake gave the likes of *Playboy* a run for its money, though it would be a damn sight harder to stash discreetly under the bed. Still, I figured it had done the trick – invigorated and my enthusiasm restored, I went back in the direction of Bhubaneswar, my mind buzzing with enough P-O-R-N-O-G-R-A-P-H-I-C I-M-A-G-E-R-Y to keep me alert and amused as far as Calcutta.

13

ROAD RAGE – Fear and Loathing in the Red-Hot Corridor

> **BODH GAYA; KM 6,352**

Whatever you do,' Reuben Abraham had told me as I drove out of the ISB campus several weeks earlier, 'don't try anything cute in Naxalite country.'

Eager to get going, I pretended to know what he was talking about, laughed and gave him and his wife Petra a chipper wave before rolling up the window and setting off. But as Hyderabad receded into the distance, his warning began to resound uncomfortably inside the Nano. Hang on, what was Naxalite country? I had never heard of it and had no recollection of seeing it on the maps. And what did he mean by cute, exactly?

Two days later, on 6 April, all my questions were answered in the news reports. Seventy-four members of the Central Reserve Police Force had been massacred in an ambush carried out by Naxals, who I learned were fearsome revolutionary Maoists who terrorized a large swathe of India through violent operations like this one. The attack had taken place in the forests of Dantewada in Chhattisgarh, near the border with Orissa and Andhra Pradesh (about 300 km from our route), and followed another incident two days earlier that saw eleven soldiers killed in Orissa when a landmine blew up a van.

The massacre in Dantewada had been the group's most deadly to date. As I reread the sequence of events on several news sites, the gut gremlins – largely absent since I banished them through the evocation of Swami Vivekananda's thunder-bolt mind back in Kanyakumari – made a dramatic comeback. I read on with trepidation about the group's continuing campaign of violence, which had allegedly claimed the lives of 6,000 people in the past twenty years. According to an Indian intelligence estimate in 2006, there were around 70,000 active Naxals in the country, 20,000 of whom were armed. Most of their attacks were aimed at police and government forces, but civilians, and especially local tribespeople, were frequently caught in the crossfire. The areas they mostly operated in – Chhattisgarh, West Bengal, Orissa, Bihar and Jharkhand – were considered 'severely affected' by Naxalite activity.

I got hold of a map of these areas and compared it with my own route. There was an alarming amount of overlap. Hyderabad itself appeared to be at the centre of an area called the Red Corridor, a rash of Naxalite-impacted territories that dropped down like a sash around India from West Bengal all the way to Kerala. So I had already been in the thick of these badlands that stretched in the other direction all the way up to Orissa and Calcutta and closed around my next destination, the sacred Buddhist town of Bodh Gaya.

From what little I knew of Bihar and Jharkhand, it made sense that they might be ripe territory for Maoist activity. Among the poorest states in India, a large majority of their population lives rurally, while the size of their middle class is negligible. Bihar has the lowest GDP per capita in India and virtually no industry, relying on its migrant workers to send money home from the big cities for a great deal of its income. The state also has a reputation for lawlessness, with a large number of criminal activities – most notoriously, kidnappings and extortion – that stick to the wall in a way that just wouldn't wash in other parts of the country. Even the guidebook was a bit iffy on the subject of Bihar and Jharkhand, grouping them into one chapter and glossing over them with the general attitude that despite the presence of some nice Buddhist sites, more discerning travellers might want to think of taking themselves off to another neck of the Indian woods.

As I crossed the border from West Bengal into Jharkhand, it immediately became apparent that something was quite different here. The most obvious sign was a massive drop in the number of private cars on the road, an indication, I guessed, of the prevailing economic situation. However, the highway that cut through the state, the NH2 – the eastern arm of the country's Golden Quadrilateral network – drove a smooth line through a landscape that, despite all the doom I had managed to monger, turned out to be beautifully and breathtakingly rugged. Making good time through sublime scenery, and not a Naxal in sight, gumption levels inside the Nano were high. That is, until we approached the frontier with Bihar.

There was the usual long line of trucks waiting at the state border. I had read that truck drivers spend an average of two to seven hours waiting at such borders, and even up to 24 hours, a chronic delay that the World Bank estimates costs India $420 million annually.[32] Still, inert boredom for the attendant truckies had the upside of providing a fun driving game for me: due to the often unruly nature of the lines, getting through to the front was like trying to figure out a maze, ducking through the spaces between stationary trucks in a bid not to hit a dead end. In the past, I had left such situations to the experts, latching on to the first SUV I saw negotiating the lines with any degree of dexterity and tailing it right to the bitter end. But on the border between Jharkhand and Bihar, there was no such opportunity. Abhilasha was the only private car I had seen in at least an hour, and when we met the giant lorry park, I had no choice but to go it alone.

I began to weave tentatively through the maze of colossal trucks, trying to gain as much ground as possible along the edges of the road. The line went on for at least two or three kilometres. The drivers were milling about their vehicles, some of them smoking, some knocking back shots of chai, some of them taking a nap in the shade underneath their trucks. Heads turned as we passed by, making me painfully aware of our exterior bright yellowness, interior single white femaleness and general excellent candidacy for high-profile kidnapping, should there be any off-duty Naxals among the fray. There was none of the friendly waves or salutes to the Nano to which I had become accustomed, just eyes that followed us in what felt like irritated suspicion.

At one point, two trucks parked shoulder to shoulder and, allowing for no passage, blocked the way ahead of me. After about a minute studying their posteriors while a small crowd of guys began to gather around us, I decided that staying still was not an entirely comfortable option. Trying not to meet the eyes of the lorry drivers for whom I was now a one-woman spectacle of bad reversing, I concentrated on getting Abhilasha out of our little Venus Fly Trap cul-de-sac and back onto the road.

I had never felt intimidated on account of my gender or the fact that I was alone – never, that was, until now. Perhaps it was all the stories and hype about the Naxalites, maybe it was the neurosis of entering an infamously anarchic part of the country, but among the horde of lorry drivers at the border between Bihar and Jharkhand that day, I definitely felt like a plump yellow pigeon among a crowd of hungry cats.

Half an hour later, after some very focused manoeuvres and a hardened commitment to not stopping under any circumstances, I managed to extricate Abhilasha from the scrum. We were out, over the border and back on the road as the sun began to drop and the hues of the jagged hills took on a deeper shade of terracotta, the spindly shrubs lining the hillsides appearing softer and increasingly fuzz-like. As if in a dream, I passed a group of Muslim men performing their evening prayers in perfect synchronicity in five rows of four on the central reservation of the highway. It was a beautiful sight of coordinated devotion in a most outlandish location that clocked the paranoia pixies out for the day. I chided myself for my foolishness and aptitude for gobbling up media alarmism as though it were the gospel truth. Bodh Gaya was only another 250 km away and if there was one thing I needed, it was a good grounding stint in Buddha's own seat of enlightenment under the most famous tree in India.

But it seemed that the ugly head of my neurosis had reared up for the long haul and couldn't be appeased, even by the presence of scores of well-meaning, shiny happy Buddhists to whom Bodh Gaya was a centre of pilgrimage and a temporary home. The heat wasn't helping: it was mid-April and the air outside was scorching. I can't say I wasn't told. When I set out in the relatively balmy month of February, vaguely planning a route that would take me in a circle around the country in three months and so through the northern plains around the time of the dreaded hot season, people with whom I discussed my itinerary pleaded with me to avoid the north in April. My cocksure dismissal of their advice doubtless rendered me demented in their eyes.

I don't know which part of 'temperatures in the north of India during April and May are usually between 40 and 50 degrees Celsius' I didn't quite process; it had seemed an abstraction, an intimation of warmness, but nothing that I assumed couldn't be easily negotiated with a bottle of ice-cold water and a blast of Abhilasha's AC. Besides, I had foolishly reasoned, the more hardship and adventure we faced as a team, the more character-building the experience would be and the more stories we'd have to tell.

If I had known that those stories would involve tedious tales of lying under a fan in a hotel room covered with a wet towel and groaning sporadically as I tried to muster the will to do anything, I might have rethought my route timings. Sweat-drenched clothing and heat-induced lethargy do not glamorous tales of the road make. And such was my first, and only, morning in Bodh Gaya. I lay on the bed in my room at the Kirti, a hotel wrapped in Tibetan flags, watching the clock drag out the minutes past lunchtime. Just outside, within a few hundred metres of where I lay ostensibly dying, was one of the most culturally and spiritually significant sites in the world: the Mahabodhi Temple, which contained in its grounds the Peepul tree under which the Buddha attained enlightenment. I had spent the morning chastising myself for being so close to a slice of living history and not having the gall to undergo the roasting necessary to see it. But after five hours of self-castigation, I decided I'd learned my lesson and that it was now or never as far as the Buddha was concerned. If he could sit under that tree without moving for 49 days, then I could surely get off the bed and go and check it out for an afternoon.

When I did go outside, the main street of Bodh Gaya was deserted. A couple of mad dogs limped by and began to follow me, howling in boiled derangement as they watched me make my way to the gates, where there was very little activity. The cluster of shops selling wooden statues of the Buddha and the many-armed Avalokiteshvara pulled their doors ajar resignedly in the taciturn sleepiness of the peak of the day's heat. At the Mahabodhi entrance, I found a guide who was willing to take me round. We wove our way through the gardens that surround the tall, monolithic structure of the main temple, among little pockets of cheerful Tibetan, Vietnamese and Bhutanese monks who were alternately meditating, taking photographs, rummaging through their satchels, or just sitting in the shade of the trees, chewing the fat. My guide, whose name I failed to retain despite his repeating it four or five times, gave an account (often way too thorough, given the effect of the temperature on my blood pressure and general patience levels) of the garden's artefacts, all of which were, according to him, either exactly 300, 1,000 or 2,300 years old. In his version of events, they were put there by Emperor Ashoka, or destroyed by the Mughals, or both; there appeared to be no real third alternative.

The tour over, I drank the entire contents of the bottle of water from my bag and sat down in the shade to make like a Bhutanese monk and contemplate the sprawling peepul tree that stood within a walled garden on the south side of the temple.

At dusk, when the temperature had dropped enough to allow the non-essential functions of my brain to kick back in, I was approached by a smiling middle-aged monk in yellow robes. We had no language in common and so proceeded to communicate mostly by way of hand gestures and the mutual exchange of detritus at the bottom of both our bags. He showed me his passport, which told me that his name was Le Van Chung and that he was Vietnamese. He then curiously insisted that I take a photo of his passport picture page; a strange request, which for some reason I felt might be insulting to refuse. I went ahead and snapped his document, before he quite rightly asked if he could return the favour.

Once again, the grizzly paw of suspicion took a swipe in my direction. Exchanging images of each other's passports was an unprecedentedly bizarre activity. My more rational intellect told me to relax, that the man was clearly a mendicant: his head was shaved, he was clad in holy cloth and his arms were dripping with prayer beads. This was most probably his way of getting to know people and gleaning the information that his language skills prevented him from doing: small-talk basics like name and country data. There was nothing peculiar about that, was there? But then the gremlins crawled out from their lair and whispered in my other ear – he could be an identity thief, a human trafficker, an undercover agent, a con artist, a (gasp!) Naxal… After all, the guise of the benevolent monk would be perfect for reeling in unsuspecting single females already batty from the heat. I kept my eye on him even after he left to meditate by the temple entrance, and didn't let him out of my sight until I decided to head back to the Kirti.

Back in bed, lungs heaving and sweat drying off under the force of the huge overhead fan, I began to come to my senses. The chances that Le Van was a mastermind criminal or local Marxist rabble-rouser were very small indeed. Occam's razor dictated that he was basically just a nice old chap with a quirky way of making friends.

That decided, I realized a problem remained: the issue here was not the über-friendly Le Van, nor was it the Naxals. The problem, as it revealed itself to me in a moment of lucidity, was the joint prongs on the pitchfork of my own predicament: namely, prolonged periods of time spent with nothing but my own paranoid ranting for company within, and all-encompassing mind-bending heat without. And on the back of that rather calming and incisive thought, Occam's razor also added that it was high time I got the hell out of the plains, before I started to have a meltdown of nerves.

I turned to Google Maps and checked out our options. We needed to get north as fast as possible, to the foothills of the Himalayas where temperatures were in the blissful 20s. I decided we would head for the state of Uttarkhand, which contained the closest highlands in the direction in which we were moving. I set my sights on the town of Nainital, a small holiday resort at the start of the foothills that, according to Lonely Planet, was an attractive and upbeat place built by homesick Brits who wanted to be reminded of the Lake District. That suited me just fine, but a few moments of measurement brought with them the grim tidings that this pseudo-Cumbrian mountain paradise was still 1,000 km away, which realistically meant at least another three days on the road. Between the Buddha tree and Nainital, we'd have to overnight in Varanasi (although, remembering how much I had loved the city the first time I visited, I was tempted to stay on) and again in Lucknow before finally escaping the oven that was the northern plains.

As I settled down to sleep, I tried to think what the Buddha might do in the same situation. He would probably use his infinite wisdom to accept the trials of the heat and see through the illusion of the pains of extreme high temperatures and lethargy, I thought, resolving to take my future cues more from the stoic Buddha and less from Scooby Doo in the face of 50 degrees Celsius. But then I remembered what Buddha, a native of this area, actually did: come the summertime, Shakyamuni would gather up his disciples, find a suitable spot of serenity and batten down the hatches for the next three months, thus starting the tradition of the annual summer Buddhist retreat.[33] Now that was smart. And so I drifted uncomfortably off to sleep in the grim knowledge that Buddha himself wouldn't attempt the journey we were about to embark on the next day: a 250 km drive to Varanasi over tarmac roads hot enough to make a thousand-egg masala omelette.

My hopeful plans for leaving before daybreak were scuppered by a slumber so log-like that not even the irritating sound of a phone alarm sustained over 45 minutes managed to scratch the bark of my deep REM.

After finally being frog-marched into consciousness by a protracted banging at the door from a shy youth who had been obliged by some higher power to ascertain that I was checking out that day, my departure was then further delayed by an email I received from Thor with the alarming header: 'Check this out and please don't explode and die!' Inside was a link to an article in the *Hindustan Times* that almost made me want to leave Abhilasha in the Kirti parking lot and take the first plane out to wherever, with nothing but a Dear John scribbled on a Post-it and stuck to her windscreen by way of explanation.

The headline, which jumped out at me from the screen bearing all the marks of a Hitchcock horror sequence, dismally read: 'Second Nano Catches Fire: Tata Motors'. With a bleak sense of foreboding, I went on to read the harrowing tale of a brand new Nano that had burst into flames a few days ago on its way to being delivered to a dealership near the town of Vadodara in Gujarat. The article only stated that a Tata spokesperson had announced that the company was sure a design flaw was not to blame. I found little comfort in his reassurance and was frustrated by the newspaper's lack of information about how the fire started. A cigarette left to burn on the passenger seat? A stray firework that made its way into the gas tank? I hoped against hope that the explanation was ludicrous and highly unlikely; that of all the things that might have ignited the flames, what it definitely wasn't was a faulty spark plug that would incite a recall of the 30,000 Nanos already on the road all over India. Or, come to think of it, anything connected with driving long distances in temperatures over 40 degrees Celsius.

I went straight to a YouTube broadcast by CNN-IBN that displayed the words 'Nano: Trial by Fire' across the screen in block letters, accompanied by a dramatic action-sequence soundtrack and the heart-rending image of Abhilasha's doppel-gänger in an advanced stage of immolation. I watched reluctantly as the report showed the charred remains of a grey Nano being loaded onto the back of a truck and covered solemnly with a white shroud. IBN's man on the ground, Varun Kumar, stood boldly facing the camera and recounted in his best Breaking News tones how the fire had started in the rear of the vehicle and worked its way quickly to engulf the whole body. He went on to interview an auto analyst by the name of R.K. Dhawan. Dhawan, sporting a huge moustache and a baseball cap that undermined his senior years by at least two decades, spoke with cloudy authority about the problems of new-fangled fuel-injection systems. Kumar concluded with the staunch observation that Tata might be seeing its dream sales figure reduced to ashes.

The readers' comments that followed the articles and videos gave me pause for thought. Posts such as 'It's a toaster oven on wheels – a piece of SHIT car!' and 'It has become devil. It should be banned' suggested that glowing national support for the little car might not be as widespread as I had assumed. The critics were harsh: 'What u expect for peanuts!' exclaimed an outraged user called Sahilkind, while Jam from Bangalore pulled no punches in saying, 'Tata Nano is crap. Please suggest your friends and family members not to go for it, if anyone is planning to. Saving li'l money at the cost of lives is not wise. Thank you.'

TheMrRajaG was hardly so polite: 'This is a bloody fucking car,' he said, before telling the story of his neighbour who had his Nano 'thrashed' by an autowala and had to have two doors replaced. He rounded off his tale with the deduction that the Nano was a 'plastic toy car fucking good for kids'.

'An expensive way to get someone cremated on slum-dog standards' was the insightful response from YouTube user Telears, while cyclops621 responded to the footage of the burnt-out car by chillingly laying open his own emotion. 'Hahahahahahahaha…' he wrote, with brazen honesty.

But the haters in turn had their own detractors: 'Shame on you whoever you are,' wrote parthakaroy, joined in his defence of the car by athjuljmatthew, who claimed, 'There is nothing wrong with the nano', and Porusable, who added his own endorsement: 'On the whole, the tatanano is a fantastic performer.' The Nano's supporters went on to point out that many makes of cars had either spontaneously combusted or undergone safety recalls, including Marutis, Toyotas, Lamborghinis and Ferraris. One user even pointed fellow commentators to a site called The Truth About Cars, which reported no fewer than 190,500 cases of cars bursting into flames in the United States in 2009, a figure that put these two Nano incinerations well into perspective.

At the extreme end of the spectrum of opinion were those who went as far as absolving Tata from all responsibility for the blaze by positing conspiracy theories that were very much in line with my own hopes. 'This is a deliberate adverse publicity by the scared competitors,' wrote parthakaroy, who went on to make the excellent point: 'In India, have you ever seen the fire tenders rushing in as soon as a car is engulfed in fire? Here you have the fire tenders, newsman, camera absolutely ready before the event happened.'

Still, the conspiracy theories could only comfort me to a certain point. I went on to read that there had been more spontaneous Nano fires the previous year, with at least three reported incidents in Delhi, Lucknow and Ahmedabad. These had been attributed to a faulty switch in the steering column and the public's mind was supposedly put at rest by a quote from a Tata spokesperson, who claimed his company had 'comprehensively checked all the Nano cars that are on the road'.

I did the math: I wasn't sure exactly when Mr Shah had taken delivery of Abhilasha prior to selling her on to Prasad, but I calculated it must have been in late 2009, which meant my beloved steed was probably of the same generation as the faulty switch brigade, and had not, to the best of my knowledge, been comprehensively checked out by Tata or indeed anyone (barring the Brahmin in Pondicherry, but the less said about that the better). The blazing cars on YouTube might well be acts of subterfuge, but the fact remained that there were now the twin spectres of faultiness and a potential singeing hovering in the air like a defective button on a steering column that was about to plough into my skull.

Eager for a toehold of optimism from which to chase the phantoms away, I navigated back to the IBN clips page and found an interview with Hormazd Sorabjee, editor of *Autocar India*, who according to the headline was about to enlighten us as to What's Going Wrong With The Nano. 'When cars are reduced to ashes, it's very difficult to find out exactly what the problem is,' he said rather darkly, though he went on to suggest a shoddy fitting in the spot where fuel comes out under pressure, or an electrical wire meltdown, which didn't mean much to me on a practical level. At that moment, the presenter echoed my own desperate petitions by asking Sorabjee, 'If I was going for a drive in a Nano, what should be the one thing I should look out for?'

'Well, keep your eye on the rear-view mirror!' the editor cheerfully quipped.

So that was that: one hour's worth of trawling the internet for some source of comfort or useful information, following the revelation that the car I was driving for thousands of kilometres through burning hot terrain had been reclassified from 'The People's Car' to 'Incendiary Death Trap', had borne no fruit. I was none the wiser than when I pulled into Bodh Gaya two days before, except that now I was condemned to carry the burden of knowledge and the millstone of paranoia for the next few weeks, or at least as long as Abhilasha didn't ignite into a big yellow conflagration.

When we finally did get to put very hesitant wheel onto very hot road, the sun was at its highest in the sky and the tarmac was so heated it was emitting a dizzying Will-o'-the-Wisp-like mirage that upped the illusion of oncoming speed bumps by about 300%. At one point I was convinced that a haystack strapped to a cart pulled by a tractor up ahead was a shackled Gruffalo on its way to the government labs. On top of the worry of a Nano inferno, I was also mildly concerned for Abhilasha's diminutive tyres: we had already seen dozens of signs along the highways warning motorists not to go over 70 kmph for fear of a blowout, and I figured that speed plus 40-something degrees plus incredibly small rubbers was a sure-fire formula for an afternoon spent accumulating heat stroke on a Bihar roadside while scratching my head and trying to figure out which end of my toothbrush was most suitable for prising off Abhilasha's rear hubcap.

14

THE RAJ BY CAR – Mr Kipling and the Henglish Drizzle

NAINITAL to McLEOD GANJ; KM 7,491–8,329

Varansi, India's most beautiful, historical, holy city, came and went like a garbled chimera: as the mercury hit 47, I was aware I was hotter than I had ever been in my life. Hotter, in fact, than I thought it was possible to be. On arriving there in the early afternoon in the middle of a power cut, I could do nothing but sit on the terrace of my room overlooking the bonfires of the Scindhia Ghat – one of the city's open crematoriums – and catch the occasional waft of flesh-scented smoke, while meditating on the sensation that even without the help of an open flame, my own organs were also on their way to a good browning.

After a circular exchange with the lad at reception precipitated by my supplication for a room with air conditioning (his argument, resting on the reasonable tenet that an airconditioned room would be a waste of money given the power cuts they were currently undergoing, stood staunch in the face of my desperate assertion that I was willing to take my chances either way), I spent the night shrouded in wet towels, cursing the intermittently spinning overhead fan until dawn, when I stepped outside to find the temperature had halved and I could once again form a rational thought. That singular notion was to get the hell out of Varanasi and up to the mountains as fast as Abhilasha could possibly go without herself combusting.

Still, before leaving I took the famous dawn trip on the Ganges in a small wooden boat that coincidentally had the TATA logo hand-painted along its side. My captain was a teen-age boy overflowing with enthusiasm for his hometown. As we paddled the length of the city, past the hundreds of people gathering at the riverside ghats to perform their morning puja[34] ceremonies, the kid pointed out and explained every last detail of the towering skyline that lined the river.

It was my second time in Varanasi (during my first visit, I had memorably spotted two dead bodies – one of a baby – and an expired cow floating past my morning tour boat) and I was in no doubt it was one of the most remarkable places on earth. The morning light and rising mist threw the mediaeval-looking buildings behind into a saturated relief, framing the colours of the bathers and their candles and flowers that floated down the river in a spectacular shifting composition. Everything I looked at was beautiful and exotic and otherworldly, and hap-pily the whole trip passed without so much as a hint of a float-ing corpse.

I could have stayed there for a month, but by 9 am, the celes-tial furnace was beginning to fire up and my survival instincts kicked in. I bid Varanasi a reluctant goodbye – it's not you, it's me; the timing's all wrong – and huffily hauled my bags into a cycle rickshaw, returning to the outskirts of the old city where I'd been obliged to leave Abhilasha; even she was too large for the centre's archaic little streets.

From ancient Varanasi, I set out westwards on the NH2, which ran the course of one of the world's oldest highways: the Grand Trunk Road. Like the Silk Road and other bygone trade routes, this was a key element in the movement of citizens, goods, defending armies and invading forces for two thousand years, and now formed part of the Golden Quadrilateral, the high-tech, high-speed highway connecting

India's four largest cities. As I cruised along the barren dual carriageway towards the town of Allahabad, I remembered Rudyard Kipling's eulogies of the road in *Kim* ('such a river of life as nowhere else exists in the world'); it was a sentiment that stuck a chord with me, though on this particular stretch there was little on the NH2 that appeared to correspond to Kipling's accounts.

As the landscape between Varanasi and Allahabad flattened into the Gangetic Plains, I tried to imagine the 'green-arched, shade-flecked' thoroughfare that, in the nineteenth century at least, would have been lined with up to four rows of trees. Today the sweep of road was more desolate, the heat having parched the land to a degree where dust clouds rose from the surrounding countryside to lift up a grey-brown haze. Kipling's descriptions of people on the Trunk Road, shrouded in orientalist fantasy as they may have been, were still vivid and sometimes even familiar: the 'long-haired, strong-scented Sansis with baskets of lizards and other unclean food on their backs'; the 'women with their babes on their hips, walking behind the men, the older boys prancing on sticks of sugar cane, dragging rude brass models of locomotives such as they sell for a halfpenny, or flashing the sun into the eyes of their betters from cheap toy mirrors'; the newly released prisoners, marriage processions, money lenders, soldiers on leave, jugglers with 'half-trained monkeys'; Akalis, the 'wild-eyed, wild-haired Sikh devotees'; the Ganges water sellers, cotton wagons and Changars, the women in charge of building the railways: 'a flat-footed, big-bosomed, strong-limbed, blue-petticoated clan of earth-carriers, hurrying north on news of a job, and wasting no time by the road'.

Spirited chronicler of the Raj, Kipling was staunchly opposed to Indian independence, believing the British colonizers should dig in despite popular feeling to the contrary, and carry out their white man's burden, or whatever it was they needed to do. Born in Mumbai and weaned in the local language of his nanny, he was sent back to the UK for his schooling and returned to Bombay at 16, with a pubescent moustache that apparently scandalized his mother. He got a job at the *Civil and Military Gazette* in Lahore and stayed on for as long as he could bear the chronic heat and disease, which was a total of seven years. Despite the brevity of his time in India, he always considered himself fundamentally Indian, and spent his later life in the UK regretting the 'blasted Henglish drizzle'[35] and yearning for the east.

In following the Great Trunk Road, I was also on the heels of the nineteenth-century Brits who were just as lily-livered as I was when temperatures pushed past 40 and 'the 'eat would make your bloomin' eyebrows crawl'.[36] When the hot season swept across the administrative centres in the plains, the likes of Kolkata, Delhi and Lucknow were emptied of their colonial governors, generals and civil servants, who nearly all bolted up to the highlands for some thermal respite and the eyebrow-raising extra-curricular activities that invariably followed a gathering of bored, affluent people many miles from home. Darjeeling, Mussoorie, Dalhousie, Nainital and McLeod Ganj were among the settlements in the foothills of the Himalayas that became Little Britain for the duration of the summer months. In fact, life in the hills soon grew so attractive that Sir John Lawrence, Viceroy of India from 1864–69, resolved to shift the entire colonial administration 1,000 miles from Calcutta to Shimla, a decision that resulted in a highly controversial budget-busting biannual footslog.

More than 60 years after the administration had disbanded, I found it difficult to ascertain how people in India now felt towards the British, and how the Raj was viewed in retrospect. As a Brit in India, I found it difficult to forget my Englishness completely and was never entirely sure whether, beneath the smiles and resolute hospitality, the Indians I met were harbouring a more inimical sentiment towards me based on the implications of my nationality. That there were hard feelings regarding the arrival of the East India Company and its associated acts of violence and political usurpation was clear; but there were traces of the Raj apparent in everyday life that India must have consciously chosen not to obliterate: the railways, the education system, some monumental buildings and an administrative infrastructure that had mostly descended into a slothful bureaucracy still functioning on many outdated laws. Queasy triumphal monuments the likes of the Victoria Memorial in Kolkata just left me feeling embarrassed, while macabre memorials like the Jallianwala Bagh in Amritsar, which marks the 1919 massacre of hundreds of Indians by the British Army, no doubt rendered the average visiting Limey flushed of cheek and low of profile.

One of the objectives of a liberal art school education like the one I enjoyed in London at the turn of the millennium was the harsh assessment of colonialism and its associated creative forms, for the most part led by Edward Saïd's *Orientalism* as the trailblazing text. In this highly analytical light, it was always hard to be able to see any artwork springing from foreign inspiration – or in fact any person who had ever left the UK and gone abroad, be it to Kathmandu or the Costa del Sol – as anything less than a patronizing and subjugating force. It was a paranoia I carried with me in backpacks and suitcases throughout my travels; every time I encountered something strange or unknown, like ant curry or temple pornography, my every politically correct instinct would kick in to over-judge my actions and attitudes in the face of this 'Other'. It's a tiring state of mind to sustain and after some time I found I was Othered out. Too much self-conscious not-finding-the-east-an-alluring-den-of-preconditioned-western-notions-of-exoticism was wearing me dry. Like old imperialist duffer Kipling, I too would sell my granny for a few days anywhere east of the Suez; it was that simple.

Whether my reasons for this passion arose from ingrained societal conditioning, or whether I just dug India, was open to interpretation. But in the meantime, I could only honestly say that I found India and its relationship to England fascinating. From raj-mances like *Passage to India* and *The Far Pavilions* to London's own Little India in Southall, things Anglo-Indian or Indo-English were generally a source of great pleasure to me. So the extra appeal of the prospect of a journey up to the hills and the summer playgrounds of the Raj was that I might find something there to lessen the gap of unfamiliarity between my host country and myself.

My route north involved following the GTR as far as the town of Rampur and then turning off up the NH25 towards Lucknow, where I would spend my last night in the flatlands before entering the Kumaon Hills. My chosen first stop, Nainital – which had the reputation among middle-class Indians as a top-notch holiday destination – was a place originally established by Europeans in the mid-1800s, particularly English traders, officers and officials who began to use the spot as a health spa and retreat from the south. The dizzying zigzag climb up the initial foothills was accompanied by a gust of mountain air, the first current in weeks that didn't threaten to roast everything in the car down to plastic-upholstered flesh-and-blood frazzle. The cool breeze penetrated the circuits of my brain, giving new life to each cerebral compartment as it dissolved through the grey matter. I felt my body and mind slowly decompress and return to a temperature in which they could function normally, while all thoughts of conspiracy, fires, Naxals and possible identity-thief monks flew out of the window and into the mountain skies. The resulting sensation was blissful. But my joy at having finally made it to the mountains was also tainted: as we slowly ascended the road up to Nainital, I huffed emphatically as I mulled over the new gash that ran along the left side of Abhilasha's front bumper.

The mishap had occurred in Rampur as I was turning off the Great Trunk Road. From what I could ascertain, the town was primarily known for its indigenous Rampuri Chaaku, a switchblade knife made famous by Bollywood baddies, and one whose prospects were on the line since the government had introduced a ban on carrying blades longer than four-and-a-half inches. I found out from an article in the *Economic Times* that although sales of the Chaaku had plummeted, according to one vendor, the wolf of a commercial nosedive was being kept from the door by 'small businessmen' and members of the Central Reserve Police Force, who were, apparently, his best customers.

Unfortunately, neither the NH2 nor the NH25 bypassed any of the town's more impressive monuments like the fort and Raza library that were built by the Rohilla Nawabs, a tribe of Pashtuns that have ruled in the area since the early eighteenth century. Instead, Abhilasha and I crawled through streets that became narrower and more congested as we approached the centre. At one point, we came to a stop at a railway crossing where, after a wait of several minutes punctuated by the anticlimactic passing of an emphysemic locomotive at walking speed, we found ourselves in the middle of a swarm of vehicles shoe-horned into every free inch of road in front of the barrier. What started as a couple of rickshaws, Tempos and a few two-wheelers soon became an outright crowd of drivers inching forward into any available space until they were literally rubbing elbows with their neighbours.

What concerned me as I waited at the crossing was that traffic on both sides of the barriers had spread to take up both lanes. What's going to happen, I thought with a degree of trepidation, when the barriers are raised? It was like the reenactment of an ancient battle; we were two armies standing at a face-off, the no-man's land of a railway track between us about to serve as a bloody battleground when the gates came up.

The railway warning lights started to blink and the barrier slowly lifted as the first line of attack – the infantry, composed mostly of bicycles and motorcycles – went forward and managed to weave expertly between their counterparts coming from the opposite direction. I was in the second line – the cavalry – along with the three-wheelers and motorbikes transporting heavy loads. Not so nimble on our feet as our predecessors, we encountered a plug of congestion going head to head with our opposite numbers. Angry horns were released into the air in mournful bellows while the vehicles shimmied left and right in a bid to get past one another. It was mayhem of the highest order, and so it came as no surprise that in the midst of the struggle, my steed sustained an injury from an enemy rickshaw. It happened in a split second: one moment I was trying to steer Abhilasha to the left of a minivan crammed with pigtailed schoolgirls who, judging from their screams and waves, were delighted to be fighting alongside a yellow Nano, and the next I felt the hardened rasp of metal on metal as an oncoming rickshaw cut a little too close to Abhilasha's anterior.

I issued a gush of barbarian obscenities. My instinct was to get out of the car, mid-skirmish, and demand that the fellow give me at least the details of his insurance company, if not full payment for the paint job his act of recklessness now necessitated. No sooner had I reconsidered in the dim light of the possibility of a Rampuri Chaaku being brought out to help with negotiations than my three-wheeled aggressor had scarpered into the fray, nixing all likelihood of being held accountable for his crimes. I cursed him again.

I didn't pause to examine Abhilasha's injuries until we finally stopped for the night in the car park outside Nainital's main mosque. Her scratch was not a pretty sight, and was more than a dab of TCP and a plaster would be able to solve. A series of black, brown and, interestingly, green scratches emanated from the edge of the bodywork above her left front wheel all the way across to her lower reflector. It was a sad sight, a wound of war, but it started me thinking about the significance of the fact that I was being shown no quarter by my fellow drivers.

The truth was that Abhilasha was my invisibility cloak; she was the perfect avatar in which I as a foreigner could really get stuck into the fray of an Indian way of life that would otherwise never be open to me. When I walked down the street, I stuck out like a sore thumb: people stared at me, pointed and even sometimes laughed, albeit all good-naturedly (I hoped). Out in public without Abhilasha to disguise my foreignness, I was always myself the Other, the exception, and would never really be able to witness India in situ as if I wasn't there. But driving in a car that for the most part concealed my identity allowed me to do just that; it let me hide inside a hunk of yellow metal and take my place among the warring factions of traffic on an equal level with every other combatant.

I'm not going to pull any punches: Nainital was a peculiar place. I had so far navigated over 8,000 km around India, stopping in 25 or so different towns, and nothing I had seen could have prepared me for this verdant, clean, quiet, Alpine whistle stop built around a pear-shaped lake and surrounded by rolling hills whose peaks afforded an amazing view of the snow-capped Himalayas in the distance. There was something really uncanny in the sheer spotlessness and order of the place, in the dozens of holidaying families sporting Western-style leisurewear and blinding white trainers, clutching cameras and bags of candy-floss and taking potshots at water-filled balloons in makeshift shooting galleries, or sipping cappuccinos on the terrace of the Coffee Day by the lake.

Mangesh Karandikar, the Mumbai professor who had been following my blog, wrote to tell me he and his wife had taken their honeymoon there, and indeed I spotted many a doe-eyed couple rowing a boat on the lake or strolling shyly along the woodland paths at the top of a white-knuckle cable-car ride. If it weren't for the exhausted stray dog and her six puppies who staidly occupied the entranceway to my hotel, warranting a lit-tle leap every time I went in and out, as well as the occasional waft from the tandoori restaurant next door (which served some of the best chicken tikka I'd had to date), I could easily believe that Abhilasha and I had been teleported to a small vil-lage somewhere near Geneva.

Shimla, on the other hand, was more akin to home, invok-ing somewhere like Hereford on a murky February after-noon: a series of neo-Gothic spires and Tudor-style timber beams stood out under a sky so dark and drizzly as to have me immediately snivelling into a hankie. The first Brits to arrive in Shimla – civil servants, army personnel and governors-gen-eral – came in the 1820s and began to build summer homes and holiday cottages under the heavy grey, but relatively exhil-arating, pseudo-English skies. The little Himalayan town that looked like it was slip-sliding slowly down the mountain had, during its days as the Empire's summer capital, been a hotspot of Victorian society. Infamy and transgression bred like wildfire in this most potent and fertile summertime Petri dish, a soap opera of love affairs and indiscretions that provided abundant fodder for the young Kipling, who wrote a series of stories and poems inspired by the goings-on he witnessed during the several summers spent there in the 1880s when he could get leave from his paper in Lahore.

In his biography, Kipling referred to his time spent in Shimla as 'pure joy'; it was, he wrote, 'another new world. There the hierarchy lived, and one saw and heard the machinery of administration stripped bare.' Verses such as 'Delilah', 'Pink Dominoes' and 'The Betrothed' laid out tales of extra-marital affairs, political intrigue and dreams of an oriental harem, while stories like 'The Other Man' and 'Cupid's Arrows' painted a world of lawn tennis, croquet and archery in which affairs of the heart were as wretched and complex as any latter-day television show. The last traces of the bygone improprieties have been preserved only by name at Scandal Point in the town centre, after an infamous incident when the King of Patiala made off with the daughter of the Viceroy, much to the shock of the upper crust in exile.

Abhilasha made her own ungracious debut when she failed to ascend the road to our hotel, the Spars Lodge, an ostensibly hand-made MDF-and-glass effort perched on an outcrop just above the local Oberoi and ahead of the distant Summer Hill that had been Mahatma Gandhi's residence when he came to Shimla (trips that were made for diplomatic reasons, I presumed, and not to join the locals in partying like it was 1939). The problem was a sharp-gradient driveway made impracticable by the weight of my luggage. Several embarrassing attempts at revving Abhilasha up to combustion point before letting go of the clutch and trying to catapult us up the hill ended in an ignominious stutter and extinction of the engine, and the annoying real-ization that I would have to take my bags out of the car and walk them up if I was to get to the hotel before midnight. It might not have been so bad if this hadn't taken place right in front of the gilded doors of the Oberoi, formerly Wildflower Hall, one-time residence of Lord Kitchener. What would the Viceroy think?

Wandering the famous Mall, imagining the high-society shopping extravaganza here that pre-dated the candyfloss stalls and other trappings of tourism that came with Shimla's cur-rent top-notch holiday-spot status, was a strange experience of juxtaposing worlds. On the outside, Shimla looked uncannily like England. The lemon-yellow Christchurch Cathedral in the main square just across from the Tudorbethan – that's a real architectural term, by the way – Municipal Corporation build-ing posed patiently for photographs, with the disgruntled air of an edifice wondering why the hell it wasn't in Penrith. A cuppa at the brilliantly old-school Indian Coffee Workers' Co-op Society was followed by a desire for an early dinner spurred on by the sight of a Domino's Pizza further up the mall. I resisted the stodgy-looking Peppy Paneer Cheese Burst Crust in favour of dining at a neon blue–lit restaurant that proffered southern-fried chicken and margaritas. Hardly the apex of cool, but here in the place that resembled home, I wanted the comfort food to match. The oily, sugary reality of the culinary experience, however, was a different matter, and within hours I was making hurried tracks to the toilet in my room at the Spars.

I dubbed those hours of intestinal upheaval the Night of Gandhi's Revenge; I imagined the ghost of the nation's father looking down on me with consternation from his place at Summer Hill as I munched on greasy chicken washed down with bogus Mexican hooch in the midst of a living memorial to the frivolities of his beloved country's colonial occupiers. The resulting emergency evacuation of the contents of my bowels came as little surprise, given the circumstances.

However, I was adamant that a sleepless night spent with bum to porcelain – well, plastic actually; this wasn't the Oberoi – would not impede our progress. We still had several thousand kilometres to go to get back to Mumbai and just under three weeks in which to do it. There was no time to be spent moping around feeling sorry for myself and the chicken that had so rapidly passed through me. Coupled with a head cold and an impending sense of all-over muscle ache, I knew the eight-hour drive through the mountains from Shimla to my next stop, McLeod Ganj, was going to be riddled with loo stops and bellyaches.

And so it went: after a few kilometres, a deep bubbling growl in the abdominal region had me screeching to a halt at the nearest petrol station, heading for the outhouse and holding my nose. One particular stop at an Indian Oil outpost a couple of hours beyond Shimla necessitated having to shout down an irate monkey – an actual Rhesus monkey – who had occupied the station's only cubicle and was drinking from the toilet bowl. It was a sad scene, bereft of the poise and glamour of a Merchant Ivory production.

I arrived in McLeod Ganj after eight or so hours spent negotiating mountain bends and trying to keep myself sensible by singing loudly and occasionally talking to an imaginary primate whom I briefly hallucinated in the passenger seat on a particularly sharp bend somewhere near Palampur.

As far as first impressions went, I felt more at home in this town almost entirely populated by Tibetans in exile than at

Christchurch Cathedral in rainy Shimla, built by my people to remind them of home. This was probably because of the fact that the Tibetans are joined in their mountain abode by a transitory population of foreigners who come to be near the Big Guy, the Dalai Lama himself, his temple and all the smaller seminaries his presence there has sparked. As I pulled up the hill and onto McLeod Ganj's main street, it became immediately clear that the town was a priority stop for the modern hippie: foreigners not shaven of head and clad in saffron were long of hair, scant of shoe and bedraggled of clothing. It appeared that the Little Britain of Shimla appealed more to Punjabi tourists, while contemporary travelling Brits – along with their European, Antipodean and Israeli counterparts – much preferred the coloured flags and prayer wheels of Little Tibet. Where there are Western travellers, there are ethnic handicrafts, coffee shops, wi-fi cafés, bookshops and even sushi restaurants. It was a strange kind of homecoming; a sudden immersion into a community specifically designed to cater to my latte-drinking, internet-using, book-reading ways.

For the first time after two-and-a-half months of driving around India, I could hear England English spoken with northern, southern, West Country and east London accents. The words 'Darren, will ye get us twenty of them Gold Flake from 't shop?' wafted through Abhilasha's window spoken in deep Lancastrian tones that never made me want more a slice of Hovis bread and a cup of Bovril.

Tired, sick and all driven out, I felt like the little town was welcoming us with open arms; or rather, the Tibetan woman at one of the hotels up the hill was. She actually did spread out her arms – in horror – when, using my last ounce of energy, I unceremoniously dropped my bag and all its contents at the threshold of her property before almost losing consciousness outside the front door. She gathered my belongings with matronly zeal and showed me to a bare-bones room that was immaculately clean with a view over the lush valley below.

'Eat charcoal!' Thor messaged me as I collapsed on the bed and thumbed news of my condition through to him.

'Argh, don't, I want to puke.'

'No, seriously, eat charcoal. It's the miracle drug.'

'What would you know? You never get sick.'

One of the few things that irritated me about Thor was his steely constitution. Being of a mildly competitive nature, I'd got annoyed at his capacity to maintain digestive equilibrium when I was often shuffling off to a loo. To boot, he was a vegetarian, which probably gave him an upper hand in protecting him from the threat of meat gone wrong.

'Trust me.'

'You mean actual charcoal, like the stuff you find in fireplaces?'

'Like the stuff you draw with.'

'Barf!'

'Yeah, but you take a tablet, you don't have to munch on a lump of coal.'

'And what does it do?'

'It absorbs all the bad stuff in your guts and turns your poo black.'

'Okay, well, there might be some in the fireplace down in reception. Shall I go and look?'

Thor, caring and well intentioned, was saved from further sarcasm by a knock at the door. It was the Tibetan woman from downstairs, who appeared like an angel in my doorway with a cup of hot ginger, lemon and honey, and a bowl of Tibetan noodle soup.

'Adopted Tibetan Mum saves the day,' I texted. 'No need to go foraging for ashes after all.'

'Good news,' Thor replied. 'Now lie back and dream of England.'

'Or Lhasa.'

'Whichever suits.'

RULE OF THE ROAD #7
Don't Drive (Too) Silly

'If you are married to speed divorce it' read the sign jabbed into the side of the road on a curve where, had the directive by the Public Works Department of Uttarakhand not been blocking my view, I would have seen a sweeping panorama of staggered hills rising from the seemingly bottomless valley below. I had been exercising my horn in the wake of a lardy-arsed coach for the past fifteen minutes, waiting for a long and straight enough stretch to afford me the visibility to pass as well as the runway to build up enough speed, but no such strip was forthcoming. Welcome to the start of the Himalayas, land of surprisingly well-paved (and, I had to admit, so far at least well-behaved) roads. Nevertheless, just like the rural highways on the plains, I was already feeling the familiar rise of frustration with the speed at which things generally moved.

The Uttarakhand PWD had obviously anticipated my impatience and was doing everything in its power, as far as erecting encouraging and creative road signs was concerned, to get me to chill out and slow down. Around the next bend flashed the words 'We like you but not your speed', cleverly playing on my personal insecurities as well as jabbing at my guilt glands for the numerous attempts I'd half-started at a perilous overtake of the coach ahead. 'Whisky is risky' declared another sign with undeniable poetic flair, after the defiant coach had pulled up to deposit its load of Korean passengers at a roadside *dhaba*.

As steep slopes gaped hungrily to the side and the road, only intermittently dotted with railings or concrete bollards, curved round at angles that sometimes felt like we were pulling a full 360, it became clear that traffic authorities in the north of India had additional reason to encourage safe driving along the mountain routes. Either that, or they had a lot more time – and possibly mind-altering drugs – on their hands, if evidence procured on a later web search was anything to go by. It seemed the most creative road-sign wordsmiths lived up in Kashmir, and displayed their work along the hazardous roads of Ladakh, especially the notorious Manali to Leh route, considered one of the most deadly in the world. A blogger called Ajay Jain had compiled a book and site on the subject called *Peep Peep Don't Sleep* (a title derived from a real sign), in which he catalogued a mass of inspired driving decrees from the Himalayan highways. My favourites had to be 'Fast won't last', 'No race no rally, enjoy the beauty of the valley', 'Road is hilly, don't drive silly' and the virtuosic 'Safety on the road is safe tea at home'. Genius.

It seemed the PWD had no qualms whatsoever in issuing quite graphic warnings to hammer the point of cautious driving home. 'Your family waits for you not for news of your accident' read another, more maudlin post, while 'Drive like hell and you will be there' held little hope of salvation for fast drivers. I thought whoever came up with 'Better Mr Late than Late Mr' displayed fine lyrical promise, while 'Darling, do not nag me, as I am driving. Instead turn your head and enjoy the nature charming' was worthy of Larkin.

I had been a little nervous about hitting the Himalayas. I imagined the madness and diversity of traffic on the sub-Himalayan highways transposed onto narrow rocky mountain passes; a frightful prospect. But it seemed, at least from Shimla going north, that the roads here were in much better nick, as were the vehicles travelling on them, which in any case were far fewer in number. But as with everything, when one headache dissipated, another reared up: while the roads were no longer congested, now they were all over the shop. They would often skirt the very edge of a rock face, as chasms yawned just centimetres from Abhilasha's tyres without a barrier to separate me from certain death by plummeting into the unknown darkness, and twist and turn with the scary turbulence of a cobra with an acute itch. At the heart of the problem were the hulking buses and trucks, for which the narrow roads, steep inclines and sharp turns were a pestilent wasp in their cloddish ointment. Once I got stuck behind a large vehicle, like the Korean tourist coach, I would be obliged to hover at its rear like the flies that hover around a horse's tail and wait there until an opportune moment for overtaking, which was usually not before the vehicle pulled over for a break.

No sooner had I got past the Koreans than I quickly caught up with a Tata lorry, whose backside was painted orange, yellow and red and emblazoned with the words 'Super-Star'. It was emitting thick clouds of grey smoke that infiltrated Abhilasha's interior to the point where I didn't know whether it was better to roll down the windows and at least mix the inevitable added rush of fumes with some fresh air, or maintain the drip-feed exhaust pipe in a Ziploc effect that was currently playing itself out. I nestled in at its rear, sighed and resigned myself to painful sloth and early-onset emphysema.

A few minutes later, I was jolted out of a creeping somnolence and mounting nausea by the ear-splitting horn of a truck that was attempting to pass me and the two lorries in front with phenomenal spunk, given that we were all struggling against a fairly steep incline while approaching a blind bend. I flinched as the truck slugged doggedly past, all the while keeping its horn pressed and flashing its headlights with the frenzy of a strobe light on speed. The whole manoeuvre took about half a minute during which I barely drew breath, expecting that a car might come bombing down the hill from the opposite direction at any second and end up battered into the truck's front grill. Call it luck, fate or good karma, the truck made out like a bandit and finished at the head of the queue, puttering off into the distance.

Looking in my rear-view mirror, I could see a line of cars gathering impatiently behind me, which also started to overtake one by one, while I pulled over as far as I could to let them pass. It was not my proudest moment, and I concluded in a rush of outraged self-righteousness that there was no time like the present to master the art of the perilous uphill, blind-corner overtake. I had to adapt to my environment and become the cool and nifty mountain driver; it was time to channel Bond.

As another truck passed me to my right at a speed that barely warranted an overtake, I caught a glimpse of a bus heading towards us from the oncoming lane. I could hear it bleat out its warning via a tremendous horn, a protest to which the truck to my right responded not by yielding, but by giving an indignant parp of its own instrument.

Reason dictated that by this point the truck that was blocking the opposite lane might slam on its brakes and settle for sliding in behind Abhilasha as the oncoming bus passed. But the driver clearly had no such plans and instead headed for the tiny space between me and the big gassy truck. I silently petitioned my maker, god, Ganesh, Remover of Obstacles, not to let it all end here; but then there was another, more stubborn part of me that thought, like hell am I letting the truck get in ahead of me just because it won't slow down. So instead of slowing down to create some space for the truck to pull in ahead of me, I kept my foot firmly on the accelerator, moving uphill with a determination mixed with the terror of annihilation and the vindictiveness of a moment of road rage.

What I didn't anticipate was what happened next: the bus that was trundling down the hill suddenly slowed down and pulled over so that the overtaking truck could pass. Headlights were still being flashed with great urgency and all horns were crying out in unison, but I realized this was in essence an act of extreme politeness and consideration, and it was taking place before my very eyes. As the truck that nearly ground me into the rocks to my left carried on puffing up the hill, I reflected on the implications of what had just happened. It was road courtesy of an ilk I had not witnessed until now, and if this behaviour was anything to go by, it went a long way to explaining the ostensible kamikaze over-taking tactics practised by all who flung themselves fanatically into the blind curves of these narrow mountain roads. If people coming in the opposite direction were on constant vigil as to the possibility of turning a corner and finding another vehicle in their lane, they would slow and swerve to accommodate. After all, the vehicles going uphill at this point were hardly breaking 30 kmph. How dangerous could it be?

My confidence began to mount as I toyed with the accelera-tor pedal and teased myself into giving it a squeeze. Abhilasha roared internally, but only moved forward marginally, due to the angle of the slope and the size of her engine, which was a few strokes short of Formula One. Still, if lardy-bum trucks could do it, so could we.

I began to indicate, probably much to the delight of the bright blue three-wheeler pickup piled high with tomatoes that was sniffing at Abhilasha's exhaust pipe. There was a curve up ahead, but wasn't there always? I pulled the Nano's nose out to the right, pushed her into second gear and floored the accelerator for all she was worth, mimicking the trucks' frantically urgent musical horns with my own psychotic bugle of beeps. Her little engine began to gather speed and soon we were neck to neck with the back tyre of Farty Pants. The giant tyre at that moment looked about twice our size.

'Come on, come on, come on!' I urged Abhilasha, leaning for-ward in my seat as though shifting my weight by a few centi-metres would make any difference at all to her acceleration. We were now parallel with the front cab and we were still making good speed. It was all over in about fifteen seconds. We were ahead of Guff Breath and behind the truck in front, which by now had accumulated at least two more vehicles at its bow. One down, three – or possibly four – to go.

Reeling from the success of my first mindless overtake around a blind bend, I went straight into the next one. Soon we were at the head of the queue and free to continue on an open road. I punched the air. 'Yesssss!'

The Russian roulette quality of this highly dangerous man- oeuvre had raised my serotonin levels past quietly confident to acutely cocky, and I was now taking Abhilasha around the snaky roads as fast as she could go. We whizzed past buses, zoomed away from gas tankers, even left the odd well-meaning SUV in our dust.

Something in me had changed: I was no longer the cautious, law-abiding driver who had first driven in India two months ago. To add to my tally of new driving vices, I was now also executing suicidal mountainside passes, blasting my horn as though my life depended on it (which, when I come to think of it, it often did) and completely disregarding the cautionary signs and signals that had been erected for my benefit. I felt like I had been possessed by a devil, a demon of the road that had just named me queen. Uttarakhand Public Works Department be damned – I was married to danger and had no foreseeable plans for divorce. After two months on the road, I was becoming a bona fide Indian driver.

15

DEFLATED IN DELHI – How Not to Deal with a Blowout

NEW DELHI; KM 8,975

You moron!' I screamed at Delilah, who seemed quite chuffed with her decision to direct me down a very crowded passage heaving with people shopping from shoulder-to-shoulder tungsten-lit booths that sold bits of ribbon and elaborate wedding hats. This was a pedestrians-only street, a fact that was clearly evident from the withering scowls and tuts Abhilasha and I were receiving. Oblivious to my pain, Delilah instructed me to hold course for another 200 metres.

'This isn't even a street, it's a frigging shopping mall!' I yelled, pulling her plug.

Thrusting the Nano into reverse, I looked behind us to see that the crowd had already closed in our rear. Through the front windscreen, it was the same view. We were trapped. All I could see were people: hands, arms, wrists and palms as they pressed against the sides of the car to get around us. I heard the word 'Nano' repeated over and over again, in slightly more irritated tones than I'd been used to so far. A man in a white tunic riding a bicycle that was stacked beyond its credible capacity with hand-stitched sacks knocked angrily on Abhilasha's roof. He made a gesture with the hand that wasn't holding up his faltering load that gave me no information whatsoever other than the fact that he and the gathering mob were growing highly peeved.

I shot him back my best effort at an equally peeved 'Well, what do you want me to do, mate?' before a kindly shop owner jumped down from the podium of his store and decided to try to take charge of the situation. He carved out a space big enough for himself to stand in front of the Nano, and beckoned me to move forward. I winced. How on earth could I shift even an inch? There were two old ladies bent over the front bumper, leaning against the bonnet under the weight of the crowd of people behind them. But the shopkeeper was insistent: I had to try to move forward or there was a strong chance we'd be there until morning. I revved the engine ever so slightly and let up my foot from the clutch as gently as I could. We started to roll. I was terrified as to what the two old ladies would do, but they seemed to take the new situation very much in their stride, rolling themselves around as the car advanced. The flow of people ahead split into two side streams as we literally ploughed through them; I felt like Moses parting the Red Sea. We seemed to be moving at about the same rate as the crowd that was stuck behind us, some of whom were actually holding on to the Nano to give them a more stable advantage against the oncoming tide of pedestrians.

The heart of Old Delhi was not, as I was fast discovering, primed for motor vehicles. That came as a bit of a surprise, given that the rest of the city had so far triumphed on my own personal scoreboard of Indian urban traffic infrastructure. I had made the journey from the mountains in the north via Amritsar, the Sikh holy city just a stone's throw from the Pakistani border, in a matter of days. Back down in the plains, the heat was once again on full blast, and I was eager to get to the capital where I knew a host of cooling mod cons would be waiting for me.

Thanks in part to a recent drive by the Commonwealth Games Committee to make it presentable to visiting dignitaries,

Delhi had become home to some of the best roads and high-ways in the country. Central Delhi had had a head start with the spacious avenues that lay between the monumental government buildings and bungalows constructed by Edward Lutyens in the early years of the twentieth century. The city was already a place of sidewalks, flyovers, roundabouts and pedestrian crossings when the Commonwealth Games Committee moved in with its budget of Rs 80 crore (&8 million), which went a long way in polishing the city's arteries into the state of a better-oiled machine. I even spotted a few signs put up by an NGO campaigning for noise reduction that pleaded with drivers to refrain from using their horns. The latter strategy, though admirable, had little effect, but the former elements came together to create a symphony of road usage that was – after almost three months of bumping over potholes, dodging goats and zigzagging between pedestrians who had nowhere else to walk but the slow lane of the highway – pure manna from the gods in driving heaven.

My two days of hiding in Delhi started as I rolled through the guarded gates of a neighbourhood called Sundar Nagar. I was staying with a friend called Paul de Bendern, who was working as the bureau chief of the regional Reuters. I basically had the house to myself, since Paul was off doing Reuters-type stuff all day and his photographer wife Lynsey was dodging bullets somewhere dangerous for the *New York Times*. While Lynsey was doing the work of a real journalist, embedded on assignment, I was embedded in their apartment, basking under the cool breeze of their many air-conditioning units, using their wi-fi and downright abusing their Nespresso machine. Aside from catching glimpses of Paul pounding the treadmill and eating boiled eggs in the morning, I saw little of him until after work, when he managed to extricate me from the house and, like a perfect host, deliver me straight to the five-star Aman

Hotel, courtesy of his Mahindra Scorpio and Rakesh, his personal chauffeur. There we drank cocktails and ate tapas with foreign hacks, before moving on to gin and tonics on the lawn at the Foreign Correspondents' Club.

It was a louche and lazy couple of days with little output and much navel-gazing. The only vaguely constructive thing I managed to attain was a transaction via the internet that ensured my passage home, one week from then. It was a tight deadline, but the apathy had to be shaken off, or I knew I could stay like this in Delhi for ever.

The afternoon before we were due to leave, I decided to take Abhilasha for a spin around Delhi's historic neighbourhood. I was hoping we would catch at least a glimpse of the iconic Red Fort and Jama Masjid, on a jaunt designed to scrape off some of my own residual guilt for having done absolutely nothing even vaguely interrogative in the last 48 hours. From Sundar Nagar we breezed along the avenues of Lutyens' Delhi: past the Imperial Hotel, the monumental India Gate, the labyrinthine Connaught Place. I kept on due north, to around New Delhi train station, where the old city mingled with the new. Here, the roads started to narrow and the traffic began to crowd in on itself. I kept going in the direction of Old Delhi Railway Station, spurred on by Delilah who seemed determined to get us there via only the most densely crowded streets possible. It was goodbye Lutyens' Delhi, hello again traffic anarchy.

However much the Commonwealth Games Committee had spent sprucing up Delhi's roads, it appeared that its plans had not quite reached the limits of the Old City. Perhaps it hoped that as long as officials and athletes kept south of Connaught Place, they'd go home with the impression that India's traffic myth was merely malicious propaganda spread by competing-venue cities. Turning into Chandni Chowk, the one-time stylish main street of the Mughal Empire, we were met with an operetta of engines, horns and human bellows set against a collage of shop signs, adverts and lights, all woven together by the tangled mess of overhead electricity lines. I was in no doubt that the usual Indian road rules were back in play.

Afternoon was turning to evening as the rush-hour traffic chugged along, interspersed at every available opportunity by people wading their way through the slow-moving stream, carefully balanced sacks bobbing above the car roofs, women lugging shopping bags or holding their children aloft out of the way of the unpredictable wheels. Pumping the clutch while crawling forward, I figured our drive-by sightseeing plans might need to go on hold. Delilah, however, seemed to have a different idea, and like the wazzock I am, I followed her traffic-dodging directions down a small alley that after a few metres thinned to about a foot from the tip of each of my wing mirrors.

After grappling to get some kind of sheepish hold on the crowd-plough technique, I continued driving Abhilasha through the market for what felt like a lifetime. We wormed our way along the entire 200 m stretch of very crowded road until finally, just when the end and a much larger intersecting street was in sight, I got a sharp rap on my windscreen from a stick-wielding policeman. I reluctantly wound down my window, and for a moment considered handing over Delilah as a goodwill bribe in a gesture that would also conveniently rid me once and for all of her pestilent poppycock suggestions. The policeman frowned when he saw my face. I'm not sure whom he had been expecting, but they certainly didn't match my description. His hesitation was my hot iron.

'Officer?' I squeaked, mouse-like and vulnerable.

'This road,' he boomed, quickly coming to his senses and pointing at where I had just come from, 'is cars not permitted!'

I looked behind me at the heaving crowd with exaggerated surprise.

'Oh really?' I blurted, trying to sound casual. 'I must have missed the sign.'

He was a big bloke with a moustache you could fit on a large broom and a pockmarked face that looked like he'd been in the firing line of a squadron of peashooters. He didn't come across as one for my usual mind tricks, so I tried another tack.

'I'm so very sorry,' I pleaded. 'I'm very, very lost. And my GPS is not working.' It was a brief sob story, bereft of drama or much cause for compassion, but ingrained with the vital element of the transferral of blame onto an inanimate object that made it almost impossible for the cop to get any angrier with me. He crumpled his forehead and wearily waved me on, eying me dubiously until I was out of sight.

Back on the roomy highways of South Delhi, we returned to speed, bombing past the signs to Defence Colony, which I imagined as a neighbourhood fortified with cannons and nuclear warheads and marksmen stationed around the encircling ramparts. But we didn't get that far: just past the Jangpura metro station, Abhilasha started to shiver, then shake, then enormously shudder with a force that was more than mere fallout from her snowplough experience in the old city. Struggling to keep the wheel straight, I pulled onto a slip road and cut her engine, fearing the worst. The source of the problem was not hard to detect: her left rear tyre was deflated and spread flat under the weight of the car.

Flummoxed, I knelt down to inspect the damaged element. The source of the puncture was a mystery: I couldn't see any lacerations in the rubber that would account for the sudden loss of air. I reflected that maybe one of the shoppers I'd nearly pulped in the Old City might have thought a quick slash of a knife appropriate retribution for the abomination we'd committed. And I wouldn't blame them. Or maybe it was simply the sheer exhaustion of nearly 10,000 km of road and Abhilasha pleading for a little R&R and attention (I was yet to take her for her third service, which was due given our lofty mileage). Whatever the reason for the blowout, the fact of the matter was that I was sat by the side of a busy slip road in the dark of the Delhi night, a lone woman in trouble intermittently floodlit for the world to see. Having only once single-handedly changed a tyre many years ago in the murky backwaters of my driving past, I figured this was not the moment to get back into practice; first back to Sundar Nagar, then this one-woman pit-stop team would kick into action.

With a nagging doubt that perhaps driving for fifteen minutes on a flat tyre might not be the wisest idea either, I set off slowly, trying to hold the steering wheel steady. I felt the Nano wobble and convulse, wincing through the pain of her deflated shank as the sporadic thwack of the edge of the hub-cap hitting the tarmac sent my shoulders up around my ears with each new strike. I imagined sparks spewing out from our left rear end as we kept sheepishly to the extreme slow lane usually reserved for cyclists and handcarts. My fellow drivers were also concerned: one rickshaw-wallah slowed down beside us and motioned urgently for me to stop while making furious gestures with his spare hand that I feared indicated some kind of firework display emanating from Abhilasha's posterior. I smiled diffidently and replied by raising my thumbs in a manner that would have confirmed his original suspicion that I was an irremediably clueless halfwit with a penchant for Nano-sadism.

We made it to Sundar Nagar, but not without having reshaped the hubcap into something resembling a battered gong. I cursed physics and damned its immutable laws as I searched under the passenger seat for the large plastic wallet I had never opened but had always suspected contained materials for the remedy of flat tyres. Sure enough, out dropped a contraption resembling a giant iron grasshopper and a metal wrench. Supplementing distant experience with online assistance from a website called artofmanliness.com, I got to work jacking up the rear of the Nano, surprised at just how simple and ungruelling a task it was. The next step, according to the site, was to remove the lug nuts, which I deduced must be the massive screws that were sticking out through the hubcap. From then on it was plain sailing; the new tyre was retrieved from the tiny space under the front bonnet and fitted, and the bolts replaced.

There was one thing that concerned me, however, and that was a diagram on artofmanliness.com illustrating the order in which these lug nuts should be refitted and tightened: the drawing assumed at least four, if not five bolts in the wheel. Abhilasha's diminutive three wasn't even brought into consideration for the complicated pentagram formations that were apparently essential for a safely attached wheel. I just pushed on the wrench until I thought I'd break it and resolved to take Abhilasha to a tyre shop in the morning for a second opinion, and to check I hadn't put it on back to front.

The next day, through a relayed chain of directions that started at the petrol station just outside Sundar Nagar and ended back in Jangpura Extension close to where the blow-out had originally occurred, I finally got to a tyre shop that was more accurately a kind of a street-side walk-in closet for all things black and treaded. There was hooped rubber everywhere, hanging from the ceiling, from hooks on the walls, piled up in wobbly columns and arranged into various combinations to make the required office furniture. Sitting on one of the tyre-loungers were a couple of barefoot lads in jeans and perfectly pressed blue shirts. Alarmed at my arrival, they jerked to attention. I pointed them in the direction of my handiwork on the rear wheel.

One of them knelt down and ran a judicious finger around the distended hubcap, grimacing. I shrugged with heavily feigned indifference and, by way of distraction, led them both around to the front bonnet, from which I produced the mangled former back tyre. The lads took it from me and one of them, all the time holding the object at arm's length as though it were blighted with the plague, began to shake it and watched with disapprobation as a pile of rubber shavings floated down around his feet. He looked up at me, trying to put a polite lid on his clear disbelief at my crackbrained behaviour. Had I driven far with the flat tyre? Um, no, I lied. Well maybe for a few hundred metres; a kilometre possibly. Two, tops. Glancing down at the pile of rubber bits that now almost came up to his ankles, I know I didn't have a case. I was no expert, but I figured this was the debris from the estimated six-and-a-half kilometres I'd driven on the expired tube. The dented hubcap was just one more piece of hard evidence piled against me.

A heated discussion ensued in Hindi between the two mechanics that threw out the odd recognizable word like 'Nano', 'tyre' and 'tube' and involved a lot of earnest head-shaking. The mechanics told me that under no circumstances could I continue to keep driving on the spare tyre. It was actually not big enough to be used as a rear wheel, being the size of the smaller, front tyres. So we would need to fix the old tyre and replace it in its original spot.

Would that be possible? I asked.

He looked down at the tyre and gyrated his head. It was a yes–no tie-breaker.

Pulled in by the irresistible magnetism of a yellow Nano, a few passers-by also stopped to get a look-in at the action, and within minutes we were Jangpura Extension's number one attraction. A friendly grey-bearded Sikh gent pulled me to one side and whispered with concerned exigency, 'I think you must have driven at least four or five kilometres with this flat tyre,' he said.

'Um, actually... yes, I did,' I confessed, suddenly mortified at what this might imply to the gent: that I was lazy, stupid or plain frivolous. I had no excuse to hide behind. I was speaking the truth, and as I did, I watched the consequences of my indolence play out before me: one of the lads was resolutely beating a mallet into the dents of the damaged hubcap while the other was refitting the tyre he thought he'd repaired, but it was refusing to inflate. He removed it again and banged it about a bit more, but to no effect.

The proceedings were being monitored by an older guy in a long-sleeved shirt – I presumed he was the manager – who had rocked up and perched himself on top of a rubber column, from where he took over the chair of the debate that was still raging over what to do about the tyres. The frequency of the word 'tube' suddenly increased and within minutes one of the lads appeared with a brand new long black inner tube.

'Really?' I exclaimed. 'But shouldn't tubeless tyres not have tubes? Isn't that the point?' Nobody understood what I was saying anyway. Barely had I voiced my protests than the inner tube was fitted and inflated, and the boy was bouncing Abhilasha's back wheel up and down the tyre-shop courtyard.

The Sikh gent returned to my side. 'I can see that you are religious,' he said to me in another whisper.

Why on earth would he think that? He pointed at Abhilasha and the now slightly faded stickers of Shiva and Lakshmi I had pasted to the rear windscreen somewhere back in Karnataka.

'Oh yes, those!' I exclaimed, deeply embarrassed at the levity with which I had attached them.

'Belief in God is very important,' he intoned gravely. 'It will keep you safe on the road.'

I nodded and mumbled something about covering all my bases. I had no intention of shaming myself further after the driving-five-kilometres-with-a-flat scandal, and I wasn't sure now was the right moment to engage in a debate about the advantages of religious faith over pragmatic caution while driving. Luckily, attention on the shop floor soon turned from the triumph of the inner tube to what seemed like a far more pressing matter around the area of Abhilasha's front wheels. It was a chance discovery that further vindicated my Sikh friend's belief in divine intervention, and my own in the power of a good mechanic. What I had failed to notice, and what might have proved a bit troublesome had it not been uncovered at that particular moment, was that both of the tyres were worn completely bald down their left-hand sides, the rubber so eroded that a network of tiny fine wires was showing through from the undertread.

The garage manager shook his head. This was not good. I mirrored him, executing what felt like my first perfect Indian head wobble, my neck joints having significantly loosened over the last few weeks. I tried to ascertain from him why they were bald down one side only, but the answer was not forthcoming. I put it down to Abhilasha's chronic steering misalignment and made a mental note to point it out to the garage where I took her for her next service.

Whatever the reason, the fact was that new tyres were clearly in order. Whether or not the right ones were in stock was a cloudy issue, but eventually two new wheels were produced and within a couple of hours we were back on the road with one tubed back tyre and two spanking new ones up front, only a couple of thousand rupees lighter of pocket. It might have been more, but the price of the service had been rigorously negotiated by the Sikh gent, as some kind of reward for my apparent spiritual diligence, and as a token of our devotional camaraderie.

16

ONE FOR THE ROAD – A Right Royal Knees-Up at the Maharaja's Table

OMKARESHWAR; KM 10,396

It was all over, sort of. On the NH47 in Gujarat, somewhere between the towns of Nadiad and Godhra, Abhilasha clocked up exactly 10,000 kilometres since leaving Mumbai.

It was an exultant moment: the trip target that had seemed like an insuperable mountain three months ago had finally been reached. I resisted the urge to slam on the brakes and perform a victory dance as the odometer's unit clock slowly turned from the expectant nine to the triumphant zero while we were crossing a bridge. Instead, I waited till we were on the other side before swerving into the dust and stones of the hard shoulder in front of a Coca-Cola–sponsored *dhaba*. I took a photo of the distance dial fronted by a very pleased-looking Ganesha and another from the outside of Abhilasha looking quietly complacent as the highway traffic passed us, oblivious to our achievement. Treating myself and half a dozen flies to a scalding chai, I reflected on our accomplishment: 10,000 big ones through the world's most notoriously barmy driving country and here we still were, rolling and, but for a few bumps and grazes, largely unscathed.

Back in the car, I held Abhilasha by her wheel. A knell sounded somewhere in the distance that I knew marked the beginning of the end. We'd done what we set out to do; in one sense it was all over, but on the other hand, we still had a thousand or so kilometres of high-octane highway to go before the end of the road in Mumbai. Not sure whether this was a happy or a sad moment, I thrust the key back into Abhilasha's ignition and decided that come what may, this called for a celebration. And I knew just the person I wanted to celebrate with: the Maharaja of Omkareshwar.

I had first met the Maharaja years ago when I stumbled on the guesthouse in his old family home by the Narmada river in Madhya Pradesh during my backpacking days. My enduring memory was of a ripe old fellow with a prodigious moustache, a penchant for hunting and an insuperable love of whisky. I remembered going on a drive with him in his old Ambassador; I spent the whole ride sitting aghast in the passenger seat as he drove at great speed through a thick crowd of pedestrians without so much as a flinch of hesitation. No injuries were sustained by the general public, but we did manage to elicit a pained yelp from a dog that failed to dodge the bumper in time and went limping off into the bushes. Memories of the Maharaja had stayed with me over the years and I was determined to track him down a second time. After a protracted online search for his phone number, I was able to call him and inform him of my advent. He had absolutely no recollection of me, but was nonetheless ostensibly pleased at the prospect of my arrival.

'I will organize a lovely cocktail party in your honour,' he hollered down the line, which sounded an appropriate event to follow up the auspicious achievement of reaching my trip target.

So it was settled: Abhilasha and I would take the longer, inland road to Mumbai via Madhya Pradesh for one last knees-up with the Maharaja. I figured we'd go through Indore, Madhya Pradesh's largest city and the nearest big town to Omkareshwar. It was a 400 km drive along the NH47 that my extrasensory faculties together with my commonsensical prowess concurred would be challenging, for no other reason than we were veering off the venerated Golden Quadrilateral and were back on the old-school national highway. For the first 200 km, however, I was proven very wrong as we skimmed the smooth B road that ran due east of Ahmedabad via Gujarat, shooting through the countryside as though Abhilasha were gliding across greased marble.

There were safety railings, cat's eyes and enough road width for seamless overtaking. I concluded quite happily that Gujarat had to be one of the best states for driving and, at least for this particular stretch, one of the most beautiful. Completely unspoiled as far as I could see, the surrounding hills undulated around the road, while the sun shone through the grass of the fields and left speckled blots through the branches of the road-side banyan trees. It was beautiful rural India, and there wasn't a scrap of debris in sight. Every so often we'd pass a tractor engulfed in a cloud of red dust, or a goat herd shooting the shit at the side of the road with a beautiful woman covered by a glittering sari. Combined with our average speed of about 60 kmph, the surroundings produced in me a sublime state of road-trip gumption that was smashed to pieces the moment we crossed the border into Madhya Pradesh.

Where one state authority left off, the other picked up; or rather didn't. It looked like the MP government had gone off to spend the road budget, if there even was such a thing, elsewhere; the NH47 stretch between the Gujarat border and Indore was truly and unequivocally the *worst* section of national highway I had driven on. There were potholes every-where. The road would sometimes even out for a couple of kilometres or so, but soon I'd be back to steering Abhilasha between the craters, or, when there was no choice, slowing her right down and having to dip through the trenches, gritting my teeth at the sound of rocks thumping angrily on the bottom of the undercarriage. My hope of continuing at our previous pace all the way to Indore was a pipe dream: the first 150 km took us five hours, while the remaining 45 km between the aptly named town of Lebad and Indore took a further three and a half. By that time the sun had long since set and I was driving with tears in my eyes, this time least of all from the pain of oncoming full beams and mostly out of pure exhaustion and frustration at the slow-moving odometer.

Finally, on the outskirts of town somewhere near the airport, I was waved down by a rickshaw driver whose fraught motioning seemed more than merely the standard salute to the nitwit in the Nano that I so regularly enjoyed. I pulled over to the side of the road and saw with the help of the rickshaw's headlight, which the driver had thoughtfully angled directly at Abhilasha's right flank, that her new front tyre had already given up the ghost. Within minutes we were joined by half a dozen more rickshaw-wallahs, who all appeared to be friends with the guy who had stopped me and were infinitely more pleased than I was at the prospect of a Nano in need.

Given the last seven hours' jolting around, the flat didn't come as much of a surprise. Probably because the road had us shuddering and shaking anyway, I hadn't noticed it and had no idea how far we'd driven with a deflated tyre. Luckily for me, Team Rickshaw were more than willing to take on the task of replacing the wheel, making me feel like it was more of a privilege than a favour. I perched on the edge of the driver's seat and watched with consternation as the volunteer mechanics ratcheted the hubcap off and back on at lightning speed. Tired and dozy from the beating we'd taken from the NH59, I was deeply grateful to them, though I could think of no other way of showing my gratitude at 10 pm on a far-flung Indore roadside than slipping a couple of hundred rupees into the pocket of the driver who had spotted me. But their service didn't end there: compelled by a sense of chivalry or perhaps a lingering paternal urge, the group insisted on giving me a full rickshaw escort to my hotel, where they waited until Abhilasha was parked in the lot and I was safely through the doors, luggage in tow, and in the capable hands of reception staff.

It occurred to me the next afternoon as I descended the stone staircase to the Maharaja's house that the old place might have suffered some infrastructural decline in the decade since I was last there. The dwelling itself was a stocky stone building whose once-white walls were blackening with the spread of a dark moss or lichen that appeared to be thriving in the humid heat. It was situated on a rocky outcrop on the banks of the river Narmada, just by the footbridge that led to the island of Omkareshwar, a place of pilgrimage for acolytes of Shiva.

As I rounded the old stone walls and came to the front of the house, my suitcase trundling loudly in tow, I saw the Maharaja sitting at a table on the terrace outside his kitchen, flanked by a couple of dogs. Although his title lost most of its political sway many decades ago with India's independence, the Maharaja, who was descended from a line of local royalty, still had a distinctly regal air about him. Clad in a white vest and pyjamas and flanked by his two dogs, he was every bit the landowner and district suzerain, living in what looked like an ailing residence said to be several hundred years old. After a fleeting moment of surprise at my arrival, he shot up out of his chair.

'Welcome, welcome!' he exclaimed, shaking my hand and calling for his daughter from the kitchen, who hurried out to complete the welcoming committee. I told them I hoped my late arrival hadn't scuppered their plans for a cocktail party, but the Maharaja waved away my concern and cut straight to the chase.

'What do you say we kick things off with a peg of whisky?'

I'd have preferred a dry Martini, but as I was to discover, the Maharaja's cocktail cabinet was limited to two substances: whisky and gin. Whisky it was: a bottle of Royal Choice marked with a stamp that read 'For sale to military personnel only' was opened by the Maharaja's daughter, poured into two glasses and swiftly necked by myself and my host.

The Maharaja suggested I take my bags to my room straight away, lest, I imagine, I should have to crawl there later under the hazy spell of military-issue whisky. Ostensibly the only guest there, I was given the best digs in the house, the highly coveted Room Number One, which the Maharaja told me had recently been vacated by a Belgian guy.

'He was a fine fellow,' the Maharaja told me. 'He stayed in this room for an entire year with a very large lingam for company.'

High ceilings and ogee-arched recesses with a double door leading out onto the precipice right above the river nonetheless failed to mask the decrepitude of a building the family told me was over 600 years old. Damp to the core, and with a layer of white paint peeling off to reveal a wash of turquoise underneath, the most striking feature of the room was its host of inhabitants. I disturbed a cockroach that scuttled across the floor as I walked in and, once inside, I heard the brief squeaks of a creature under the bed, which also made a run for it but was caught mid-flight in the unforgiving jaws of the largest member of the Maharaja's pack of dogs, who had stealthily snuck in behind me.

Disturbed at the cold-blooded kill that had just taken place, I managed to ascertain as the dog trotted triumphantly out onto the porch that the animal between his jaws was not a rat as I had hoped, but the limp body of what had been a cute little squirrel. Two other squirrels raced out in the wake of their deceased brother, as a gecko shot past me, climbing up the nearest wall and into a crack by the doorframe. Later, to compound the zoological congregation, I also saw an enormous – what I would call Jurassic Park–sized – snake slither across a rock about two metres past the doors of my room that opened onto the river.

The hapless squirrel's corpse was subsequently toyed with for two hours by the happy hound, who was compelled to parade his prey to and fro across the main terrace. His royal master was largely oblivious to this display, far more focused on his Royal Choice and deciding what we were going to eat for dinner. I was invited to join him as more pegs were poured and his daughter and another woman worked in the kitchen, peeling garlic and shallots cross-legged on the floor while a television set in the back of the room beamed out a 1980s Bollywood movie in fuzzy analogue.

The last decade hadn't changed the Maharaja one bit; at 78, he cut a stout figure. He smoothed his moustache while losing himself in stories about hunting, shooting tigers, the various excellent fellows he had known and other chronicles of what he made sound like the good old days of the Raj (though I calculated he had been just a teenager at the time of Independence). He spoke about the Holkar dynasty and their palace on the opposite shore of the island, and how his own portrait hung there in the hall of fame, but try as I might, I couldn't quite fathom where the Maharaja stood in the greater scheme of the royal family tree. As the whisky began to take its toll on both of us, I could have sworn his accent grew thicker, or my ears grew more cabbage-like, and I had increasing difficulty making out what he said. Swathes of incomprehensible utterances were interspersed with very clear phrases like 'I stood facing the beast with my rifle; it was my life or his…' Still, I was hanging on to every expression. The Maharaja had an incredible knack for storytelling, and even if I couldn't quite discern every word, it didn't matter. We were just getting drunk, having a chunter and eating his daughter's incredible chicken curry, which, although apparently tempered for my western buds, still had the effect of torching my palate and made for fireworks on the loo the next day. Mouth burning from the spices, I drank more whisky, and so the evening passed until the Maharaja doubled in my vision and I figured it was time for bed. He bid me good-night and drained the last dregs of the bottle. Who was this guy, Hunter S. Thomson?

The next morning I woke up with a feeling that Godzilla had tunnelled into my brain and was performing star jumps while roaring into a megaphone. The bed was so damp I could have been sleeping in a paddling pool, and I had to shoo a tiny frog away from the toilet bowl before folding over it in a very uncomfortable squat. As the fog of unconsciousness began to lift, I realized the noise I thought was a Japanese monster roaring ferociously from inside my skull was actually coming from outside. Gunfire.

I opened the double doors of my room to find the Maharaja brandishing his shotgun.

'It's a little early for hunting, isn't it?' I mumbled, fumbling for my sunglasses.

The Maharaja was unmoved. Wearing a long-sleeved grey vest and pyjama bottoms, he stalked the rocky ground outside my room, aiming the barrel of his rifle into the overhead branches of the surrounding trees.

'Damn monkeys!' he cried as he fired off a couple of shots. Satisfied that the gun was pointed high enough for the bullets to miss the top of my head, I stepped outside. Sure enough, the branches were occupied by at least half a dozen primates who were showing the old man their teeth like they were egging him on. Incredulous how anyone could even think about engaging in armed conflict with a group of monkeys only a few hours after draining a bottle of Royal Choice, I concluded that the Maharaja was three times the man I could ever hope to be.

An hour or so later, as I was still lying on my bed, trying to pick up the will to finish the final leg of our trip back to Mumbai, I discovered the source of the Maharaja's monkey misgivings. I noticed a figure standing in the doorway that I had left open for the breeze; it was a primate, about one metre tall; from a quick look at its genitalia, I deduced it was a bloke.

There was something extremely disconcerting about being in the presence of an animal about half my size with whose genus I had little hands-on experience. I immediately stood up, grabbed the nearest weapon I could find, which was a water bottle, and made threatening gestures towards the monkey, who eyed me with the nonchalance of a bored audience considering a mid-show exit. Instead of legging it back out of the door as I had anticipated he would, the monkey turned instead to face me full frontal and opened his mouth to bare his teeth in a sort of terrifying yawn.

Sweet Bubbles, how was he not scared of me? Faced with a creature twice my size, making strange noises and swinging an empty bottle of water around in the air, I'd have run for the hills. There was a moment of silence in our face-off when I put down the bottle and watched as his eyes darted slightly to the right. I knew exactly what he was looking at. On a chair in the corner was a green plastic bag containing several bananas, some biscuits, nuts and possibly an apple. The monkey had identified his target, and he was willing to risk a pummelling by plastic to get it.

Disheartened by his indifference to my earlier intimidation tactics, I began to feel a twinge of panic at the sheer force of the creature's determination. Where was the Maharaja with his shotgun when I needed him? I thought about lobbing the bottle in the monkey's direction, but decided it might start an all-out war that would most likely end in my being quarantined to the rabies unit at an Indore hospital. I figured the best plan to get him out of the room was to take away the thing he had come for. I started to sidestep slowly towards the bag at exactly the same time the monkey decided to go for it. We moved towards each other with duel-like intensity. I grabbed the bag and he shot back. Without giving it another thought, I leapt into the bathroom and locked the door, hoping the monkey wouldn't decide my camera or laptop was a sufficient booby prize.

A few minutes later, I emerged to find the simian out on the porch in front of my room, engaged in an act of self-stimulation that I presumed was intended to show me the greatest gesture of disrespect a primate could bestow on a human. I watched aghast from behind the door as he finished himself off before making for the treetops, leaving nothing but a small pool of monkey spunk to remember him by.

'You're leaving already?' The Maharaja blinked at my suitcase as I brought it clunking back over his porch. I nodded, trying not to let the combination of my hangover, the fact that I was embarking on my last journey with Abhilasha, and the close encounter I'd just had with the degenerate primate reduce me to tears.

He suddenly brightened. 'How about a peg of gin before you go?'

I protested that I couldn't possibly imbibe another drop and that to do so before the 600 km final push down to Mumbai would be downright imprudent.

The Maharaja raised a pedagogic finger. 'A colonel friend of mine – fine fellow – once told me that a peg of gin before a journey keeps you focused on the road.'

I wondered if it was the same colonel fellow who was supplying him with military-issue whisky. Conceding his point, I continued to stand firm on the grounds of common sense.

'I just... I've really just had enough.'

Finally consenting to my departure, the Maharaja thoughtfully fingered his moustache and pulled me in for one last word.

'That car of yours...'

'The Nano?'

'Yes, the Tata Nano... What will you do with it at the end of your trip? Will you sell it?'

Actually, I had no idea. I was leaving the country in a matter of days and had no plan for Abhilasha's wellbeing, other than leaving her in Akhil's capable hands. I hadn't had the time to find a buyer, although it seemed that now, at the last moment, one was making himself known to me.

He smiled and stepped in closer. 'If you decide to sell it, then please call me. I would like to buy it.'

I tried to imagine the Maharaja behind the wheel of a Nano instead of his grand old Ambassador, and realized I'd misconstrued him: despite the antiquated India of royalty and palaces and tiger hunts that the old man embodied, he obviously had his finger on the pulse of the nation as much as any of his younger countrymen. If the Maharaja was ready to make the transition from Ambassador to Nano, then everyone was.

It occurred to me that of all the potential bidders I had met, the Maharaja was the person I would most have liked to bequeath Abhilasha to. But I wasn't really sure if I could knowingly subject her to the same fate as his Ambassador. I wondered if he'd try to take her out hunting, and if he'd always down a quick gin before hitting the road. The last thing I wanted was for her to get on bad terms with the dogs of the village after some unfortunate incident with her bumper. Though who was to say that after a peg or two of gin, the Maharaja wasn't a far better driver than I was anyway?

I was 200 km from Mumbai, the end within my grasp, when the effects of a third Red Bull on an empty stomach began to kick in. The decision to drive 600 km after a night's whisky-swilling was a questionable one from the outset. I was tired, hungover and frankly a bit naffed off that I was on my way home. The NH3 that led down from Indore to Nashik and then continued all the way to Mumbai was not a bad road: not the Golden Quadrilateral by any stretch of the imagination, but the traffic flowed in an orderly manner with only a few roadblocks and one overturned lorry to disrupt the stream. Still, things moved slowly. The distance dial seemed to be dragging its digits to Mumbai as I fought to ignore the thumping in my brain and keep my eyes open, despite their insistence on closing and sending me into a deep and peaceful sleep at 50 kmph.

With better planning, I could have spent the night in Nashik, but given that my flight left the day after tomorrow, I wanted to be back in Mumbai that night. With the finishing line just over four hours away, I began to feel the composure sift out of me. The nauseous effect of the hangover had prevented me from eating, and the will to get to Mumbai with as few pee stops as possible meant I had drunk very little, with the exception of the three Red Bulls I had necked in order to stave off the Sandman at this very crucial stage in the journey. After eight unbroken hours at the wheel since leaving Omkareshwar, I was beginning to feel a strange numbness in my limbs, my heart was beating fast and I had difficulty focusing on the road.

Deciding it was time for a break, I pulled into the first petrol station that presented itself. Its garish green lighting did nothing to ease the growing panic in my veins, as I stared at the pump attendant down the barrel of the long, dark tunnel that now framed my vision. I had to work to breathe. My body was cold and disconnected and I could barely discern my extremities as I sat dumbly watching the guy fill Abhilasha's tank. When he was finished, I thrust a handful of rupees at him from my wallet and, without waiting for the change, hauled the Nano over to a quiet corner of the station forecourt and turned off her engine.

I realized I was having some variety of panic attack. Sharp, prickly adrenaline coursed through my body; I felt beaten, utterly powerless and terrified, in a petrol station miles from anywhere at 10pm on a very dark Indian night. It was like I'd suddenly been dropped into the middle of a nightmare, from where my now overactive paranoia was telling me that the two attendants were about to forcibly eject me from the forecourt in accordance with station policy that forbade single foreign females to have a meltdown on company property. I cursed Red Bull, and all of the world's caffeine and sugar. I cursed military-issue whisky. I cursed the roads, the cars, the stones and every inch of tarmac that now separated me from comfort and safety.

I thundered through my options with the grace and rationality of a charging hippo. What the hell was I going to do? How was I going to get out of this? I feared that if I stayed put, undefended in the butthole of nowhere, I would end up with my face in *Mid Day* for reasons other than my quirky driving exploits. But there was nothing I wanted to do less right now than go back to the blinding lights and dodgem manoeuvres of the highway, which I honestly thought would be the end of me.

Disoriented, panicked, knackered, I was ready to throw in the towel. So I did what any other daredevil in my situation would have done: I called my mum. On hearing her voice, the childish tears began to flow. Sir Edmund Hillary might not have blubbed to his mother just minutes before reaching the summit, but had he done so, he would have been bolstered in his final steps.

'Come on,' she pep-talked me, 'you're so close. Just 200 km – that's like two hours!'

'Make that four,' I whined. 'It's so far. I just… just can't do it…'

'Yes, you can!' she insisted. 'Drink lots of water and keep going.'

I wiped away the tears and after a few turns on shaky legs around the forecourt and the fast ingestion of half a litre of water, I decided I had no choice but to set back out on the road. I took a very deep breath, turned on the engine and nudged Abhilasha towards the station exit. By now it was completely dark and all I could see were the bastard bright lights of oncoming vehicles. They were moving towards me quickly, almost haphazardly, as I stared out to my right for a breach in the flow. The intensity of concentration sparked off another wave of jitters, and I told myself that if I was going to make it to Mumbai tonight, I had to release every clamp in my nerves and joints and float my way back to the city.

I rejoined the stream almost unconsciously. I slowed down and veered to the side of the road, where I could take shelter from the traffic rumbling past me to my right, and from there I counted my deep breaths and locked into a steady 50 kmph, keeping my eyes only on the one tiny bit of road I could see in Abhilasha's headlights. I held the wheel at its lowest point, barely tapping it with my fingers when we needed to budge a little to the left or the right. And when the cars coming from the other direction blinded me, I didn't swear at them and curse the lack of road markings, I simply steered on in the darkness, pushing Abhilasha forward with the blind faith of the deeply religious or the clinically insane.

It was the final surrender. As though I hadn't tempted the fates enough these last three months through my allegiance with an economy vehicle on the world's most deadly roads, I had raised the stakes for the finale by first intoxicating myself with large amounts of Royal Choice, and then trying to repair the damage with excessive energy drinks, while driving an inordinate distance that I would not have previously attempted even on a good, sober, sunshine-happy day.

I stopped looking at the clock; I stopped counting the kilometres; I stopped worrying about how fast I was going. Instead, I allowed myself to be overtaken by some primeval version of myself whose only concern was getting me to Mumbai, eventually, in one piece. All the will and effort drained out of me, leaving a blinking, breathing, driving automaton. Lights danced in front of me, cars moved around me, trucks blocked me on all sides, and all I did was keep moving forwards, slowly, steadily, as though in a dream.

It must have been about two o'clock in the morning when Abhilasha caught up with a crowd of bullocks moving languidly by the side of the road, plodding forward through the night on their way to god only knew where, led by a pair of crooked women, one bent at the waist and the other brandishing a staff about twice her height, both of them harbouring a strength that went beyond their years and appearance. Where they could be taking the animals at the dead of night I had no idea, but I felt like riding with them for a few minutes, so I slowed down and joined the herd, ploughing forward at bullock miles per hour.

I wound down the window and heard a couple of low drones that I hoped were bovine approval of our presence and not a groaning consensus to run us off the road.

As we moved together with the beasts, I began to feel the sensation of once again inhabiting my own body. I reached out to a small calf whose head was bobbing along right by my window and gave it a little scratch behind the ear. I was coming back.

RULE OF THE ROAD #8
Mind the Bullocks

The last few hours of driving on autopilot back to Mumbai demonstrated that a certain Indian road prowess had cemented itself into my subconscious. Although driving with my eyes shut, jedi-style, was still not quite an option, I realized that steering Abhilasha through this confusion of vehicles actually required little in the way of will and effort and much more in the way of opening myself up to the innate rhythms of the road. Becoming one with the car, as my father had once said, meant more than merely driving it as fast as possible. It meant finding my own number within the great traffic marathon.

By the end of the journey, my overall cruising speed was something in the region of 35–40 kmph. At the beginning of the trip, this sluggish rate would have inspired in me the wrath of a woman scorned by her Sat Nav. Had I been driving blindfold? Or had I gone in reverse the whole way? Did we just make the journey with four flat tyres, or had I switched the engine off, cut a hole in the floor and walked us there, Flintstones style? It seemed that no matter how focused I was on the road, I could never pick up our average velocity above crawling speed. And no matter how hard I tried to chill out and enjoy the scenery, I couldn't stop that fact from irritating the living daylights out of me. I had spent several weeks in a state of sustained denial, stuck on a learning curve that would have scuppered all of Pavlov's theories of repeated conditioning in intelligent animals.

The animals themselves were a large part of the menace. One of the most common causes of delay was the sudden appearance on a country road or highway of a mob of sheep, goats, cows or bullocks, with the odd elephant or camel thrown in, depending on the region. They would surge around Abhilasha in an orchestrated pincer movement that quickly engulfed us and forced us to a standstill. The animals may have been low down on the pecking order but in some ways they wielded more power than any other road user.

This was especially the case for the cow and her gelded husband the bullock. As the weeks wore on, I came to believe that the sacred bovines were probably the most intelligent road users of all, imbued as they were with confidence, stability and ethereal traffic-stopping powers of which Abhilasha could only dream. After three months of battling against the tide of Indian traffic, of swimming upstream in my attempts to figure out the rules and carve out for myself some kind of knowledge base that would give me an advantage over other drivers and get me to my destination in half the time, I began to grasp that instead of looking to the rickshaws and truck drivers for tips on how to stay on top in the road race, I should have been looking down the line to the oldest and most experienced travellers around. The bullocks, I finally fathomed, were the guardians of the unwritten rules of the country's roads: they had been lumbering along them for millennia, aeons prior to the rumble of the first motor engine. The noisy new machines of the twenty-first century are a blip on the bullocks' epic timeline, one they tolerate with enduring dignity.

The castrated workers of the bovine world, bullocks are variously employed as farm hands – pulling heavy ploughs to till the fields – or as a form of transport, hauling people or carts piled with hay between fields and villages and marketplaces. Late in the afternoon, on their way home from work, they spread out along the route, kicking up dust with their cloven hooves and heading forward in a single-minded drove, mob-handed, horns painted and sauntering from their skinny shoulders and haunch bones, their tails swinging like pendulums, indiscriminately slugging passing objects with a flick of their snaky appendages.

They were invariably unhurried; whether in the thick of urban chaos or on a small country road holding up a mile of traffic, they were amblers, less concerned with their speed than with the concentrated, easy plod of putting one foot in front of the other. Their calm bearing and phlegmatic eyes blinked away the flies and put to question any concept of speed or hurry. They were the true champions of the road because only they really knew how to travel.

It occurred to me that for the past three months, as though employed by the Graces to protect me from myself, the bullocks had been slowing me down. Every time I'd run into them, I was induced to stop and take a breath. Why was I always hurrying? What did an extra hour on the road matter, when there was so much ground to cross and such a wealth of watering holes along the way? When there were centuries – behind us and up ahead – and hundreds of roads to explore and leave our hoof prints on, where was the necessity to keep running today?

Make like a bullock, the bullocks said, and enjoy the ride.

STARTING OVER – From Nano to Pixel

'$hit!' Thor gave the gearstick a brutal rattle and, kicking his feet at the pedals below, turned the key in Abhilasha's ignition for the third time. For the hat trick, she did exactly what she'd done on the two previous attempts, lurching forwards with a hacking whine as the engine exhaled and cut out once more. I piped the squeak of a far more radical reaction withheld; Thor vengefully thumped the steering wheel. Rain pounded down while the cars and buses surrounding us crooned their disapproval of the Nano's standstill. Bicycles and pedestrians ploughed through the pools of brown water on the ground and slipped by, filtering out around Abhilasha in a fugitive stream.

This was extremely delicate territory and I had to proceed with caution.

'Was your foot on the clutch?'

'Yes, it was on the clutch,' he said peering down into the footwell, 'unless that's the brake.'

Thor sneezed violently and swore into the tissue he held up to his mouth. A colony of mushrooms that had grown around the base of the gearstick during the monsoon, along with the mysterious demise of the car's air conditioning, had rendered the atmosphere inside so murky that it set off his allergies and inflated his sinuses to red-hot levels.

'And was the gearstick in first?'

He shoved it again. 'Probably not. What the hell do I know? Why can't everyone just drive automatic cars?' Sneeze.

'Because manual ones are much more fun. Once you get the knack of them.'

A very loud horn of ear-shuddering decibels entreated us to move. Thor rolled down his window and tried to follow the direction of the noise. 'Okay, I'm trying! Just give me a break will you, asshole?'

The crowd was ruthless. Their honking threw us deeper into a vicious circle of failure. The mounting sense of performance anxiety had all but completely dashed Thor's hopes of ever being able to start the car again, and the longer we stayed in the middle of the junction, the more I felt the urge to throw my dupatta over my head and bury myself deep in the passenger seat, in a bid to convince myself that none of this was really happening.

'Okay, gearstick in first…'

'Before you do that, maybe turn the engine on? Leave the gearstick in neutral for now?'

I discovered that if I framed my commands as questions, the effect was not nearly so ignominious. The loud horn from behind resumed its campaign. This time Thor directed his wrath at the rear-view mirror.

'What? What? What do you want from my life? Why's everyone getting so pissed?'

'I think he wants you to move a couple of feet out of the way?'

'I'll move a couple of feet up his…'

Another sneeze and we finally began to move forward, this time at the rate of a mercifully controlled crawl.

Thor and I were back in Pondicherry, contending with the three-way challenge of monsoon rains, sharing Abhilasha and our first few weeks of cohabitation in a flat we rented on Cazy Street, among the tinny-voiced mosques of the Muslim

Quarter. On returning to Europe and sizing up the diminutive dimensions of Thor's Berlin bachelor room, I had suggested we return for a six-month sabbatical in India, where I would begin to write this book, Thor would write programming code and together we would live the life of Monsieur et Madame Riley among the finer fripperies of France's former fiefdom.

By the standards of a small German Hoff-crib, our apartment in Pondicherry was near-palatial: two bedrooms, three living rooms – one of which was a study with a delightfully large oak desk – and a terrace that housed a jungle of creeping plants that the monsoon had defibrillated into life and that I felt I needed to keep a vigilant eye on lest they devoured us in the night. Large fans hung from the ceiling of every room and spun constantly in an effort to dry out the fibres impregnated with the dampness of the seasonal rains. The colonization of all soft furnishings and fabrics by sharp-smelling dusty white fungi, as well as the clear evidence of rats and cockroaches inhabiting our abode, sealed the conviction that for me, housekeeping in India would be a similar experience to driving; namely, fraught with challenges.

Our landlady took pity on me and sent help in the form of an immensely powerful woman by the name of Elisa, who arrived every morning and spent two hours washing the floors, airing any cloth that was susceptible to fungal infestation, cleaning the kitchen to within an inch of its life, and storing everything gastronomically appealing to the rodent race in large glass jars in the larder.

On Cazy Street, Abhilasha rested her wheels by the road-side. Figuring I had had enough long-distance driving in India for one year, I had shipped her over from west to east, tacking her onto the back of a consignment of brand new Marutis that were also crossing the country. While stationary, she provided a roof over the head of a stray dog we named Muttley, who took up permanent daytime residence in the drier, shadier confines of her undercarriage, occasionally popping up to our flat after mealtimes to see whether he could profit from any leftovers.

Abhilasha was an indispensable accessory to our south Indian existence: while the rains lasted, she was our shelter for trips to the supermarket; when the weather got better, we took her on excursions to the beach, on trips up to the nearby visionary kibbutz-like community of Auroville, and even on weekends to Chennai via the verdant East Coast Road that runs along the side of the Indian Ocean.

In the expanding spirit of our new relationship, Thor and I both made extensive efforts in the direction of self-betterment: he applied himself to the task of driving a stick-shift car on what was for him unequivocally the *wrong* side of the road, and I put my mind to dispelling the demons of my own domineering nature. Progress was slow for us both: he accidentally ground the gearstick to a rough snarl and I inadvertently sighed; he had trouble with a parallel park or came close to another vehicle and I lunged for the door handle, in spite of myself. Thor maintained (and continues to do so) that the root of the problem was not his shaky driving skills, but my own inexhaustible opprobrium, which is a credible theory and is still a work in progress for me.

When we weren't locked into a driving power deadlock, neither of us could fail to notice that Abhilasha was no longer basking in the same light of congeniality cast by her fellow countrymen as earlier in the year. By the time we arrived in Pondicherry, the Nano wasn't selling nearly as well as Tata had predicted. In fact, the future looked increasingly bleak for the little car. The last weeks of that year were among its most ignominious, marked by a piece in the *Hindustan Times* about Nanos offered as stimulus to health workers in Bhopal to inspire extra incentive in the city's vasectomy drive. 'Get someone neutered and win a Tata Nano!' was one of a rash of sardonic blog headlines that chronicled the wheels-for-balls trade-off that was the insult following injury a month after it had been announced that the Nano's sales had dropped to a paltry 509 in November 2010 – almost seven times fewer than at the same time the previous year. The I-told-you-sos began to rain down: what had once seemed like the poster car for the Indian dream was morphing into something much less covetable: a sales flop with an embarrassing association to the neutering of Madhya Pradesh.

Why was the rest of India not buying into the dream that Tata was trying to sell? Safety concerns and spontaneous fires aside, to me what was really at the core of the Nano's shortfall was the way it had been launched and marketed. It had been touted as the People's Car set to change the face of motoring in India, which was no small claim. Whether or not the car's instant entrance into the limelight was a deliberate move by Tata, worldwide attention on launch was unavoidable and meant that the car's post-launch mechanical, financial and promotional tweaks had to be performed under a great deal of scrutiny. Too much publicity might have set the Nano up for a fall.

Its catchy price tag shot it to global fame as the World's Cheapest Car, which is a wonderful achievement if you're an engineer, but perhaps less impressive if you're the person on whom a cheap car confers the stigma of a skinflint. In its attempts to carve a niche in the car market by producing a more affordable product, Tata had paradoxically alienated its target customers by making them feel that driving a Nano would be a humdrum and even degrading experience. If it's true that a person's choice of car stands for what he aspires to, it follows that only an individual with very low self-esteem would pick his wheels from the bottom of the pile.

It was my opinion that if Tata wanted to revive the fate of the Nano, it needed to revise radically its idea of who the car would be aimed at. Hip-looking, low-cost city cars were not going to go down well with practical-minded country dwellers, supposedly the target market. Instead, Tata needed to look to the people who were initially seduced by the Nano – cityfolk. More specifically, I thought it needed to appeal to the new generation of drivers: the kids with smartphones, iPods and iPads who had enough cash to buy a cheap car, but fell short of that chauffeur-driven Hyundai. The Nano's social mission was completely incongruent with the car itself.

A new, improved Tata Nano was in fact launched in 2013 to the strains of a freshly engineered tagline: 'Celebrating Awesomeness'. Out went the demure adverts showing happy families driving through the countryside, and in came a new campaign of bright colours, loud music and fashionable kids dancing in the streets with an air of reckless consumer abandon. Celebrity designer Masaba Gupta and model Sarah Jane Dias were called in to bear witness to the car's new-found 'epicness' and 'kickassness', while the company rebranded the range in a fresh palette of colours ('mojito green', 'papaya orange') and added youth-friendly features like a Bluetooth-enabled MP3 stereo and keyless entry.

Whether the Nano's revamped image will boost sales remains to be seen, but it appears that *celebrating awesomeness* has notched up a bit more cred than the car's original incarnation, with the ad getting upwards of 5 million hits on YouTube within the first month of airing. The promises keep coming: a diesel version of the vehicle in 2014, and the prospect of an international launch some time in the future. The European Nano has been on Tata's drawing board for years, but still seems to have got no further than a mouth-watering promo for a super-space-age car called the Pixel, which was revealed at the Geneva Motor Show in 2011.

A recognizable cousin of the Nano, the Pixel in its current concept form is all CGI flare and futuristic design: the doors flip up into the sky like rabbit ears, the front wheels turn at 90 degrees to allow for effortless parallel parking and U-turns in narrow streets, and the interior details are controlled by a smart tablet sleekly placed on the dashboard. The website and company promo video have had me literally salivating into my laptop, while secretly nurturing the hunch that no vehicle that cool could actually ever be real *and* affordable.

Thor and I returned to India to get married. The date of our wedding was almost two years to the day since I had bought Abhilasha and conceived of the madcap notion of driving 10,000 km around the country. Prior to meeting Thor, I had never seriously entertained the prospect of marriage, and so my reaction in the face of his proposal (I cried solidly for two hours between bouts of trying to convince him I was shedding tears of joy) came as something of a shock to us both. It was an unequivocal yes, made all the more emotive by the speed at which our circumstances had turned around. Two years might be a long courtship by some standards, but in my own contemporary world of long engagements and perennial relationships that segued into parenthood long before vows were even verbalized, it was a shotgun wedding.

We had decided our union would best be sealed in Chennai, at Thor's ashram, under the authority and with the blessing of Mr Rajagopalachari. We emerged early one January morning to join no fewer than ten other couples who were all tying the knot the same day, and together we sat at the front of a large auditorium filled with the friends and families of the other newlyweds, who numbered in their merry thousands. One by one, the couples were called up onto the stage, where they were festooned with heavy garlands of flowers and given large boxes of sweets to hand out to the exuberant crowd. Our number came up last and Thor got up and strode towards the stage, while I waddled behind him, tripping over the hem of my inexpertly arranged sari and jingling from my hennaed wrists and ankles like the village cow. Our vows were said for us at lightning speed and Chariji held our hands together while we exchanged rings to seal the deal.

After the ceremony we were set upon by hordes of well-wishers – mostly complete strangers – as we basked in grinning post-nuptial delirium, sweating under the weight of the pounds of roses hung around our necks and taking pictures with people we'd never met before whose families had adopted us in a brief moment of wedlock rapture. The Marceaus held a party for us that night in their garden, complete with disco lights and a Franco-Indian soundtrack that was everything I would never have imagined, but had me dancing in my sari till I thought I'd collapse.

The next day, we rode off in Abhilasha. Hénoc had bought her from us before we left Pondicherry and now gave us back the keys for a honeymoon burn. A faint rattle from her under-carriage provided the traditional newlywed tins-and-cans ditty as we waved off the Marceaus and their mini-zoo and set out on Highway 55 towards the sea and the beautiful East Coast Road.

Abhilasha's AC had been fixed and she was in fair fettle, given the number of miles she now had to her name. Her shiny yellow surface was clean, but only I knew that behind her wheels and compounded into her nooks and crannies were the remnants of thousands of miles of road: the black fumes from the hallucinogenic lorries, the particles of dirt we threw up every time we flew over a speed bump or dipped into a pothole, the smut of the evening bonfires or the dust that hovered in the air above the scorching earth. It was the same sooty blanket that hung over the shoulders of all the itinerants we had passed: the rickies and truckies, the bus drivers and motorcyclists, the suited professionals driving their clientele in black cars with tinted windows, the cart pushers, the boy racers, the cyclists and the walkers; the guys at the pumps and the roadworks crews, the diggers, dumpers and layers; the farmers, the cattle herders, the quick sly dogs, the impervious camels and heavy-footed elephants, the shepherd boys with their armies of goats and the women hiking home at dusk with cloth-bound stacks of firewood balancing on their heads; the yelling kids, the cho-rus of hellos, the traffic light hawkers and the people sleeping, eating and praying by the sides of motorways; the crowded towns and the placid villages, the cities under construction and the locked-up gates of the bubble communities; the vast ocean beaches and the starry skies, the wide-open fields and the flat and arid landscapes, the mountains that were monumental and lush and the rivers that ran rugged brown, foamy and fertile, or just plain dry. Everything and everyone was flecked with the identical road dirt, and the splattered forms of dead insects and bird poo that now covered Abhilasha and undeniably me and my husband too, and the great big, lumbering bullocks.

EPILOGUE

$\mathcal{S}$ ome bonds are hard to break, others are locked in a pattern of eternal return. In the autumn of 2013, I regained official custody of Abhilasha from Hénoc Marceau, who was having trouble selling her following his decision to move back to France. At around the same time I was by chance due to return to India for a month-long publicity tour; it seemed to me that the stars were aligning and that this was a sign from the cosmos that Abhilasha and I were due an encore.

We were reunited at 6 am in a parking lot in Andheri West, a suburb of Mumbai just a few miles from the airport. Thor and I had just landed there a couple of hours earlier, and were still drowsy from the flight. Hénoc's friend who had been looking after Abhilasha had broken his leg in a car accident a few days earlier. He'd had Abhilasha's keys in his pocket at the time and now they were bent out of shape.

But they still worked. As the Nano rattled into life, I was assailed by a sense of amazement at the 10,000 kilometres I'd attempted in this little car that, after the bulked-out 1993 Audi Cabriolet I'd been driving in Rome for the past two years, felt more like a mobile jerrycan. Abhilasha's Frisbee-sized wheel was very heavy to steer, her gearstick seemed stiff and her brakes were incredibly sensitive.

We spent several nostalgic days together driving around Mumbai and, as soon as I got used to the traffic again, we were back on our old form, weaving in and out of jams, honking for all we were worth and rather ignominiously running out of petrol in the full flow of evening rush hour by the Flora Fountain.

My departure loomed and still I couldn't bring myself to think about selling Abhilasha again. I toyed with other options: the most appealing was to palm her off on one of my friends or acquaintances in the city who'd take temporary custody of her, but (understandably?) none was biting. A man I met at the British Council offered to raffle her off at his office Christmas party, but that plan also eventually fell through. Up to the evening before my departure I was in a sustained state of denial about where I could leave Abhilasha (the airport car park seemed as good a last resort as any), when the day was saved by a photographer friend of a friend who happened to have a spare parking space at his apartment in Bandra, Mumbai's hipster neighborhood of the north.

I dropped the Nano off at her new home just hours before my flight and was pleased to see that this particular part of Mumbai, right next to the sea and with the quiet air of a fishing village, was possibly one of the nicest parts of the city I had seen to date. Sea air corrosion notwithstanding, Abhilasha was in a beautiful spot and in good hands.

She now spends her days bombing around Mumbai on photography assignments. I draw comfort from the knowledge that she's being put to good use, that she's there for me should the need ever arise, and that our partnership is sealed until the day I'm made an offer I can't refuse.

NOTES

1. Back in 1994, this was an easily forgeable folded pink slip with a glued-on passport picture, stuffed into a plastic sheath. My only form of portable ID for many years, it got me duly laughed out of pubs and clubs the world over, and flatly denied entry into some of the more pedantic drinking venues in the US.
2. http://www.nytimes.com/2010/06/08/world/asia/08iht-roads.html?pagewanted=all
3. This was the figure in 2009. The number of road deaths in 2011 jumped to over 140,000. http://articles.timesofindia. indiatimes.com/2012-06-08/india/32123122_1_road-accidents-road-fatalities-road-deaths
4. *WHO Global Status Report on Road Safety*, 2009.
5. http://www.topgear.com/uk/car-news/Tata-Nano
6. http://www.thedailybeast.com/newsweek/2008/01/09/how-green-is-a-mini.html
7. http://green.blogs.nytimes.com/2009/03/23/worlds-cheapest-car-boon-or-bane/
8. http://ibnlive.in.com/news/ratan-tata-will-be-a-hero-if-he-made-a-bus-like-nano/56973-11.html
9. http://www.business-standard.com/india/news/sunita-narainisright-right/353011/
10. http://articles.timesofindia.indiatimes.com/2012-04-20/mumbai/31373302_1_lifeline-poles-accidents
11. Indian National Crime Records Bureau.
12. Ministry of Road Transport and Highways, 2011.
13. World Bank.
14. I later discovered that five vehicles per kilometre of road is a national average made from wildly disparate statistics. In fact, the number of vehicles per kilometre of road in

Mumbai stands at 674. http://www.hindustantimes.com/India-news/Mumbai/Mumbai-has-674-vehicles-for-every-km-of-road/Article1-829604.aspx

15. My Mumbais and Bombays were in a perpetual muddle; and not just here, but in every city that had recently changed its name in India. What I realized was that within the cities, opinion was split as to which name to use, and so a mixture of both appeared to be the norm. Hence, Bangalore can be Bengaluru, Madras can be Chennai and Calcutta can be Kolkata, depending on your (or my) mood and/or political inclination.

16. Pavan K. Varma, *Being Indian*, Penguin India, 2005.

17. One crore = a hundred lakhs or 10,000,000.

18. Though not cows. I was beginning to understand that cows were a whole different story, exempted from the directives on account of their divine standing.

19. http://articles.timesofindia.indiatimes.com/2010-01-14/ahmedabad/28122955_1_inter-state-gang-gang-of-highway-robbers-gang-members

20. A popular clothing and fabric chain.

21. Persons of Indian Origin.

22. I'm not counting the rather outlandish and clearly erroneous results for Dadra and Nagar Haveli, a Union Territory squished between Maharashtra and Gujarat whose death rate is 100% based on a reported 45 accidents in all 45 of the state's registered cars that resulted in 45 fatalities, or the Lakshadweep Islands' 200% based on a single accident in 2009 that killed two people.

23. It could also mean quite simply that Malayalis are more diligent in reporting minor accidents to the police.

24. http://www.businessweek.com/news/2012-10-11/india-to-pay-for-highways-for-first-time-in-14-years-freight

25. http://washpost.bloomberg.com/Story?docId=1376-MBQ2AW0D9L3501-03KFPD9FO6DULNCQ08IA3IP0CL

26. In my defence, the light was a superfluous item placed in an inconspicuous (I could almost say hidden) spot along a one-way, intersection-less road that had no discernible reason to require traffic to stop at that particular point. I sensed a crafty fundraising drive on the part of Chennai's traffic department.

27. He is now India's Prime Minister.

28. http://news.bbc.co.uk/2/hi/south_asia/55427.stm

29. http://www.telegraphindia.com/1080111/jsp/nation/story_8769282.jsp

30. http://www.businessweek.com/stories/2008-05-09/inside-the-tata-nano-factorybusinessweek-business-news-stock-market-and-financial-advice

31. http://timesofindia.indiatimes.com/business/india-business/Engineering-the-Nano/articleshow/2693758.cms?

32. http://www.bloomberg.com/news/2012-08-28/lingerie-delayed-as-517-billion-india-jam-idles-trucks-freight.html

33. I later found out that by 'summer', historians in fact meant the time of year we in the West traditionally refer to as summer – that is, from June to September – and not the actual hottest time of the year on the subcontinent, which would be April and May. This means that Buddha and his buddies were escaping the incessant rains of the monsoon (for the sake of not harming any wee beasties during the course of their travels) and not the ferocious summer heat; so Buddha was infinitely more hardcore than me, as we all initially suspected.

34. A religious ritual, in this case performed in the waters of the sacred river Ganges.

35. 'Mandalay'.

36. 'Gunga Din'.

ACKNOWLEDGEMENTS

Thanks to Akhil Gupta in Mumbai and his assistant Prasad CG, without whom the journey would not have been possible.

And then to everyone who made a donation to the Nano Diaries project: Mum and Dad, Steve and Hannah Shellswell, Jon Meldrum, Dom Goodman, Olly Lambert, AOMAC, Charles Strasser, Robb Ellender, Ljilja Lainovic, Dijana and Dobrica Vukcevic, Mike and Jean Barnes, Dorothea Evans, Chris Gothard, Sacha Lainovic, Jason Sanchez, Can Esenbel, Balamurugan Manoharan, Jan Pearse, Richard Norman and Vamsi Mohun.

Another big shout-out to my agent Sherna Khambatta and the team at Nicholas Brealey, as well as the very talented Hiromi Suzuki Asakura who drew that lovely map on the front cover.

Thank you to the friends who softened the blows of long-distance travel and who provided support and advice, or allowed me to share their homes and the delights of creature comforts. Special big-ups to the Korgaonkar family, as well as Reuben, Petra, Hénoc, Marion, Hadleigh and Paul.

I'm grateful to Ratan Tata and to the folks at Tata Motors who have shown encouragement and cooperation, and who have refrained from filing any legal action against me.

Thanks to my parents and my husband Thor for all their support and patience in the face of my refusal to get a proper job.

Thanks to everyone in India. You truly deserve your title as the most hospitable nation on earth, as well as the mantle of the country of the craziest drivers. Yes, you lot who drive like your pants are on fire: just take care and watch how you go.

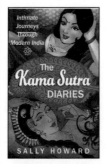

Around India in 80 Trains

Monisha Rajesh

"A promising debut from a writer to watch."
—Giles Foden, *Condé Nast Traveller*
"Crackles and sparks with life like an exploding box of Diwali fireworks."—William Dalrymple

To understand India you have to see it, hear it, breathe it and feel it. Living through the good, the bad and the ugly is the only way to know where you fit in and where India fits into you.

In 1991 Monisha uprooted from Sheffield to Madras in the hope of making India her home. Fed up with soap-eating rats, severed human heads, paying bribes, and the creepy colonel across the road, she returned to England with a bitter taste in her mouth. But twenty years later, she turns to a map of the Indian Railways and takes a page out of Jules Verne's classic tale, embarking on an adventure around India in 80 trains, covering 40,000 km, the circumference of the Earth.

Indian trains carry over twenty million passengers every day, plowing through cities, crawling past villages, climbing up mountains and skimming along coasts. Monisha hopes that 80 train journeys up, down and across India will lift the veil on a country that has become a stranger to her. And with a self-confessed militant devout atheist in tow, her personal journey around a country built on religion isn't quite what she bargained for...

Paperback ISBN 978-1-85788-595-8
eISBN 978-1-85788-948-2
PB £10.99 UK / $17.95 US
www.nicholasbrealey.com